Architectural Press Library of Planning and Design

Hospitals

HOSPITALS

Design and Development

W. Paul James DipArch FRIBA, William Tatton-Brown CB MA ARIBA AADip

The Architectural Press: London

First published in 1986 by the Architectural Press Ltd,
9 Queen Anne's Gate, London SW1H 9BY

British Library Cataloguing in Publication Data

James, W. Paul
    Hospitals: design and development.
    1. Hospitals – Design and construction
    I. Title   II. Tatton-Brown, William
    725'.51   RA967

ISBN 0-85139-299-7

The Architectural Press wish to make known that any
royalties earned by William Tatton-Brown will be given
to St Thomas' Charitable Trust.

Typeset by Crawley Composition Ltd.
Printed in Great Britain by
BAS Printers Ltd, Over Wallop, Hampshire

CONTENTS

Acknowledgements and photographic acknowledgements

The authors would like to take the opportunity of acknowledging help, information and material so generously given by the following:

American Medical Internation (Europe) Ltd
Ahrends, Burton and Koralek, UK
British Architectural Library, UK
Building Design Partnership, UK
Caudill, Rowlett, Scott, USA
Department of Health & Social Security, UK
Eukelenboom Geiritse & Middelhoek, Netherlands
Fernando Florez Plaza, Spain
George, Trew Dunn Beckles-Wilson, Bowes, UK
Hospital Design Partnership, UK
Itten and Brechbuhl, Switzerland
Krohn and Hartrig Rasmussen, Denmark
King Edward's Fund Library, UK
Llewelyn-Davies Weeks, UK
Medical Architecture Research Unit, UK
Percy Thomas Partnership, UK
Powell & Moya and Partners, UK
PRC Engineering (UK) Ltd

Pütseps Arkitektkonter, Sweden
Rosing, Koln, Polos, West Germany
RIBA Library, UK
Salling-Mortensens, Tegnestue, Denmark
R. Seifert and Partners, UK
South Western Regional Health Authority, UK
SPRI, Sweden
Stone Marracini & Patterson, USA
St. Thomas' Hospital, UK
Trent Regional Health Authority, UK
Watkins Gray Woodgate International, UK
White Arkitektkonter, Sweden
Weber, Brand & Partner, West Germany
Yorkshire Regional Health Authority, UK

Additional help was given to us by some of the organisations listed in Appendix 2, and is also gratefully acknowledged.

Illustration copyright is acknowledged wherever it has been possible to ascertain it, but the authors apologise for any omissions. The authors wish to acknowledge copyright of illustration material supplied by the following:

Source	Figure number	Source	Figure number
Architectural Press Ltd, 9 Queen Anne's Gate, London SW1H 9BY	1.17, 1.22, 1.61, 1.79, 2.21, 2.90, 3.22, 3.31, 4.42	J. H. Kent, 74a Montague Street, Worthing, West Sussex	2.92
John Arthur Studios	1.65	Middletons, Nottingham	3.3, 3.11, 3.19, 3.20, 4.2
Aspect Picture Library	1.90, 3.1, 3.2	Thomas & Poul Pedersen, Norre Alle 446, 8000 Arhus, Copenhagen, Denmark	1.26, 1.56, 3.15, 4.8
Aerofilms, Station Road, Boreham Wood, Herts	1.126		
British Architectural Library, London	1.1	Malcolm Pendrill, Amen House, Church Street, Reigate, Surrey	1.122, 1.141, 2.35, 2.65, 2.66, 2.80, 4.47
Balthazar Korab, PO Box 895, Troy, Michigan 48094, USA	1.100	R. W. Park, Moorlane, Preston, Lancashire RR1 3PQ	1.139
Caudill Rowlett Scott	1.98	Gerald Ratto, San Anselmo, California 94960, USA	1.130
A. Clarke, 17 King Street, Maidstone, Kent	1.112, 1.113	John Rawson	1.101
John Dewar, 2 N.E. Circus Place, Edinburgh 3	1.105	Powell & Moya & Partners, 21 Upper Cheyne Row, London SW3	
John Donat	1.114		
Ahrends Burton & Koralek		Henk Snoek, 44a Pentonville Road, London N1 9HF	1.134
Norman Dutton, 42 Castle Street, Guildford, Surrey GU1 3UQ	4.33	John Slater, Newmarket, Suffolk	1.118, 1.123, 2.32, 3.9, 3.10
Fox Photos	1.8	St Thomas' Hospital Library, Lambeth Palace Road, London SE1	2.4, 2.5
Handford Photography, 82 George Street, Croydon CR0 1PD	1.23, 4.44		
Jiminez, Serrano 31, Madrid, Spain	1.59, 4.41	Sybolt Voeten, Baronielaan 1 bis, 4818 Breda, Netherlands	1.86

GENERAL INTRODUCTION

General Introduction

Rational discussion of hospital design is complicated by the fact that hospitals are connected with matters that affect life and death. Once these absolutes are mentioned, normal methods of evaluating results become difficult to apply; when life is at stake people naturally feel that 'only the best is acceptable.' Any form of financial limitation is apt to be seen as an inhuman restraint. Escalating costs are accepted as a matter of course. It is assumed that more sophisticated modern procedures automatically justify a correspondingly heavier investment in building and engineering.[1] The latest technology is embraced, even if it affords no economies in output and the efficacy of treatment has yet to be proved.[2] Only when there is no more money in the bank are people prepared to look at results achieved.

In 1983 the British Secretary of State for Health and Social Security invited a successful businessman to conduct an independent enquiry into the management of the UK National Health Service.[3] Roy Griffiths was Deputy Chairman and Managing Director of Sainsbury's, a large chain store and supermarket network in the food industry. (The connection between nutrition – the supply of good food and drink – and health was purely incidental). Griffiths and his team spent six months visiting clinics, offices, institutions and hospitals, talking to people on the shop floor and listening to what they had to say. He was struck by the enthusiasm and dedication of the men and women working at all levels of the organisation. But he observed that 'if Florence Nightingale were carrying her lamp through the corridors of the NHS today, she would almost certainly be searching for the people in charge.' Accordingly, one of his key recommendations was the appointment of a general manager for every unit of the service, with the maximum devolution from the centre to the periphery.

A primary task of management is the organisation of physical resources and capital assets. Managers are not only concerned with people, but with the surroundings in which they work and attend to the needs of their customers. Managers are inevitably involved in building or rebuilding. It is for them and their architects that this book is written.

Griffiths suggests that managers can be drawn from many different disciplines: from accountancy, estate development, engineering and so on, as well as from medicine, nursing and hospital administration. Much of what we say will be already familiar to them. Some of it will be controversial.

We have attempted to give an overall view of hospital building during the last eighty years with an emphasis on the state of the art that has now been reached. Each section comprises an introduction and illustrated examples. The introduction presents the problems as perceived by contemporary planners working at that particular moment in time. The illustrations show the solutions arrived at by their architects. More than 60 examples have been selected from all over the world from 20 different countries, including USSR. The text points up the physical consequences flowing from the policies adopted, and the advantages and disadvantages of the strategies employed. The reader is given a clear, factually based insight into the design lessons which emerge for future application. These are equally applicable to developing and developed countries. We believe that any manager and any architect will be able to recognise his or her own predicament, pinpoint their problems and find indicators (often not more than that) of the cost of alternatives open to them.

There is now an enormous volume of literature on hospital planning. All the subjects that we have touched on are dealt with in far more detail in the professional and technical press and official publications. But until quite recently, authors concentrated on innovations. Each new discovery or technique tended to increase the complication and add to the cost of design. This book seeks to do the opposite. We have tried to take the mystique out of the subject, and to provide the reader with commonsense guidelines for containment as well as for growth.

Griffiths emphasises that one of the managers' major tasks will be to 'promote realistic public and professional perceptions of what the NHS can and should provide as the best possible service within the resources available.' Television programmes have shown the immense public interest in what goes on behind closed doors in operating theatres. This book attempts to do the same thing for hospital planning. It takes the reader behind the scenes, before a new hospital is built. It leads him backstage to the drawing board, the research bench, the consulting room and the corridors of power.

Coming at a time when hospital building is thought to be out of reach in developed and developing countries, we believe it has a message for Ministers of Health, for insurance companies organising schemes of hospital cover for paying patients, for civil servants, members of hospital committees and all those who are concerned with securing better hospital provision in the future for themselves and those whom they love. It would be ironical if, just at a moment when surgical and clinical intervention in hospital has proved to be most effective, new hospitals were to become so expensive that none could be built. The aim of this book is to show that the sort of hospitals people really need *can* be built, at a price they can afford to pay.

PLANNING THE WHOLE HOSPITAL

Chapter 1

Planning the whole hospital

Changing expectations

People's expectations from hospitals have changed over the centuries. In the middle ages they were primarily associated with death. Some of the finest hospitals were built for pilgrims. Far from home, they had nowhere to go when they fell sick. They were often cared for in cruciform halls with the nuns' nursing station at the centre and an altar at the end.[1] The aim was to protect healthy pilgrims from infection and to prepare the sick for death. They were called 'patients' because they were patiently awaiting the course of events.

The same idea of course lay behind the old fever hospitals and leper colonies. Even lunatic asylums and poor-law institutions were built primarily to protect those outside, rather than for the benefit of those within. Custodial care offered little hope of recovery. The only exit was normally the grave. Even the great teaching hospitals in the centres of European capitals had such a high mortality rate that Florence Nightingale writing in 1859 asserted 'It may seem a strange principle to enunciate as the very first requirement of a hospital is that it should do the sick no harm'.[2]

Key dates

Gradually the idea that hospitals were about life rather than death began to dawn. The key dates may be said to be:

1846 The discovery of anaesthetics, which spread throughout the Western world within a few years.

1866–9 Lister's use of carbolic sprays for antiseptic surgery, which by combating infection enormously reduced the number of post-operative fatalities.

1886 Von Bergman's introduction of aseptic techniques, the sterilising of instruments and the use of autoclaves.

The use of anaesthetics permitted carefully planned deliberate procedures instead of 'smash and grab' operations. Barber-surgeons were replaced by men with medical training. An operating theatre became a part of every hospital, and more beds had to be provided because of the need to accommodate an increasing number of survivors. The successes of Lister and Von Bergman gradually extended the range of surgery and the area of ancillary accommodation associated with it.

Then in 1895 Roentgen used X-rays as an aid to diagnosis. Instead of relying solely on their five senses, doctors now had the possibility of confirmation in black and white. Laboratories similarly added a new dimension to medicine and enormously extended the use of pharmaceuticals. The primary function of hospitals turned slowly from custodial care to active intervention. They became places where life could not only be saved, but the quality of life improved. With this realisation, more and more people sought to take advantage of the new facilities provided in the old institutions and the new specialist voluntary hospitals that proliferated at the beginning of this century.

Ownership

After two world wars the ownership and control of hospitals assumed a different pattern in each country.[3] In Belgium and Holland most hospitals were run by voluntary and charitable organisations. In the USA too, voluntary non-profit-making bodies were responsible for three-quarters of the beds provided, and only one quarter were built by state or municipal authorities. Whereas in France, where the Revolution of 1789 had taken away all charitable foundations and conferred them on the "Commune" or municipality, only one-sixth of the beds were privately owned. But whatever the pattern of ownership, most Western countries inherited from the past a small number of large well-equipped hospitals of 600–1000 beds, associated with universities and providing all specialist services, a sprinkling of district hospitals of 150–600 beds and a large number of small local hospitals of 20 beds and upwards.

Inevitably their location was haphazard. Some areas had very little cover, while others had empty beds. Everywhere there was a chronic shortage of funds. In the USA the Hill-Burton Act of 1946 sought to remedy this by giving federal aid on the basis of one dollar for every two dollars raised by the local community. Between 1947 and 1970 some 10,584 projects were approved for grants. These provided nearly 500,000 beds as well as out-patient, public health and rehabilitation facilities.[4] But all too often they were placed in new and flourishing suburban areas. Some isolated communities had nothing, while the bulk of the population in the inner cities had to rely on what public authorities could provide. Non-revenue-generating patients could only be cared for in large antiquated buildings funded from local taxes. A similar situation confronted most of the developed countries of the west, while the developing countries suffered from an overall shortage of beds, combined with a spiralling increase in population.

Rationalisation

An opportunity of planning health care on a more rational basis arose in Britain with the passing of the National Health Service Act in 1948. The Minister of Health took over more than 2,000 hospitals and began the mammoth task of reorganising health care facilities on a nation-wide scale. The corner-stone of the service was to be the District General Hospital. In 1962 Enoch Powell, the UK Minister of Health, published his famous *Hospital Plan for England and Wales*,[5] which was 'to give the hospital service both the physical equipment and the pattern and setting which will everywhere place the most modern treatment at the service of patients and enable the staff who care for them to exercise their skill and devotion under the best possible conditions.'

District General Hospitals

Originally the UK plan envisaged a District General Hospital of between 600 and 900 beds. But this was doubled, partly as a result of criticism of the tiny US hospitals, and partly under the influence of the very impressive Scandinavian university hospitals. A committee set up in Britain in 1960 under the chairmanship of Sir Adrian Bonham-Carter[6] recommended that the new hospitals should serve at least 200,000–300,000 people, or more in major concentrations of population. This meant a complement of between 1000 and 2000 beds. The huge increase was inspired by the ideas of Professor Thomas McKeown.[7] He believed that the District General Hospital should mirror the pattern of morbidity of the community it served. Thus it should contain in addition to beds for medicine and surgery, a much larger proportion of beds for psychiatry, mental subnormality, geriatrics, and the chronic sick. Facilities normally housed in isolated institutions were to be brought within the confines of the District General Hospital. In addition there should be not less than two consultants in each speciality, so that there would always be cover at consultant level when one was off duty. Ideally no consultants would have patients at more than one hospital. If private patients were being treated, they too should be in the same hospital. Training facilities should be incorporated for all medical, nursing and paramedical personnel. This meant the inclusion of libraries, lecture halls and residential accommodation with reasonable provision for recreation. There would also be facilities for postgraduate education and research, as well as a base for specialised community health services, such as medical or psychiatric social work, occupational therapy, and some components (child guidance and speech therapy) of the school health service. The office for the appropriate departments of the local health authority would also be provided, in order to facilitate the prompt deployment of domiciliary health services. In short, all the hopes and ideals of all the members of the committee for an integrated national health service found a place in the report. Its intentions were admirable but its influence disastrous.

Unprecedented expansion on all fronts

Hospital planners in the 1960s found themselves at the centre of an intellectual ferment, which extended far beyond the buildings they were called upon to design.[8] Architects, like the artists of the Renaissance, were involved in many-sided activities for which their previous training had not prepared them. But unlike those artists, who had a private patron, they were enveloped in a web of bureaucracy: a bureaucracy rapidly expanded to cope with a building programme which it too had never been designed to handle.

The first problem they had to come to terms with was one of scale, the sheer bulk of building envisaged. The rate of increase both in the complexity and the size of hospitals was unprecedented. A typical nineteenth-century hospital had had a gross area of about $20m^2$ per bed. Wards accounted for more than half this space. In the inter-war period this was increased to $40m^2$. Now they were being asked to provide 75 to $80m^2$. The nursing area had doubled; the other areas had increased fourfold.

Three zones: nursing, clinical and support

It may be helpful to pause here and look at these areas in more detail. There is first of all the *nursing area* or zone; here patients are fostered throughout their stay in hospital. It deals with people, and in temperate climates is usually naturally ventilated. Then there are the working areas, which can be divided into two – the clinical and non-clinical or support zones. The *clinical zone*, consisting of diagnostic and treatment facilities, is often artificially ventilated and is primarily associated with the technical equipment required for procedures on patients. The *support zone*, comprising kitchens, cafeteria, staff changing, stores, laundry, boiler house, transformer station, workshops and other industrial plant, accommodates all the supporting services necessary for running the hospital. Nurses' homes and other residential accommodation are excluded from this classification because they are often catered for off-site. This simple three-zone classification is described in detail on pages 15–21. The key to hospital planning is the manipulation of these zones and their relationships to produce a fully functional, integrated hospital.

Given this analysis, the earliest response to the problem of scale was to stack all the accommodation in a tower rising from a podium. The clinical zone was placed in the podium at street level with the supporting zone in the basement below, and the nursing zone in the tower. Very economical solutions were designed on this formula, particularly in the USA[9]. It was the logical answer for a 'one-shot' hospital, where all the ultimate goals could be foreseen, defined and achieved at a single point in time.

Changing rates of growth

But when hospitals took longer to plan and build, architects were faced with another problem: the expanding brief. The different zones were not only growing in front of their eyes, they were growing at different rates. In Holland, for instance, it was estimated that in a decade the nursing zone increased by 20 per cent, the clinical zone by 40 per cent[10] and the support zone, combined with the plant rooms and duct space required for the provision of air-conditioning to a whole hospital, by as much as 100 per cent.

Indeterminacy and obsolescence

The first architects in Britain fully to grasp the situation were Llewelyn-Davies and Weeks. They produced their classic theory of indeterminacy, an architectural principle enabling buildings 'to grow with order and change with calm.' A complex organisation, they said, should never be housed in a finite symmetrical building. It should be a series of loosely-knit independent structures, each capable of separate growth in response to changing demands. In his masterly summary of the changes in his planning philosophy, John Weeks makes the revolutionary point that 'user studies of function are not by themselves a sound basis for hospital design. Functions change so rapidly that designers should no longer aim for an optimum fit between building and function. The real requirement is to design a building that will inhibit change of function least, and not one that will fit specific function best'.[11] So at Northwick Park Hospital, London, he designed a "hospital street" along which were placed blocks of buildings which could expand at right angles. Both the blocks and the street were open-ended.

This strategy proved very influential. But it required a great deal of land. What could be done on urban sites where land was at a premium? This was the problem set to the Hospital Building Division of the UK Department of Health, under the leadership of its chief architect William Tatton-Brown and his successor Howard Goodman.

Universal space

Their answer was a building providing 'universal space': that is, a series of structurally uninterrupted floors, to which any services such as electricity, gas, water, could be brought from above, and from which all wastes could be taken from below. 'In agricultural terms', as Richard Crossman, the Secretary of State for Health, said, 'it is like a Dutch barn. The building is permanent, but its uses are constantly changing.' Starting with the premise that the whole building would be air-conditioned, it followed that the zones could be placed anywhere at any time. At Greenwich

Hospital, London, the nursing zone was placed along the periphery so that the patients could have a view out of the windows. The clinical zone formed an inner core, while the non-clinical zone occupied the basement. In all, 800 beds and full supporting areas were accommodated within a highly compact, fully air-conditioned four-storey building (page 18). Air-conditioning at that time (1962) was accepted, indeed welcomed, because of the part it was hoped it would play in reducing airborne nosocomial (hospital) infection. At Greenwich[12] the designers accepted its full implications. Instead of treating services as additions and concealing them in ducts and behind false ceilings, complete engineering sub-floors nearly 2m high are provided. These are sandwiched between each nursing, clinical or support floor, and are connected to four vertical shafts that run from top to bottom like a vast ship's engine room. Calorifiers, pumps, sub-stations and so on, are stacked in these shafts and cat-ladders give access to the engineering floors. Blue-collar maintenance men can thus circulate on their rounds without inconveniencing the white-collar staff and patients on the clinical floors. This was a real break-through and it has been widely copied abroad. Some 70 hospitals have been designed on the engineering floor sandwich principle pioneered at Greenwich.

Combating obsolescence

A common taunt that a hospital planner has to face is that every new hospital is out of date the moment it is opened. Hospitals take so long to design and build that this is often the case. Zeidler in designing the McMaster Hospital, Ontario, Canada[13] was one of the first to see the advantage of a universally serviced space in combating premature obsolescence. He persuaded his clients that it was not necessary to wait for final approval before letting a contract. Once his budget had been agreed he could go ahead and build the carcass and main service runs, knowing that they would be adequate for any functional demands. Construction proceeded in parallel with decision-making and the choice of equipment could be postponed until the last possible moment, for with rapid advances in technology, the latest piece of equipment is often the most cost-effective. The possibility of obtaining the latest model and plugging it in without incurring the penalty of contract variation orders is an important consideration.

Plug-in departments and systems development programmes

A further attempt to combat obsolescence was developed by the UK Department of Health, working with Regional Hospital Boards. They produced an array of standard building envelopes, housing different departments which could be selected and assembled into a whole hospital to meet varying demands and site conditions. They were designed on a modular basis with 15m clear spans, so that they could be plugged in to the mainly horizontal network of corridors and ducts serving the hospital. This communication and energy network is like an electrical harness in a motor car: it provides a flexible link between interchangeable components which can be installed or replaced, to keep pace with technological progress. The Harness[14] system as it was called, was due to start with a pilot project at Dudley Hospital UK in 1974. It was a highly sophisticated computerised programme involving the production of some 70 hospitals planned to roll off the production line by the year 2000. A similar Building Systems development programme was devised by George Agron of Stone, Marraccini and Patterson for the Veterans' Administration Hospital in USA.[15] But unlike Harness it used the interstitial floors of Greenwich, because for climatic reasons air-conditioning was essential. The prototype, Loma Linda in California, was completed in 1977.

A brave new world

The ways in which hospital planners attempted to solve the problems of growth, complexity and obsolescence must be seen against the background of the times. The 1960s and early 1970s were a period of great optimism. The enormous growth of population, the increase in the gross national product and the rise in the standard of living encouraged everyone to think big. The ways of handling very large and complex organisational problems, the theory of indeterminacy, interstitial space (the engineering sandwich floor), the computerised systems for combating premature obsolescence must be seen as heroic experiments to meet unprecedented demands. They may now have been temporarily superseded. But that does not detract from their permanent value, and future generations will return to them with interest and advantage.

B   Containment

In 1973–74 came the energy crisis, accelerating inflation and the hint of economic recession. Enormous increases in construction costs brought hospital building almost to a standstill.

Some countries were hit sooner than others. But even the strongest economies in the Common Market countries of Europe could not afford the spiralling cost of health care, and higher and higher standards of hospital construction. A yawning gap opened up between new buildings and those completed only ten or twenty years before. There is now no way out of the vicious circle. As it becomes ever more costly to bring old buildings up to standard, in order to meet new fire regulations or provide intensive care units or energy saving devices, there is even less left to spend on new building. The higher the cost of building, the fewer new hospitals reach the drawing board. In every country of the world there is a reversal of the expansionist thinking of the 1960s, and people are turning their minds to ways of reducing or at least containing the cost of hospital care.

Changing need for beds

As the most expensive element in health care is the hospital bed, the most obvious way to economise is not to have to build any beds at all! Today the nursing zone, and those supporting areas (kitchens, stores, plant) associated with it, is the zone most likely to contract. If the patient can be treated at home in his own bed (with his own kitchen and stores), then there is no need to provide a second bed in a hospital.

Preventive medicine and early diagnosis have already almost eliminated the need for beds for tuberculosis, polio and venereal diseases. Whole sanatoria and infectious diseases hospitals have been closed or put to other uses. But once the patient is admitted, the number of beds required depends on a variety of considerations. In an international study of hospital utilisation in 1979 Dr Bridgman[16] says the demand for hospital care will depend upon such things as accessibility, availability of beds, prevalence of disease, the reputation of the hospital, the attitude of the doctors, and the cost of utilisation. This in turn will depend on whether the cost is borne by individuals or the community, either directly or through financing agencies, the state, social security, sickness insurance funds or other institutions.

The number of beds available varies surprisingly in different countries. In Western Europe for instance, there are some 5 or 6 beds per 1000 population in Spain, about 8 in Britain, 11 in France and 15 in Sweden. The disparity in numbers is not entirely due to the climatic differences between the Mediterranean and the North Sea, nor is it very closely linked with the gross national product. Parkinson's Law applies to some extent: if a bed is available it will be filled. How soon it will be emptied depends on various factors such as the rapidity of diagnosis and the success of the treatment prescribed, where the patient will go on discharge and who is available to look after him. Social and financial considerations often play a more important part than medical ones.[17]

Throughput of patients

The number of beds needed depends on the throughput of patients. The shorter the length of stay and the quicker the arrival of the next patient, the fewer the beds required. Brian Abel-Smith[18] drew attention to this in 1967. He contrasted the 'high-pressure workshop' atmosphere of the 7–9 day average length of stay in USA (in both private and public sectors) with the 'rest and recuperation' spirit of European hospitals, with their average length of stay of 15–20 days. Since that time substantial progress has been made; in Britain, for example, the average length of a patient's stay has been reduced from 11 days for surgical cases and 15 for medical in 1969, to 8 days for surgical cases and 10 for medical in 1979. The total number of occupied beds over the same period fell from 350,000 to 300,000.[19] France and West Germany have been slower to achieve a reduction. The natural tendency there, is for hospitals to keep patients as long as possible, in order to increase their income. Hospitals are reimbursed on a patient/day basis. The heaviest costs, for diagnosis, treatment and nursing, naturally occur on the first few days and tend to fall off as the patient recovers. Hotel costs on the other hand are constant throughout the stay. The easiest way to recoup high initial expenses is therefore to prolong the number of days at the cheaper end of the scale.[20] The doctors and nurses are happy, and the patient seldom complains unless he has to pay.

Alternative strategies: planning from the base upwards

But these administrative anomalies are unlikely to remain for ever. The question that has to be asked is; how can the number of beds required be reduced still further? One answer is to shift some of the functions performed in the larger hospitals into less sophisticated but adequately equipped places nearer to the community served. In 1970 the UK Office of Health Economics published *Building for Health* no 35, in which they argued 'To the consumer of medical care, the advantages of access to specialist advice and modern equipment are obvious. The disadvantages, however, of travelling perhaps long distances and being treated in unfamiliar surroundings can be equally obvious. The continued policy of concentrating resources within the grounds of the District General Hospital will increase the size of the institution, the time spent in travelling and probably the number of cases dealt with there. Any change of this nature must rely largely on an effective system of primary medical care which can filter patients through to the appropriate level. For these reasons, one of the most promising alternative strategies may be to think of planning the health services from the base upwards rather than from the District Hospital downwards.' Using the analogy of local, neighbourhood, district and regional shopping centres, they proposed a hierarchy of medical facilities from a base of general practitioners and group practice Health Centres up to District General Hospitals and Regional or Metropolitan Teaching Hospitals.[21]

Better value for money

This strategy was successfully put into practice in the UK in the two Best Buy hospitals at Frimley and Bury St Edmunds opened in 1974.[22] The two hospitals are carefully fitted into the existing pattern of community care. By closely integrating the services provided by family doctors and local authority nurses and health visitors, with an efficient ambulance service, many more people are cared for, at home or in less sophisticated surroundings such as cottage hospitals. An effective day-care unit has been devised. Patients arrive in the morning for minor surgery, treatment or investigation, and after rest and supervision return to their own homes the same evening. The beds they occupied during the day are available for emergencies at night, without disturbing patients in the general wards. This flexible use of space is extended to the whole hospital. Wards are planned as at Greenwich, in a continuous band, so that the number of beds allocated to each speciality can ebb and flow according to need. Gynaecology can expand into post-natal for instance, just by opening or closing a set of doors across a corridor. There is no empire-building by department heads, and with close co-operation between hospital and community, admission and discharge procedures are streamlined, bed occupancy is increased and the length of stay significantly reduced. Applying these policies throughout the country, using specially designed accommodation, would open the way for the number of acute beds to be reduced from 3.3 to 2 or less per 1000. This would make it possible to close a further 50,000 beds. But it must be appreciated that this strategy is only applicable in countries already possessing well developed community health care facilities.

The UK Best Buy hospitals cost two thirds the price of the average hospitals being built at that time in Britain. As the name implies, the intention of the planners was not to aim at producing the best possible hospital, but while maintaining acceptable medical and nursing standards, to produce the best value for money; the bulk of the savings were made in medical planning, as described above. But important economies were made in every field. These are described in detail in subsequent chapters. Here it is only necessary to mention the reduction in on-costs. On-costs are defined as the percentage addition which has to be made to take account of pecularities of site, additional foundations, height allowance, air-conditioning etc., (chapter 5). At the two Best-Buy hospitals this figure was halved.

Careful choice of site meant that the building could be contained in two storeys. Courtyards provide natural light and ventilation. Communications – the corridors and ducts linking the departments together – are reduced. Instead of the conventional boiler house with its factory chimney, distributing steam to all parts of the hospital, small interconnected rooftop boiler houses are located near the centres of demand. Artificial ventilation is restricted to the clinical zone at the core of the hospital.

Nucleus

To a large extent these economies resulted from the strict application of zoning principles, and planners began to look again at the need for flexibility. Some zones might never expand; indeed, they might even contract. The cost of universal space (as at Greenwich) could not now be afforded, and some of it might never be needed. Unknown future demands might perhaps be met more easily by providing facilities on another site. Waiting until they could be predicted with more certainty, and only building now what could be brought into immediate use, seemed a more sensible course. Accordingly the idea of building hospitals in self-contained phases was re-examined. In 1975 Howard Goodman, now chief architect at the UK Department of Health, and his team set to work on this new strategy. Using much of the material from the Harness programme, which had been abandoned following the energy crisis, and scaling it down in accordance with Best Buy principles, they evolved the Nucleus concept.[23] As its name implies, this aims to build a hospital in phases. The first phase is a 300-bed nucleus, capable of expansion by further self-contained phases to 600 beds. The Nucleus system is described in detail on pages 55–57. It is a highly versatile and economical answer to the problem of growth and change. Some 50 hospitals or parts of hospitals were already in the pipeline by 1982 and the number has since doubled: total value 1 bn pounds.

In the UK new hospitals of the 1980s have brought down the gross area per bed from 75–80 m^2 to 50–60m^2. Similar reductions in area can be seen elsewhere in Europe. Some might argue that the process has gone too far and that small is not always beautiful. It is too early to judge. What is certain is that the new smaller hospitals have eased a number of problems. Access is better for patients and visitors. Catchment areas for part-time labour are widened. They are quicker to build, less capital is tied up and they are far less of an intrusion on the rural landscape or urban scene. At the very lowest, little mistakes will be easier to correct!

Renewal based on local initiative

The move away from the very large hospital that has occurred in recent years can be summed up by the change in attitude of the Department of Health in the UK. The rigid pattern outlined in Enoch Powell's Hospital Plan has been replaced by a more flexible approach. The arguments set out in this chapter may be summed up in the words of Gerard Vaughan, the UK Minister of Health in 1980.[24] 'There is a real risk' he said, 'of concentrating services more heavily than the advantages strictly justify, to the detriment of other considerations such as the accessibility of hospitals to patients and visitors, and the sense of identity which many local communities have with their local hospital.' He went on, 'It would generally be better to concentrate on making the best of what exists . . . So I have no intention of producing a blueprint to be applied everywhere . . . Our aim is to establish a set of broad policies acceptable to the professional and other interests concerned, and then to give Health Authorities the greatest possible discretion within these policies and within their financial allocations to arange their services in the way best suited to their local circumstances.'

This change in policy may mean two or more District General Hospitals in one district and the retention of many local hospitals for geriatric and similar functions. Instead of replacement there will be

renewal. Renovation and remodelling call for different approaches from new construction. There is more room for local initiative, unfettered by rigid regulations applicable to new buildings. Savings can be made if there is a certain amount of give-and-take on areas and standards and schedules of accommodation.[25] Rapid decisions can be taken on the spot and there is less likelihood of newly built space remaining empty for lack of revenue funds to staff it.

In 1979, the Development Group of the UK Department of Health, in collaboration with the Regional Architect, undertook a demonstration project at the Nelson Hospital in south London. It showed how a small under-used hospital could be converted into a modern unit, providing a valuable service to its local community and a supporting role to the District General Hospital; the work was done at a fraction of the cost of new building. Finance was provided by revenue savings arising from the transfer of patients from a neighbouring hospital and the sale of the site.[26]

In 1983 Ceri Davies conducted an enquiry into under-used and surplus property in the National Health Service of the UK.[27] The amount of land owned is some 50,000 acres (20,000 hectares) worth perhaps £20,000 million, with all the buildings that stand on it. Roughly one quarter have been built since 1948. But an even larger proportion was erected before 1900.[27] Much of this stands on valuable land in central areas. The Davies report makes two key recommendations. The first is that each Area Health Authority should put a value and a notional rent on all its property. The second is that it should be allowed (subject to certain safeguards) to dispose of any surplus and keep the assets. The proceeds of the sale can then finance the renewal of the property retained.

Need for a businesslike approach

This very cursory summary shows the enormous range of problems that have confronted hospital planners over the years. No two countries see their priorities in the same light. The differences that exist between USA and Europe and even between neighbouring countries in western Europe, mean that there can be no such thing as an 'ideal hospital' to which all must conform. Once this is accepted, then the secret of success lies in controlling demand and allocating resources to achieve the best balance between the two. The recognition that local needs are best satisfied by making the most of what can be found on the spot, holds promise of much greater variety in the future. It will be especially welcome in developing countries where the need for a businesslike approach is even more important.

Professor G.L.S. Shackle, discussing the nature of business success, suggests the desirability of two types of mind in management. 'One type is the truth-seeker or scientist. Management has been deeply and rightly sold on mathematical methods. The manager trained in such methods can see ahead of him "the one right answer". But we need also the poet-architect-adventurer who sees a landscape inexhaustibly rich in suggestions and materials for making things . . . We need the radical as well as the axial type of mind'.[28]

In the following pages we look in more detail at some of the radical ideas that are emerging in the planning of the nursing, clinical and support zones and the procedures adopted for putting them into practice.

C   The planners' response 1900–1985

Service zones and departments: key to drawings in chapter 1C only

1   Nursing zone

1A	Medical/surgical ward	1E	Psychiatric ward
1B	Geriatric ward	1F	Plastic surgery/burns ward
1C	Paediatric ward	1G	Renal ward
1D	Obstetric ward	1H	Day care ward

2   Clinical zone

2A	Accident and emergency department	2O	Nurse training school
2B	Administration department	2P	Nuclear medicine department
2C	Anaesthetic department	2Q	Operating theatre department
2D	Central treatment department	2R	Out-patient department
2E	Clinical investigation department	2S	Obstetric delivery unit
2F	Day surgery unit (endoscopy)	2T	Opthalmic department
2G	Dental department	2U	Paediatric department
2H	Intensive therapy unit	2V	X-ray department
2J	Laboratory (service)	2W	Radiotherapy department
2K	Laboratory (teaching)	2X	Rehabilitation department
2L	Mortuary	2Y	Reception and records
2M	Medical illustration department	2Z	Research department
2N	Medical teaching unit		

3   Support zone

3A	Central kitchen	3G	Plant
3B	Central sterilising department	3H	Staff cafeteria
3C	Central stores	3J	Staff changing
3D	Maintenance/works department	3K	Staff residences
3E	Laundry and linen stores	3L	Receiving/despatch
3F	Pharmacy (manufacture)	3M	Vehicle parking

▨	Main corridor	◹	Staircase
M▶	Main entrance	↰	Ramp
E▶	Emergency entrance	CT	Courtyard
▮▮	Lifts		

1.1 University College Hospital, London, UK; designed by A.W. Waterhouse in 1903 and still in operation after some alterations over the years. A highly ingenious plan provides approximately 250 beds within an urban site 75×75m. A four-storey cruciform ward block rises from a single storey rectangular base covering the entire site. An early example of the 'tower on podium' strategy.

1.2 Maidstone District General Hospital, Kent, UK: completed 1984. One of a number of 300-bed hospitals now being constructed in the UK based on a standard modular plan. Extended courtyard development, mainly of two storeys, on a large parkland site on the outskirts of a country town.

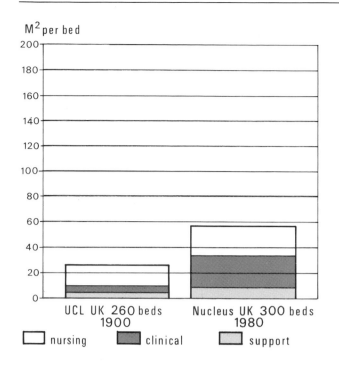

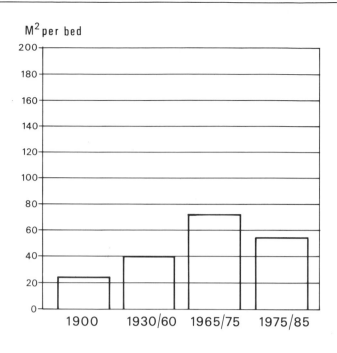

1.3   Comparative space per bed for hospitals in 1900 and 1980: based on analysis of areas in examples 1.1 and 1.2.

1.4   Comparison of space per bed in sample of general hospitals in the UK, 1900–1985.

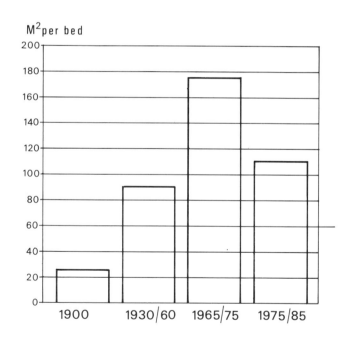

1.5   Comparisons of space per bed in sample of teaching hospitals in the UK: 1900–1985.
Note peaks during growth period 1965–1975 and the response to containment efforts from 1975.

Hospital space programmes

1.6, 1.7 In recent years considerable research and development work has been undertaken, with the aim of reducing both the cost and time-scale of hospital building. Space, previously visualised as a series of self-contained departmental units, is now viewed as a resource which can be programmed over time and shared between adjoining or associated functions. In addition, more flexible design solutions have opened up the possibilities of reduced functional content, and of construction and commissioning in stages. Today general hospitals (similar to the UK Nucleus Hospital: see 1.111) and university teaching hospitals are being planned to accommodate up to 900 beds within average areas per bed of $60m^2$ and $110m^2$ respectively.

1.6   Teaching hospitals 500–900 beds. Based on examples in UK, Belgium, W. Africa, USA and Far East.

	500 beds	Net Space m²	600 beds	Net Space m²	700 beds	Net Space m²	800 beds	Net Space m²	900 beds	Net Space m²
A In-patients wards										
Medical/surgical	364 beds	6190	420 beds	7140	504 beds	8570	580 beds	9860	644 beds	10950
Paediatric	69 beds	1360	92 beds	1810	92 beds	1810	115 beds	2265	115 beds	2265
Obstetric	50 beds	815	75 beds	1185	75 beds	1185	75 beds	1185	100 beds	1550
		8365		10135		11565		13310		14765
B Out-patients										
Consulting clinics	All depts	3190	All depts	3825	All depts	4460	All depts	5100	All depts	5740
Emergency department	1 dept	1125	1 dept	1125	1 dept	1500	1 dept	1500	1 dept	1500
		4315		4950		5960		6600		7240
C Diagnostic/treatment										
Regional specialities*	–	–	–	–	1 dept	500	1 dept	500	2 dept	1000
Radiodiagnostic	7 r/d rms	825	9 r/d rms	1060	11 r/d rms	1300	13 r/d rms	1535	15 r/d rms	1770
Operating/endoscopy	6 tables	990	8 tables	1320	10 tables	1650	12 tables	1980	14 tables	2310
Intensive treatment unit/ recovery	25 beds	415	30 beds	495	40 beds	660	45 beds	745	50 beds	830
Clinical service labs	All depts ⎫		All depts ⎫		All depts ⎫		All depts ⎫		All depts ⎫	
Mortuary and post-mortem	1 dept ⎭	3080	1 dept ⎭	3700	1 dept ⎭	3850	1 dept ⎭	4110	1 dept ⎭	4625
Functional diagnosis	1 dept	1000	1 dept	1200	1 dept	1310	1 dept	1500	1 dept	1600
Rehabilitation	1 dept	1000	1 dept	1280	1 dept	1400	1 dept	1600	1 dept	1600
Obstetric delivery	1 dept	750	1 dept	800	1 dept	1050	1 dept	1200	1 dept	1600
Day care (endoscopy)	2 tables	110	3 tables	165	4 tables	220	5 tables	275	5 tables	275
		8170		10020		11940		13445		15610
D Administration										
Central administration	500 beds	750	600 beds	960	700 beds	1050	800 beds	1200	900 beds	1350
Admin units	500 beds	940	600 beds	1200	700 beds	1310	800 beds	1500	900 beds	1690
Social medicine	1 dept	1000	1 dept	1200	1 dept	1200	1 dept	1200	1 dept	1200
Social services	500 beds	1810	600 beds	2320	700 beds	2540	800 beds	2900	800 beds	3260
		4500		5680		6100		6800		7500
E Industrial										
Kitchen	500 beds	700	600 beds	760	700 beds	885	800 beds	1010	900 beds	1135
Laundry	500 beds	560	600 beds	560	700 beds	655	800 beds	750	900 beds	840
Stores	500 beds	750	600 beds	900	700 beds	1050	800 beds	1200	900 beds	1350
Sterilising	500 beds	340	600 beds	340	700 beds	340	800 beds	450	900 beds	450
Pharmacy	500 beds	450	600 beds	450	700 beds	525	800 beds	600	900 beds	675
Workshops	500 beds	480	600 beds	525	700 beds	615	800 beds	700	900 beds	700
Plantrooms	500 beds	500	600 beds	600	700 beds	700	800 beds	800	900 beds	900
		3780		4135		4770		5510		6050
F Teaching/research										
Teaching units	150 student	1250	180 student	1500	210 student	1750	240 student	2000	270 student	2330
Teach/research labs	150 student	1500	180 student	1800	210 student	2100	240 student	2400	270 student	2700
Lecture/classrooms	150 student	690	180 student	825	210 student	960	240 student	1100	270 student	1285
Library/TV/cloaks	150 student	1810	180 student	2175	210 student	2535	240 student	2900	270 student	3260
		5250		6300		7345		8400		9575
G Dental										
Hospital and school	N/A		N/A		N/A		100 student	2120	100 student	2120
								2120		2120
H Circulation (percentages are of net space)	(60%)	20495	(60%)	24555	(60%)	28430	(60%)	33535	(60%)	37500
Total gross space		54875		65775		76110		89720		100360
Space per bed	508 beds	108	617 beds	107	711 beds	107	815 beds	110	909 beds	110

*Regional specialities: radiotherapy, nuclear medicine, haemodialysis, burns

1.7   General hospitals 100–400 beds. Based on recent examples in UK, W. Germany, Switzerland and Middle East.

	100 beds	Net Space m²	200 beds	Net Space m²	300 beds	Net Space m²	400 beds	Net Space m²
A In-patients wards								
Medical/surgical	84 beds	1210	140 beds	1870	196 beds	2825	252 beds	3630
Paediatric	–		46 beds	730	69 beds	1100	69 beds	1100
Obstetrics	20 beds	290	25 beds	365	25 beds	365	50 beds	730
Psychiatric	–	–	–	–	–	–	30 beds	480
		1500		2965		4290		5940
B Out-patients								
Consulting clinics	12 C/E rms	350	18 C/E rms	505	24 C/E rms	670	30 C/E rms	840
Emergency	1 dept		1 dept	590	1 dept	590	1 dept	590
		350		1095		1260		1430
C Diagnostic/treatment								
Radiodiagnostic	2 rooms	220	3 rooms	310	4 rooms	415	5 rooms	520
Radiotherapy/ nuclear medicine	–	–	–	–	–	–	–	–
Operating/endoscopy	2 tables	290	3 tables	580	4 tables	620	5 tables	790
Intensive treatment unit/ coronary care	4 beds	140	6 beds	210	8 beds	280	8 beds	280
Laboratories incl. post-mortem	1 dept	110	1 dept	260	1 dept	390	1 dept	390
Functional diagnosis	included	–	included	270	included	–	1 dept	160
Rehabilitation	1 dept	135	1 dept	270	1 dept	405	1 dept	540
Obstetric delivery	1 dept	180	1 dept	365	1 dept	365	1 dept	480
Day care	1 dept	120	1 dept	235	1 dept	355	1 dept	450
		1195		2230		2830		3610
D Administration								
Central administration	100 beds	290	200 beds	320	300 beds	345	400 beds	460
Medical administration	100 beds		200 beds		300 beds	60	400 beds	80
Admission/reception etc.	100 beds	110	200 beds	225	300 beds	340	400 beds	450
Staff facilities	100 beds	140	200 beds	280	300 beds	425	400 beds	560
		540		825		1170		1550
E Industrial								
Kitchen	100 beds	260	200 beds	410	300 beds	445	400 beds	480
Laundry	100 beds	260	200 beds	–	300 beds	–	400 beds	480
Stores	100 beds	150	200 beds	170	300 beds	255	400 beds	340
Sterile:/disinfect:	100 beds	100	200 beds	160	300 beds	280	400 beds	280
Pharmacy	100 beds	80	200 beds	160	300 beds	240	400 beds	420
Workshops	100 beds	120	200 beds	200	300 beds	300	400 beds	420
Plantrooms	100 beds	230	200 beds	250	300 beds	280	400 beds	370
		940		1350		1800		2790
H Circulation (percentages are of net space)	(60%)	2715	(60%)	5080	(60%)	6810	(60%)	9190
Total gross space	108 beds	7240	217 beds	13545	298 beds	18160	409 beds	24510
Space per bed		67m²		63m²		61m²		60m²

1.8

Development of modern planning strategies

1.8 St Thomas' Hospital, London UK 1867, by Henry Currey; photograph taken before the extensive redevelopments (pp. 34, 110). Over 600 beds in six 3-storey pavilions linked by wide ground floor corridor 900 ft long. This simple spine and pavilion plan proved ideal for the static custodial care of the time when bedside nursing was the prime activity.

1.9 Block plan of St Thomas' Hospital in 1950. The original design covered the whole of the site. The courtyards provided the only available sites for extensions (shown black) to house demands for clinical space following World War II.

1.10 Demands for more space on restricted urban sites and important technical innovations – structural frames, air-conditioning, automated elevators and conveyors, central storage and processing of food and supplies – all contributed to the development of the tower-on-podium strategy.

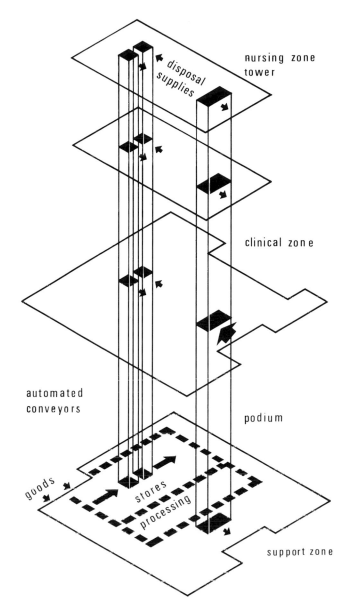

1.10

1.9

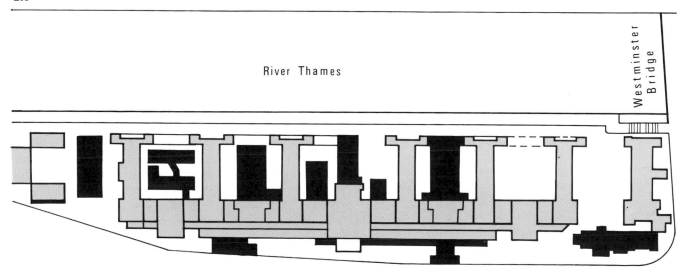

1.11   The shape of the nursing tower was primarily influenced by the design of the modern wards: see chapter 2.

The tower-on-podium design enables a precisely defined programme to be realised in one complete building operation on a restricted site within a low budget. However it is argued that this can result in buildings which do not readily respond to the need for growth and change during their lifespan, nor can they be delivered in a series of self-contained fully operational phases.

1.12, 1.13   In the early 1960s Llewelyn-Davies Weeks, the planners of Northwick Park Hospital and Clinical Research Centre, London, developed an alternative strategy which combined modern high-rise and deep-span construction with a traditional spine and pavilion layout. A number of separate open-ended buildings of varying heights and widths, to suit the requirements of the different zones, are linked at ground and basement levels by a wide corridor, or street, along which people and supplies circulate. The subdivision of functional zones into a series of separate blocks could limit the possibilities of change by means of ebb and flow between zones.

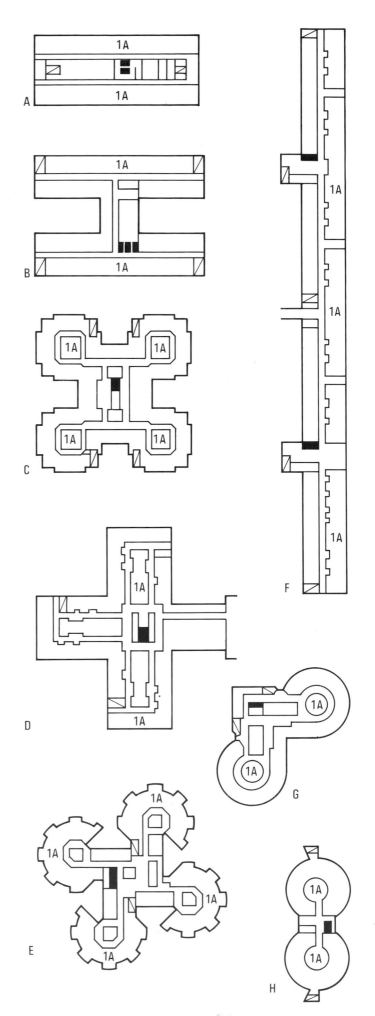

1.11

A   Etobicoke Hospital,
       Ontario, Canada
B   Mercury Hospital,
       California, USA
C   Lincoln Hospital,
       Nebraska, USA
D   Charing Cross Hospital,
       London, UK
E   Goeppingen Hospital, West
       Germany

F   Medizinische Hospital,
       Hanover, West
       Germany
G   University Hospital,
       Muenster, West
       Germany
H   Kaiser Foundation
       Hospital, USA

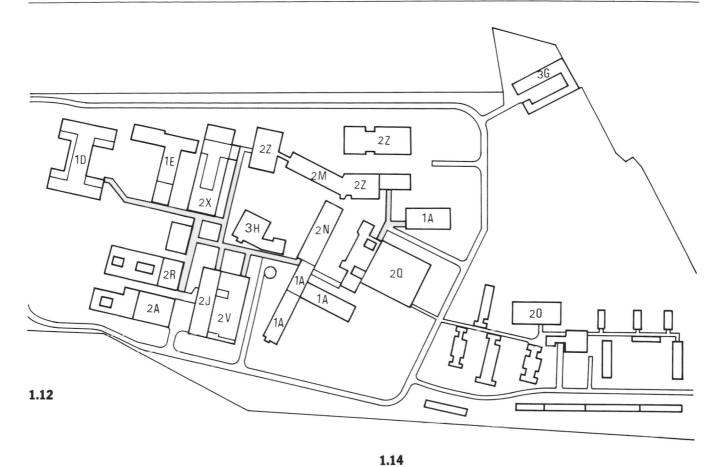

1.12

1.14

1.13/1.14 Later versions of this strategy at the
Medical Centre, Flinders University, Adelaide,
Australia, and at the Institute of Cancer Research,
UK, use more compact courtyard forms incorporating
net or lattice street systems.

1.13

Indeterminate, loose-fit building strategies are justified by the complex and ever-changing requirements of specialist teaching and research hospitals. They require large sites with plenty of space available for future expansion if needed. However, general hospitals serving large urban populations often need to be located on restricted city-block sites. With the aid of modern air-conditioning and by deep-span frame structures it becomes possible to plan a hospital like a department store, in one continuous floor occupying the whole of the site.

1.15   A typical floor of Belle Vue Hospital, New York. The space zones, nursing, clinical and support, are merged into one continuous floor of 6000m^2.

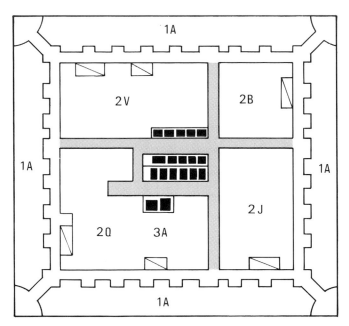

1.15

1.16

1.16   This 'universal space' system was further developed in the UK at Greenwich General Hospital, London. Here interstitial spaces accommodating engineering plant and services are sandwiched between the deep-span functional floors: 1.17. This, it is claimed, will enable the allocation of space to ebb and flow between zones according to changing need: 1.19 and 1.20. The use of interstitial services floors has influenced hospital design throughout the USA and in Europe: pages 64–67.

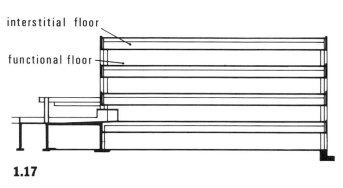

1.17

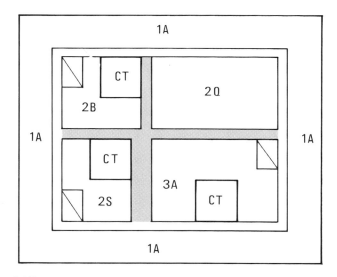

1.18

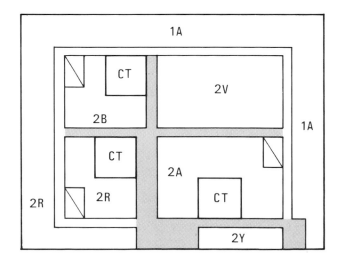

1.19

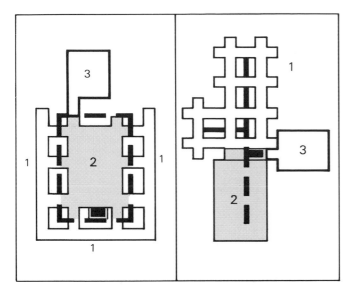

1.20

In an attempt to contain the high costs of building hospitals in multi-storey and deep-span forms a horizontal courtyard strategy was developed in the UK during the 1960s: 1.20. Instead of the vertical arrangement in the tower-on-podium the zones are related horizontally, in the form of simple two-storey structures tailored in plan and section to the particular functional and environmental needs of each zone. Two basic layouts have been developed; extended courtyard (Airedale Hospital, Yorkshire: 1.21) and compact courtyard (Frimley Park Hospital, Surrey: 1.22). These horizontal strategies have proved very influential in the UK and they are enshrined in the DHSS standard hospital development projects – Best Buy, Harness and Nucleus: pages 55 to 63. Recently a number of new hospitals elsewhere in Europe and in the Middle East are being designed using similar layouts: pages 59 and 63.

1.21

1.22

1.23   Diagram showing the relationships between the three zones and indicating approximate proportions of space allocations in a typical modern general hospital. Hospital planning is primarily concerned with putting together the 30 or more separate departments to form a functional and viable whole. Functional zoning can facilitate this process. It will permit the tailoring of plan shape, volume, structure and environmental services to suit the needs of groups of departments with similar characteristics. The clinical zone requires deep-planned, high volume, uncluttered and hygienically finished spaces suitable for sophisticated equipment and support systems. The nursing zone needs an appropriate environment for fostering sick people during their brief stay in hospital. Storage and processing areas can be housed in separate structures with industrial-standard finishes, to form the support zone. Fire safety may require the separation of such high life-risk areas as the nursing zone from other high fire-risk areas such as the support zone.
Each zone should be free to grow and change without affecting the integrity of the other zones.

1.24   Since the beginning of this century various planning strategies have been devised to meet the

1.23

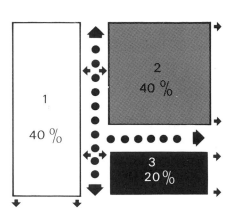

requirements of differing health needs, cultures, climates, sites and budgets. Most of these can be classified into two main groups: vertical and horizontal.
In vertical strategies (1–5 inclusive) the zones are arranged one above the other so that the movement pattern is mainly vertical.
In horizontal strategies (6–10 inclusive) the zones are linked together laterally, so that movement is mainly horizontal.

1.24

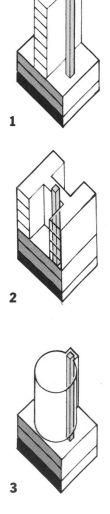
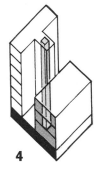

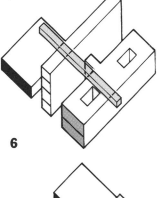
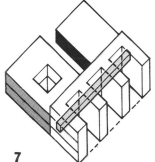
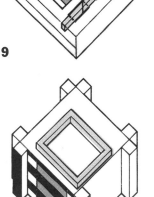
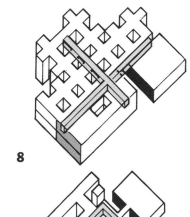

VERTICAL	HORIZONTAL
1 Simple tower-on-podium	6 Independent linked slabs
2 Complex tower-on-podium	7 Spine and pavilion
3 Radial tower-on-podium	8 Extended courtyard
4 Articulated slabs-on-podium	9 Compact courtyard
5 Vertical monolith	10 Horizontal monolith

1.25 A recent example using strategy 4. Fredriksborg Hospital, Denmark: page 32.

1.26 Desert Samaritan Hospital, Arizona, USA uses a variation of the spine and pavilion layout – strategy 7 pages 50–51.

On the following pages we illustrate examples of each of the above strategies from all over the world.

1.25

1.26

Simple tower-on-podium

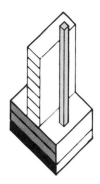

1.27

1.27   Etobicoke General Hospital, Toronto, Canada: completed 1972. 500 beds, 38,000m² on a 10.1ha site. 8-storey simple rectangular tower (1.28) on 2-storey deep-plan podium (1.29). Typical Friesen hospital designed around a highly automated materials handling system. 72 beds per floor arranged in 4-bed, 2-bed and single rooms. Very compact clinical zone includes combined obstetric delivery suite and operating theatre suite.

1.28

1.29

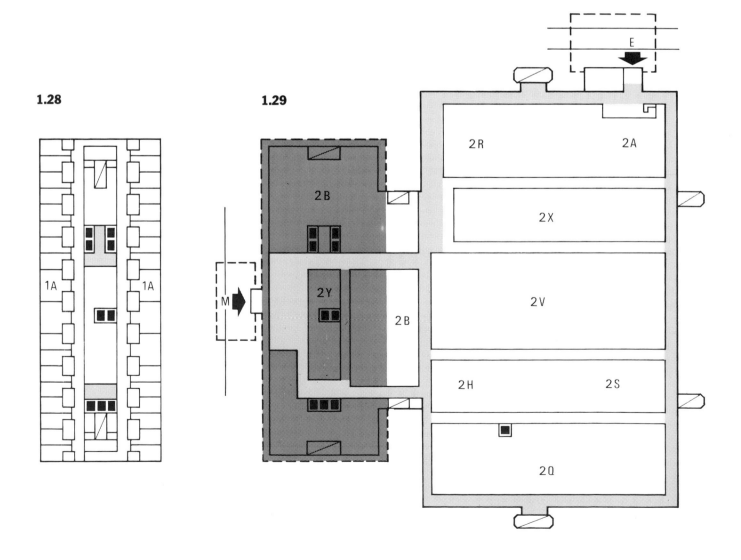

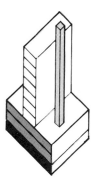

1.30

1.30 Marienhospital, Gelsenkirchen, West Germany: completed 1977, 600 beds. Gross floor space per bed 68m². 7-storey tower (1.31) on 3-storey podium (1.32). 78 beds per floor arranged mainly in 3-bed rooms.

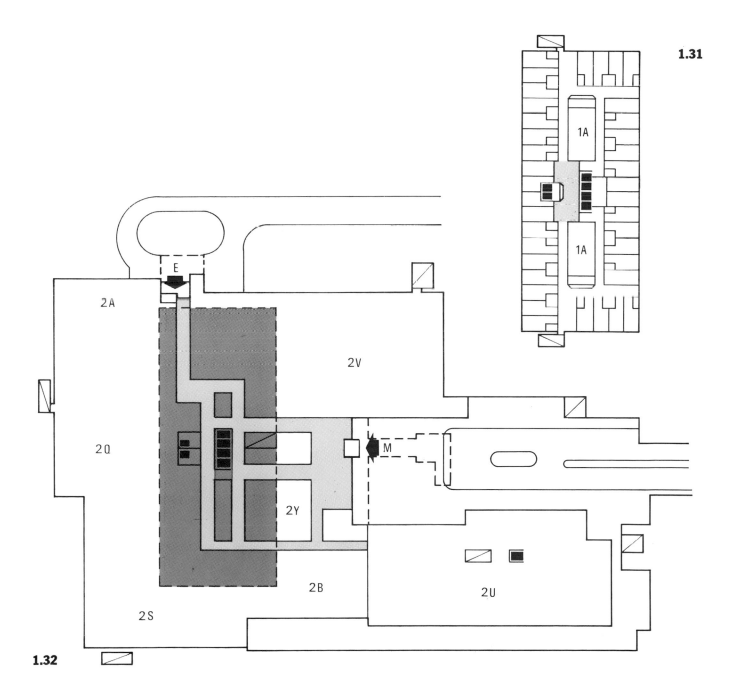

1.31

1.32

Complex tower-on-podium

1.33   Lister General Hospital, Stevenage, UK completed 1972: 543 beds; gross area per bed 75m² 7-storey, 4-winged nursing tower (1.34) with 60 beds per floor. Extensive 2-storey podium (1.35) accommodates clinical and support zones.

1.36, 1.37   Lincoln General Hospital, Nebraska, USA: here wings are deep-planned to form four separate radial ward units, each of 20 beds. Typical compact, economical, tower-on-podium layout on a small urban site.

1.33

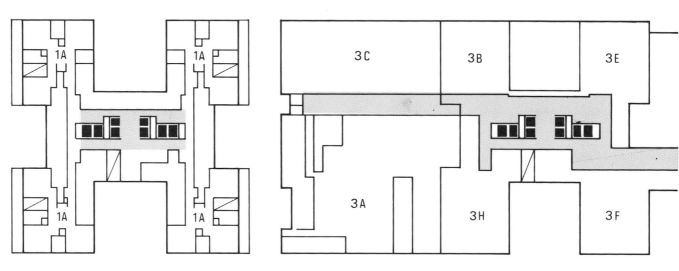

1.34

1.35

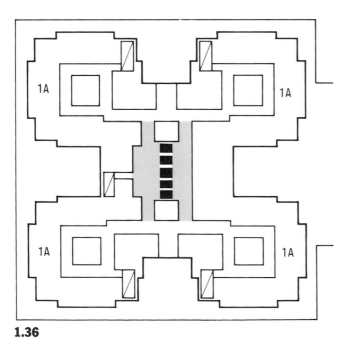

1.36

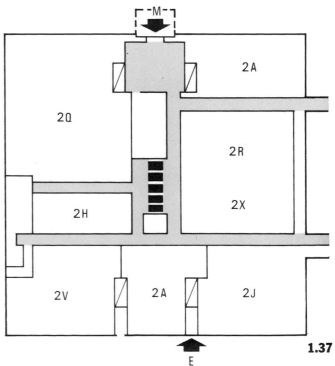

1.37

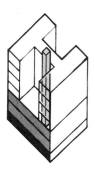

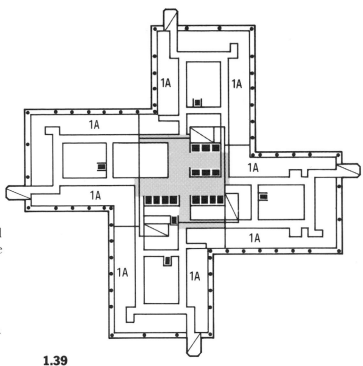

1.38   Royal Free Hospital, London, UK: completed 1976. 843 bed teaching hospital on a high density site in central London. 9-storey cruciform tower (1.39) accommodates up to 112 beds per floor. 5-storey podium houses clinical and support zones. One of a number of large teaching hospitals planned during 1965–75, the period of growth in the UK. Gross area per bed 170m².

1.39

1.38

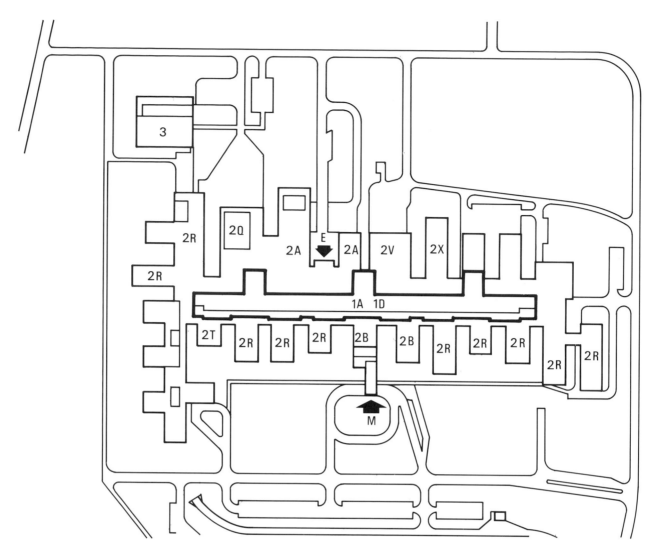

1.40

1.40   Sundsvall Hospital, Sweden: completed 1975. Huge State General Hospital serving 268,000 population. 1084 beds in 8-storey slab. Podium accommodates clinical and support zones arranged in a series of open-ended sections at right angles to main slab. Planning, design and construction covered a period of nearly 20 years.

1.41–1.43   Varberg Hospital, Sweden: completed 1973. 747 beds, gross floor area 59,166m². Long slab block accommodating nursing zone over extensive podium arranged around garden courts.
Sundsvaal and Varberg are typical examples of large-scale general hospitals built in Northern Europe in the period of rapid expansion (1965–1975) in response to the demand for a high concentration of all specialities (including psychiatry) on one site serving very large population catchment areas. The capital costs of building these vast institutions are now becoming unacceptable.

1.41

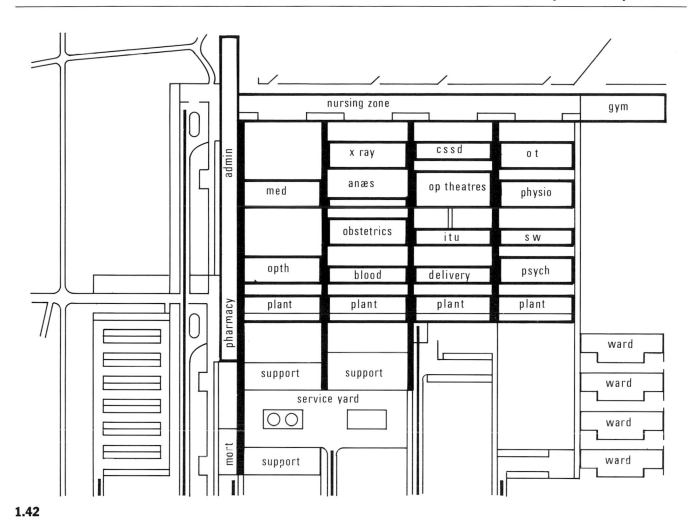

1.42

1.43

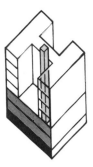

1.44, 1.45 Hvidovre Hospital, Copenhagen, Denmark: completed 1978. A successful attempt to break down the scale and visual impact of a very large (94,000m^2) 1200-bed general and teaching hospital.

1.46, 1.47 Instead of a 10-storey nursing tower the designers have placed five 2-storey slabs over a sunken 2-storey podium landscaped into the ample site. A sixth 2-storey block accommodates teaching and research facilities.

1.48 Section showing vertical relationship of nursing, clinical and support zones. The subway houses the automatic transport system for distribution of all supplies.

1.44

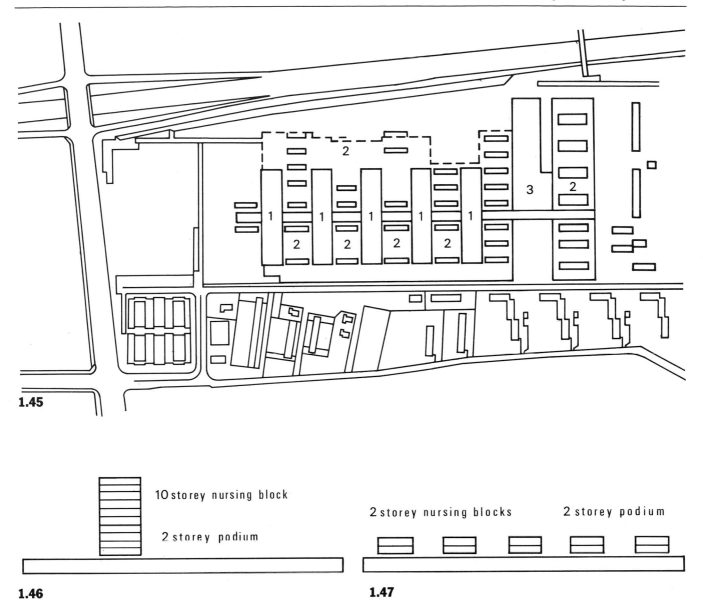

1.45

10 storey nursing block

2 storey podium

1.46

2 storey nursing blocks   2 storey podium

1.47

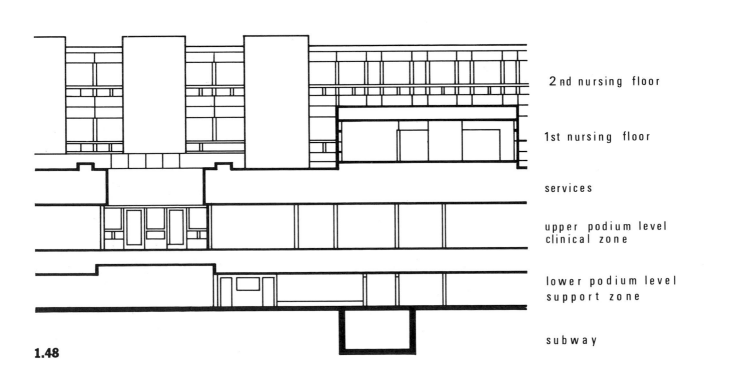

2nd nursing floor

1st nursing floor

services

upper podium level
clinical zone

lower podium level
support zone

subway

1.48

Radial tower-on-podium

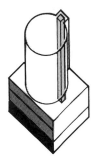

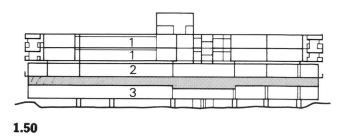

1.50

1.49   Kreiskrankenhaus, Nordenham, W. Germany: completed 1974. Compact, highly ingenious plan with four interlocking radial ward units providing 247 beds on two floors above a two-storey rectangular podium housing clinical and support zones.
Note interstitial service space (1.50) separating the tower from the podium, (1.52) thereby freeing the clinical zone from the services and structure of the nursing zone (1.51).

1.53, 1.54   Fraubrunnon District Hospital, Jegensdorf, Switzerland: completed 1978. Small, very compact and economical 100-bed hospital; 59m² per bed. 1.53: Nursing tower, 1.54: podium.

1.55   Model of Sion Hospital, Switzerland, now under construction. Larger 300-bed version of Jegensdorf using identical floor plans for nursing zone.

1.49

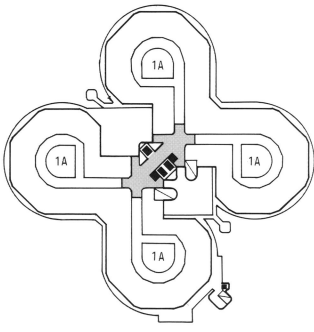

1.51

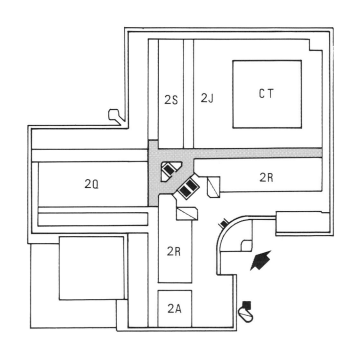

1.52

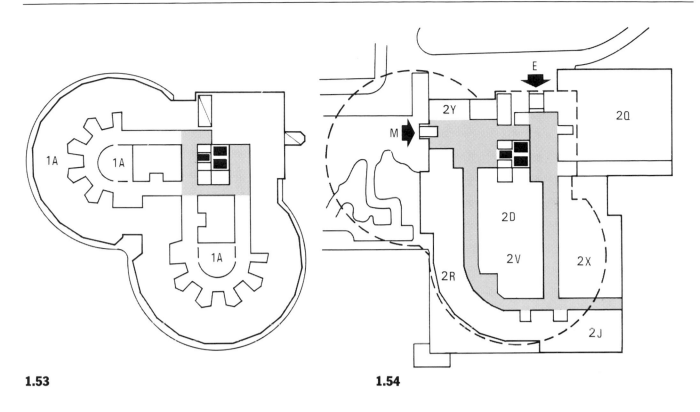

1.53

1.54

1.55

Articulated slabs-on-podium

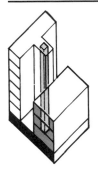

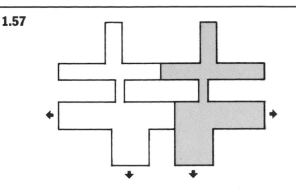

1.57

1.56   Frederiksborg Hospital, Elsinore, Denmark: first phase (1.57) completed 1976. 180 beds with clinical and support services for 240 beds (1.58). Gross floor area 37,600m². The hospital is planned to be extended up to a total of 720 beds.

1.56

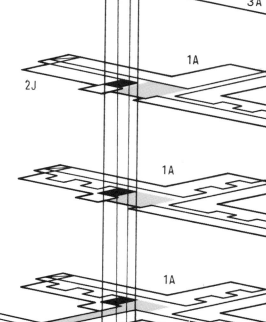

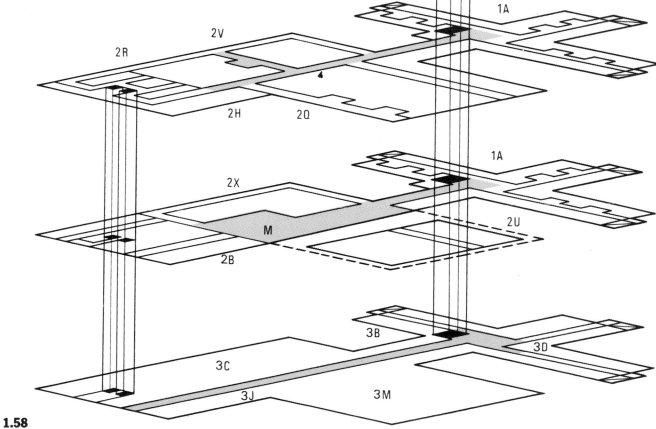

1.58

1.59   Santa Fe Hospital complex, Valencia, Spain: view and first floor plan (1.60) of the central acute care block accommodating 1100 beds and full supporting services. Part of a central campus of hospitals providing comprehensive specialist services (including maternity, paediatrics, burns, orthopaedics etc.) for 1.5 million insured workers and their families: a total of 2,200 beds on one site. This remarkable development was completed in a period of 4 years and at a very low capital cost. Gross area per bed 50m^2.

1.60

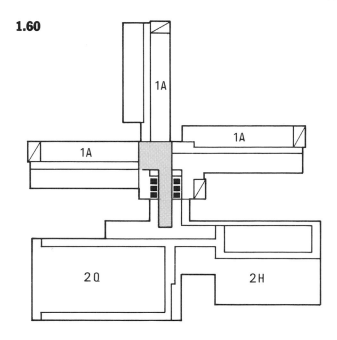

1.59

1.61

1.62

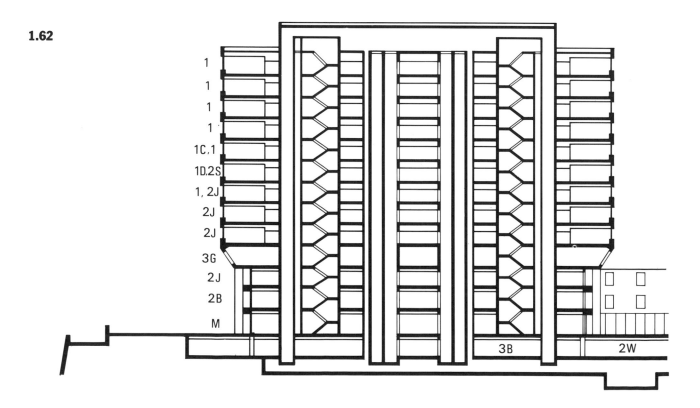

Vertical monolith

1.61, 1.62 St Thomas' Hospital, London, UK: main phase of major rebuilding scheme completed 1976, 630-bed teaching hospital (over 100,000m^2 gross floor area) on 3.6 ha site.

1.63, 1.64 St Mary's Hospital, London, UK: model and block schematic plan of first phase. 300-bed teaching hospital (33,500m^2) now under construction.

These are high density solutions to the problem of rebuilding two of London's famous teaching hospitals on very restricted sites. The tower and podium merge into one deep-planned monolithic form. The vertical relationships of the zones are preserved by the insertion of a continuous floor of plant between the nursing and clinical zones. Distribution of services is arranged by means of large vertical shafts at regular intervals. Compare with horizontal monolith.

1.63

1.64

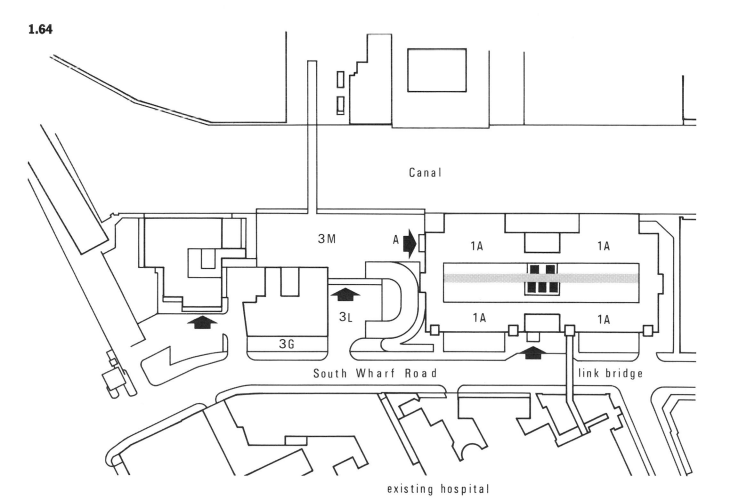

Canal

3M   A   1A   1A

3L

3G

1A   1A

South Wharf Road   link bridge

existing hospital

1.65 Alexander S. Onassis Memorial Cardiac
Surgery Centre, Athens, Greece: 100-bed specialist
hospital. Vertical arrangement of nursing, clinical and
support zones planned in a monolithic block around a
central atrium (1.66, 1.67).

1.65

1.66

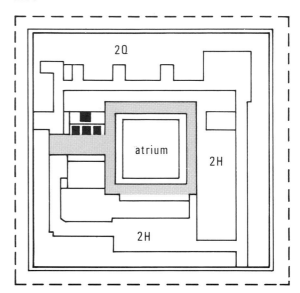

1.67

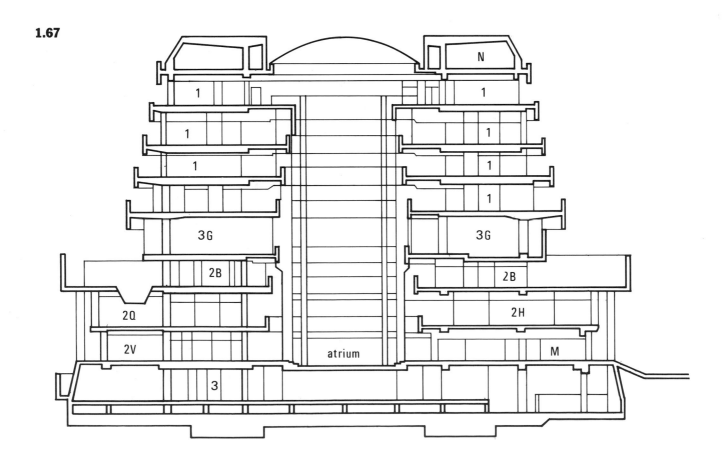

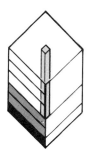

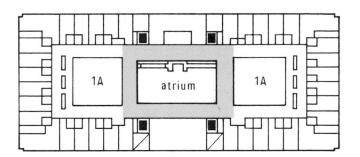

1.68

1.68–1.71 Eisenhower Memorial Hospital, California, USA. Prestigious 140-bed (10,500m²) private hospital funded by Mr Bob Hope, the American comedian. 4-storey monolith with central atrium.

1.69

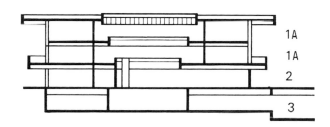

1A
1A
2
3

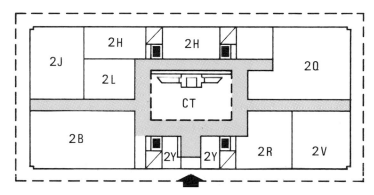

1.70

1.71

1.72

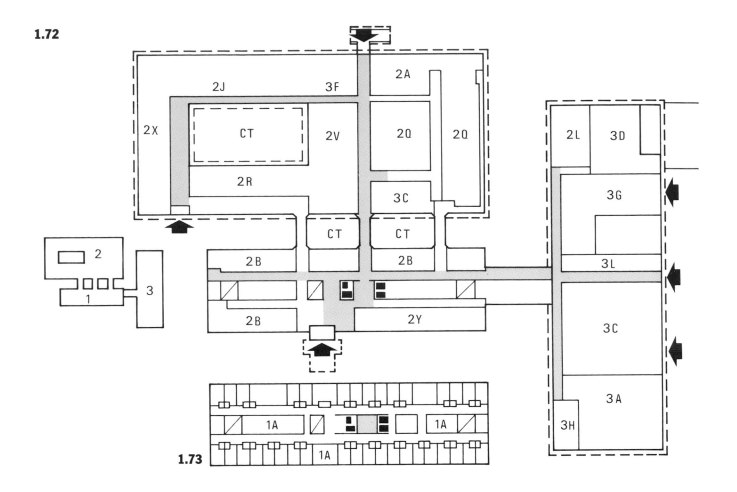

1.73

1.74

Independent linked slabs

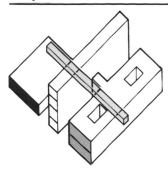

A simple strategy which allocates each of the three basic zones, nursing, clinical and support, to a purpose-designed structure. The three elements are linked horizontally, usually at ground level, by means of a wide corridor.

1.72–1.74   Beaune Hospital, France: completed 1970. 309-bed (18,850m²) general hospital. Planned and built in a total period of 20 months by a turnkey

building and engineering contractor briefed directly by the State Government. Became the model for a number of hospital projects in France and overseas.

1.75   Standard 240-bed acute hospital, Algeria: similar to the Beaune plan; approximately 100 of these small economical hospitals (60m² per bed) are being built throughout Algeria.

1.75

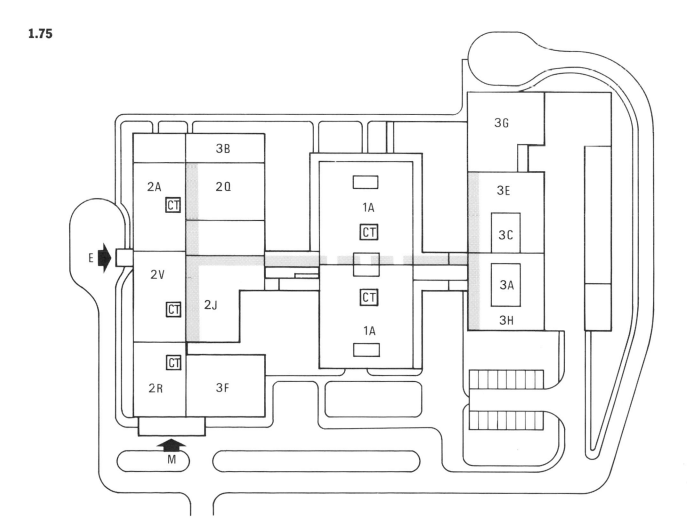

1.76

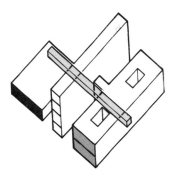

1.76 Khon Kaen University Hospital, Thailand: phased development up to a total of 700 beds. Parallel slabs of linear form and varying storey heights orientated to face north/south away from the low sun and into the prevailing winds (1.77). Air-conditioning is confined to certain parts of the clinical zone. Most buildings are naturally ventilated. Central spine corridor (1.78) with easy gradient ramp system allows free movement of people and goods without dependence on lifts. Large site will permit most buildings to be extended independently.

1.77

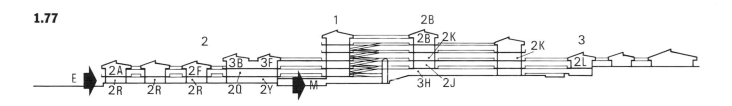

1.78

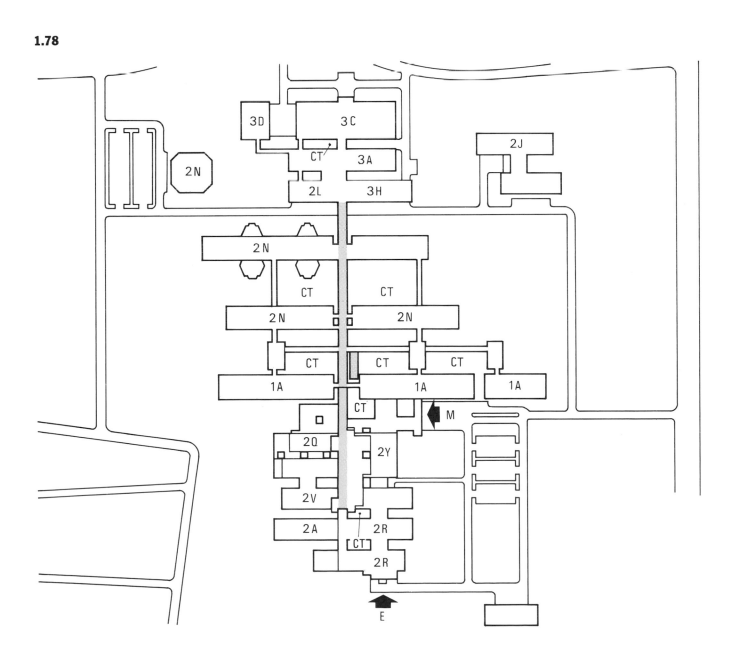

1.81

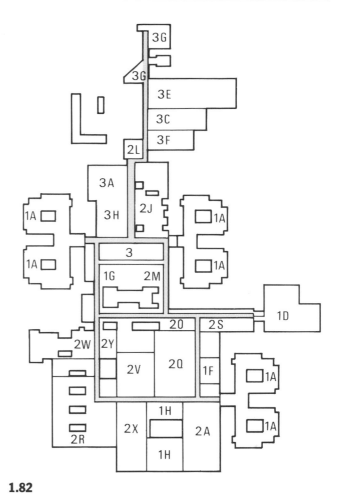

1.82

1.80

Spine and pavilion

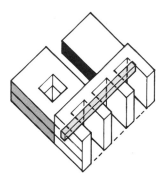

The growth period (1965–1975) saw the demand for large hospitals which could rapidly double in size to accommodate a comprehensive range of specialities serving up to 300,000 population. In the UK the 'one-shot' compact, tower-on-podium layout was soon abandoned in favour of horizontal strategies, like the spine and pavilion, which envisaged future extension of all zones, limited only by the 30–40 acre sites. This type of layout was exported overseas, particularly to the Middle East.

1.79   York Hospital, UK: completed 1975. 800-bed general hospital. Multi-storey nursing zone incorporates the spine (1.80) from which project open-ended pavilions containing the clinical zone.

1.81, 1.82   South Teeside General Hospital, UK: first phase completed 1983; 1200 beds. Nursing zone consists of a number of separate multi-storey pavilions (1.83) linked together by the clinical zone which forms the spine.

1.79

1.83

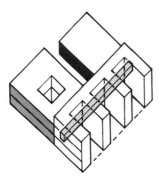

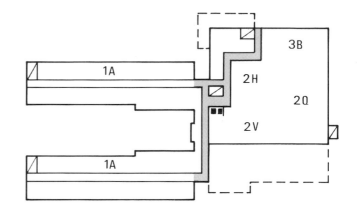

1.84, 1.85 Alexandra Hospital, Manchester, UK: 150-bed private hospital, completed in 1982 in a period of 12 months. Simple spine-and-pavilion layout. Contrasting built forms (linear, naturally ventilated pavilions; deep-plan spine) clearly reflect differing environmental needs of nursing and clinical zones. First floor above, ground floor below.

1.86, 1.87 Academisch Ziekenhuis, Utrecht, Holland: 1000-bed teaching hospital, currently under construction. Multi-storey spine-and-pavilion strategy envisages future growth for this already vast institution ($190m^2$ per bed). Today there are few nations which can afford to build hospitals of this size in one operation.

1.88–1.90 King Faisal Specialist Hospital, Riyadh, Saudi Arabia: completed 1974. 240-bed private hospital. Nursing zone consists of single bedrooms, each with en-suite bathrooms arranged in a series of pavilions, some projecting from and some parallel with a main spine corridor incorporated in the clinical zone.

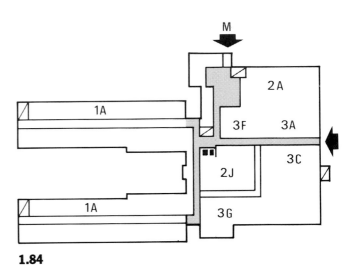

1.84

1.85

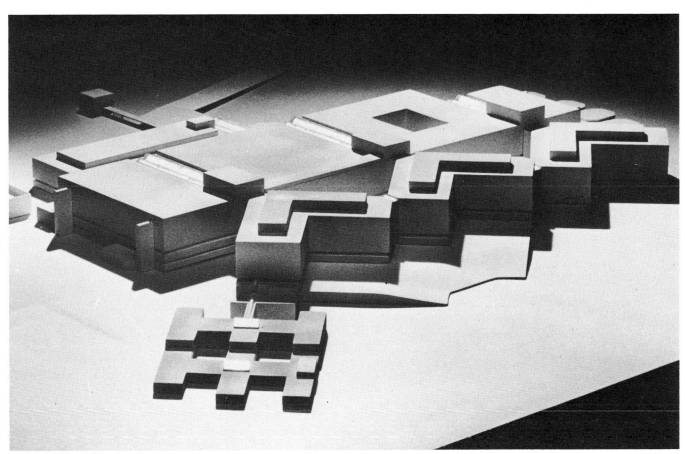

1.86

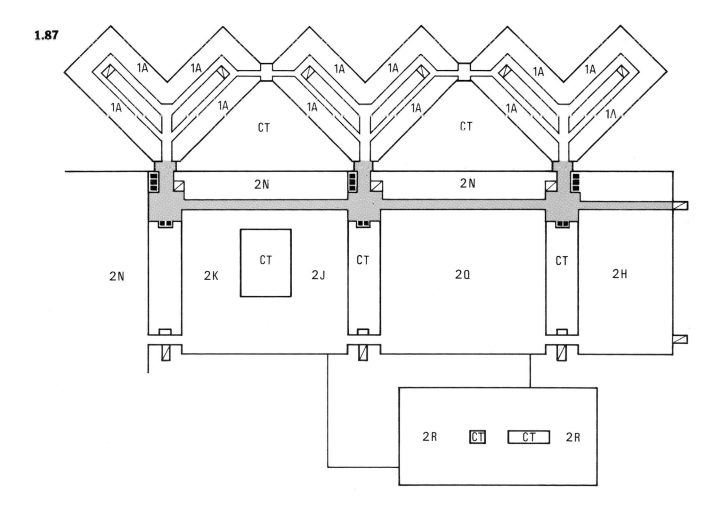

1.87

1.88

1.89

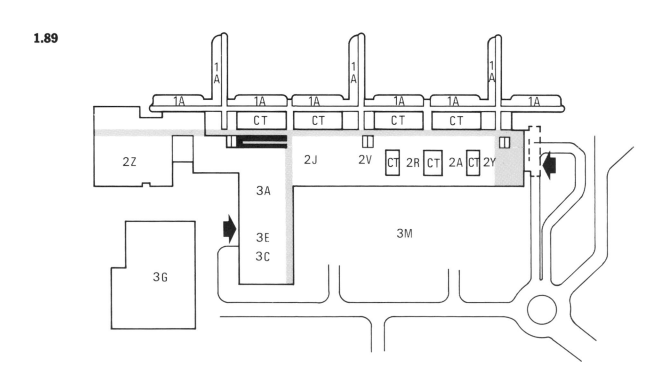

1.90

1.91

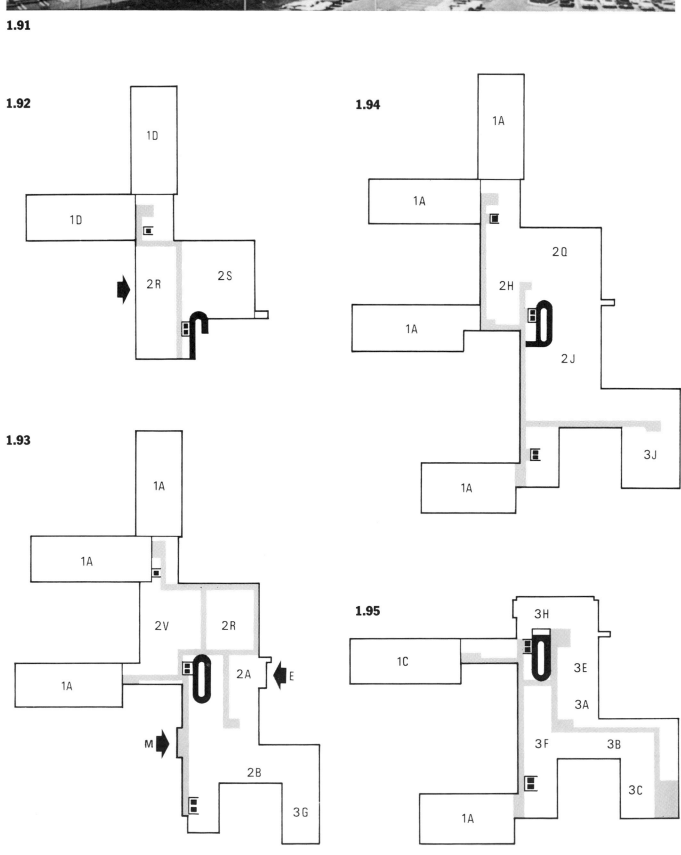

1.92

1D

1D

2R   2S

1.93

1A

1A

2V   2R

1A   2A   E

M

2B

3G

1.94

1A

1A

2Q

2H

1A   2J

3J

1A

1.95

3H

1C   3E

3A

3F   3B

3C

1A

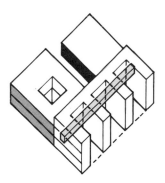

to 600 beds. In the past most hospitals in USSR have been designed using tower-on-podium or vertical monolith strategies. Compare with the previous example.

1.91 Greater Baltimore Medical Centre, USA: completed 1966, 400 beds, extendable up to 600 beds. Area per bed 70m². Large sloping site permits separate access to each zone at various levels (levels 1–4: 1.92–1.95). A rare example of this type of horizontal development in the USA. Compact four-storey deep-planned spine contains the clinical zone. The support zone is located at the top level. Three to four-storey pavilions housing the nursing zone are arranged around two sides of the spine. This will permit further pavilions to be added as well as extensions to the clinical zone. Instead of the usual automated supplies system the scheme features distribution of goods by locomotive trains using a spiral ramp.

1.96, 1.97 Kapsukas Hospital, Lithuania, USSR: experimental 360-bed general hospital with expansion

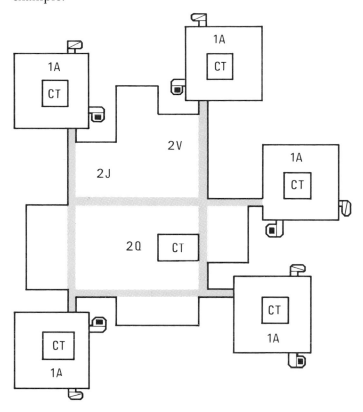

1.97

1.96

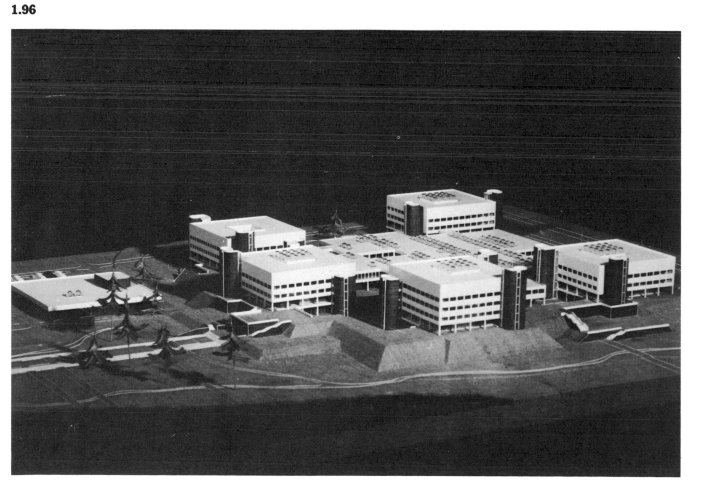

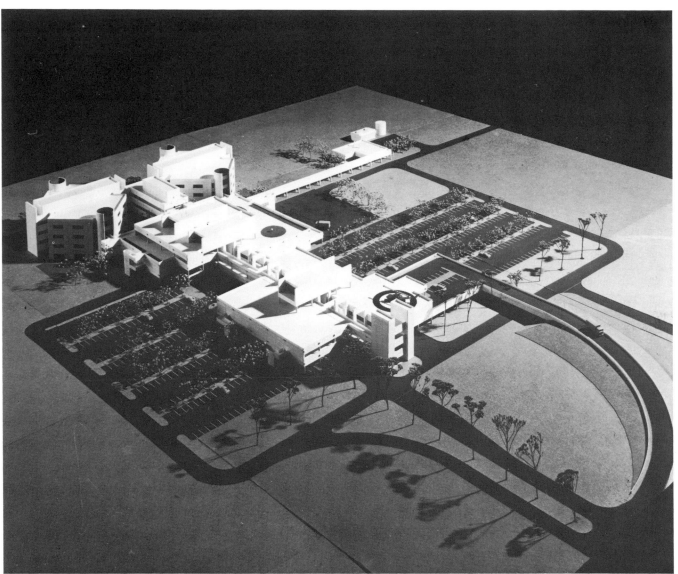

1.98

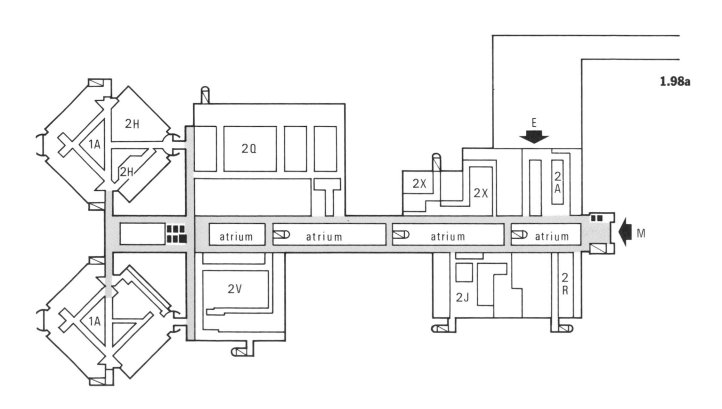

1.98a

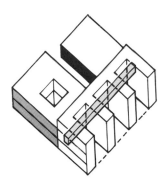

1.98–1.100   Desert Samaritan Hospital, Arizona, USA: first phase, 275 beds, completed 1977. Provides for expansion up to 1100 beds. Recent American example of the use of the spine and pavilion strategy to provide for open ended incremental growth; 1.98a shows first floor, much influenced by the British approach. However at more than 90m^2 per bed the space standards are 30 per cent higher than in UK.

1.99

1.100

Extended courtyard

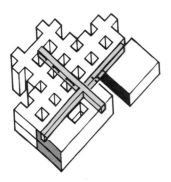

Similar to the spine and pavilion layout but the accommodation is planned around open courtyards instead of separate pavilions. The height is normally limited to 4 storeys; few examples exceed two storeys. The zones are linked horizontally at upper levels as well as at ground floor level, via a central spine corridor system which affords easy access for patients, visitors and goods to all departments. Dependence on lifts is much reduced.

1.101, 1.102 Wexham Park Hospital, Slough, UK: completed 1966; 300-bed general hospital. Fully exploits advantages presented by this type of single-storey layout: natural light and ventilation from rooflights and landscaped courtyards, domestic scale, ease of evacuation in case of fire, provision for future extension, simple load-bearing structure.

1.103 Ninewells Hospital and Medical School, Dundee, Scotland: 800-bed teaching hospital, planned in 1963, opened in the late 1970s. 175m^2 per bed. The extended courtyard layout cleverly exploits the large sloping site (1.104, 1.105) to give close horizontal relationships between the functional zones. The implementation of this project was beset by most of the problems discussed in chapter 5.

1.101

1.102

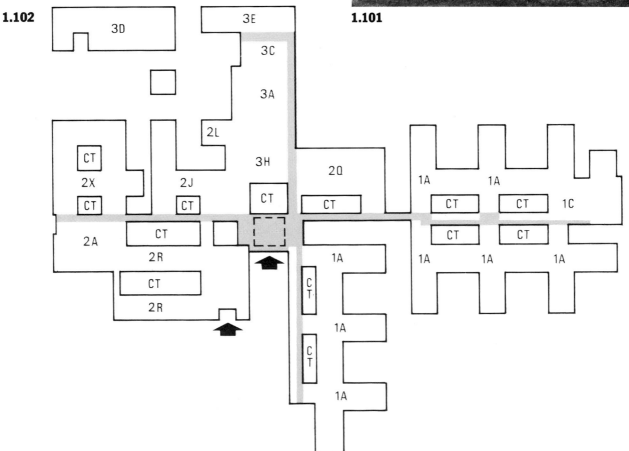

1.103

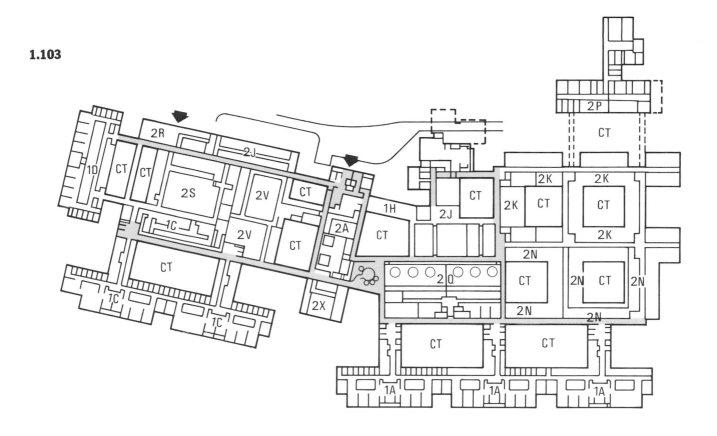

1.104

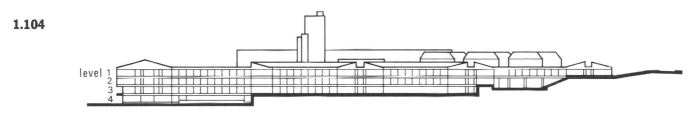

1.105

1.106

1.107

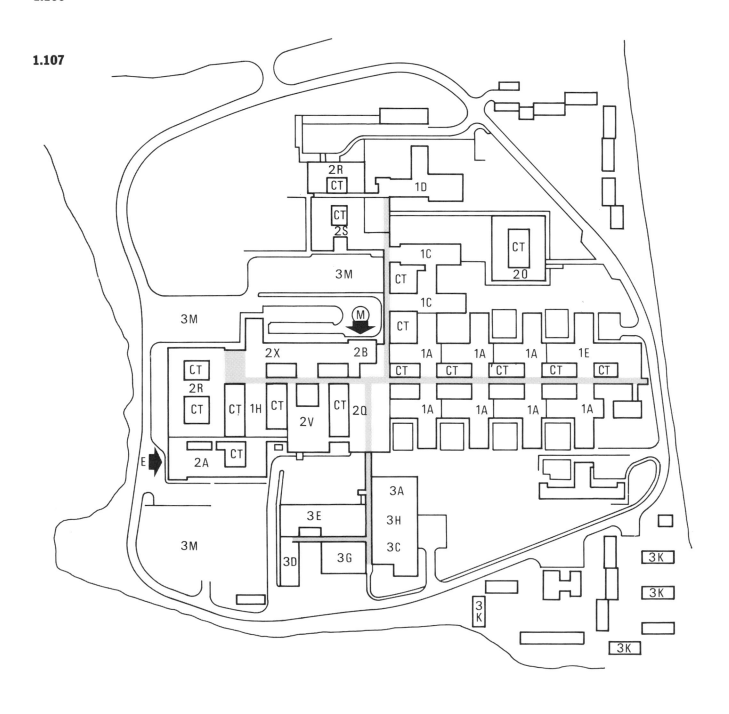

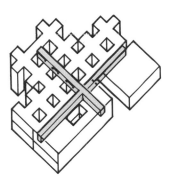

1.106   Airedale Hospital, Yorkshire, UK: completed 1971; 600 beds. 42,000m² excluding staff residences. Movement of patients to and from acute wards and the clinical zone (emergency, operating, X-ray and rehabilitation departments) takes place at the upper level without the need for lifts (1.107). Goods and services from the support zone are routed at the lower level.

The Harness concept was an attempt by the UK Department of Health to standardise hospital planning and building on a national scale rather like a giant game of Lego. Pre-planned departments are hung on a horizontal 'harness' of main corridors and service ducts (similar to the Airedale scheme). This massive programme, devised at the peak of the growth period, proved too ambitious and was superseded by Best Buy and Nucleus.

1.109

1.108   Stafford General Hospital, and Southlands Hospital, Shoreham, (1.109), both 300 beds, were among the few schemes executed under this programme in the UK.

1.108

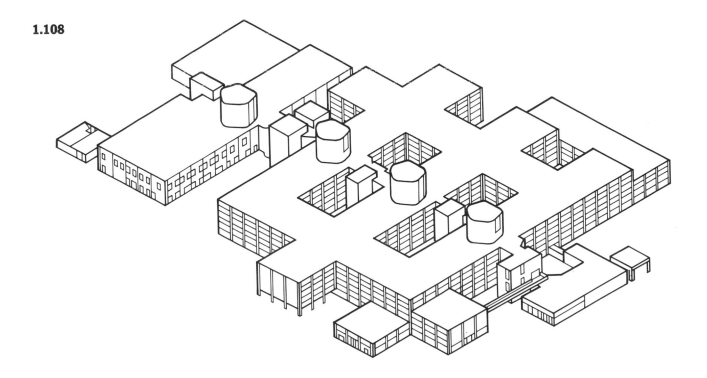

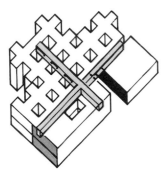

The Nucleus programme was developed in response to the demand for containment of the scale and cost of acute care hospitals. It provides nationally for a largely pre-planned initial phase, or nucleus, of a general hospital, which could subsequently be extended if required. The size of the nucleus is limited to around 300 beds (18,000m²) and it is designed to be fully operational in its own right.

1.112, 1.113 Maidstone General Hospital: completed 1983. Ideally the nursing zone is located on the upper level to take maximum advantage of natural daylight.

1.114 St Mary's Hospital, Isle of Wight, UK: under construction; 200-bed general hospital. Fan type layout of standard nucleus templates enables length of spine corridor to be reduced.
In addition to the 50 hospitals completed, under construction or projected using the Nucleus standard modular plan, there are a number of examples in the UK and overseas which show the influence of the Nucleus strategy.

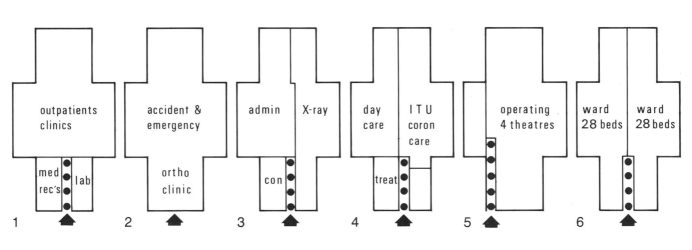

1.110 Cruciform templates contain standard departments; each template is approximately 1000m² in area and is based on a 16.2m module.

1.111 Block schematic plan of Maidstone General Hospital, UK illustrating how the templates, numbered 1–6, are assembled into a two-storey courtyard development arranged on either side of a central spine corridor system which also carries the main services distribution and plant rooms. Unnumbered templates indicate how the hospital can be extended up to 800 beds.

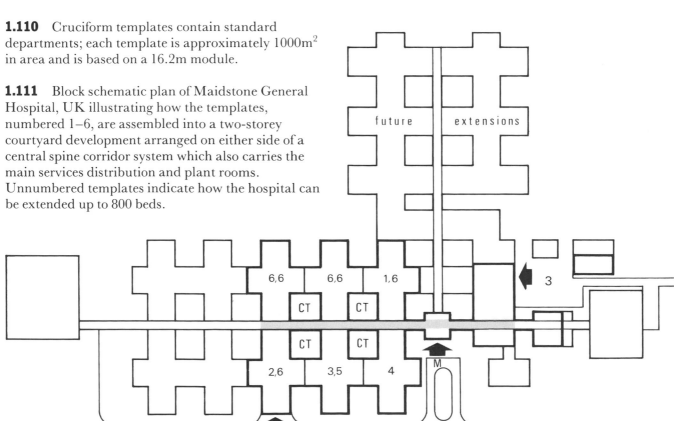

1.112

1.113

1.114

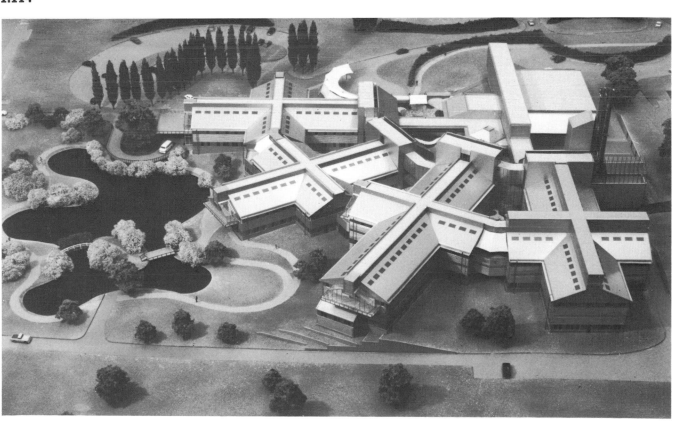

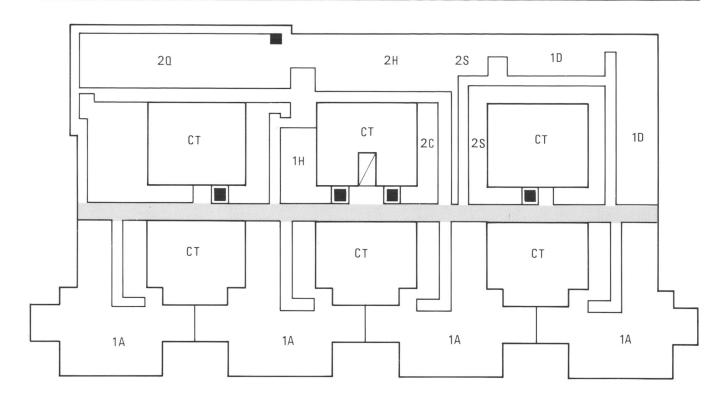

1.115

1.116

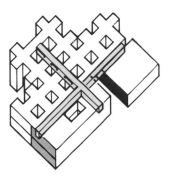

1.115, 1.116 Weston-super-Mare, General Hospital, UK: 250 beds (20,000m²); three-storey complex with nursing zone on one side of central spine corridor and clinical zone on the other.

1.117, 1.118 Central Emergency Hospital, Abu Dhabi, UAE: 250-bed specialist hospital linked to an existing 300-bed general hospital. Influence of Nucleus can be clearly seen.

1.117

1.118

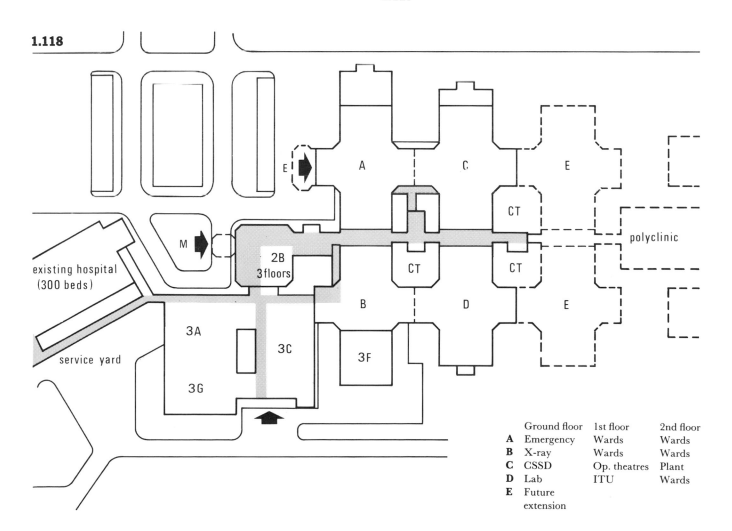

existing hospital
(300 beds)

service yard

2B
3floors

3A

3C

3G

3F

M

E

A

C

E

CT

CT

CT

B

D

E

polyclinic

	Ground floor	1st floor	2nd floor
A	Emergency	Wards	Wards
B	X-ray	Wards	Wards
C	CSSD	Op. theatres	Plant
D	Lab	ITU	Wards
E	Future extension		

1.119

1.120

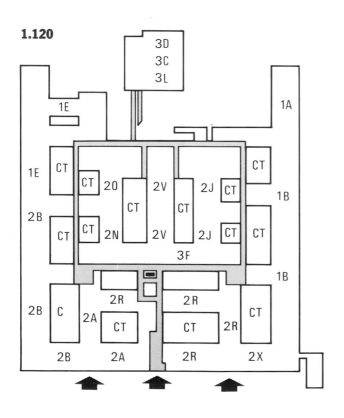

1.121

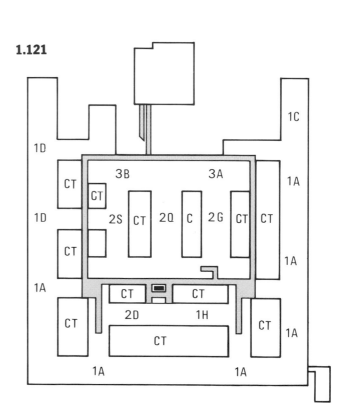

Compact courtyard

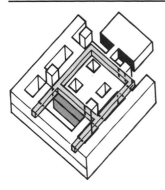

1.119–1.123   In 1967 the UK Department of Health initiated a development project which deliberately sought to reduce the content, size and cost of the typical general hospital needed to serve a population of 170,000. The resulting design concept, known as Best Buy, was built simultaneously in two separate regions of the UK: at Frimley, Surrey, and Bury St Edmunds, Suffolk. Both hospitals contain 550 beds and full supporting services (30,000m²). The compact two-storey courtyard layout (135×135m) was achieved by wrapping the nursing zone around three sides of the clinical zone. Between the two zones is a square ring-main corridor. Ramps, one up, one down, connect the two levels to the separate single-storey support zone.

1.122

1.123

1.124   Level A

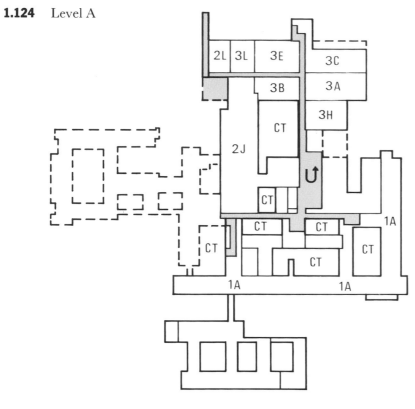

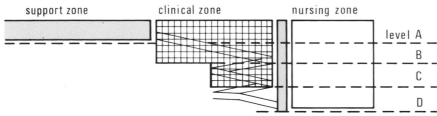

1.125   Level

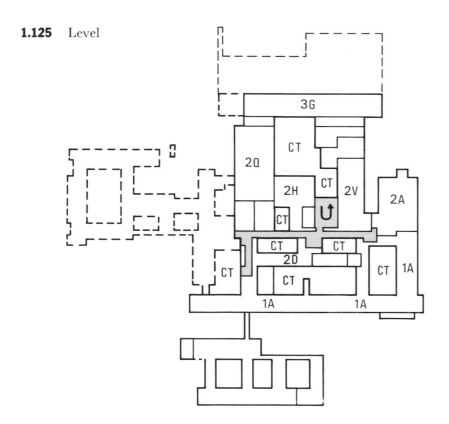

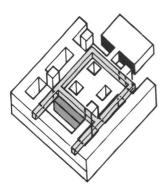

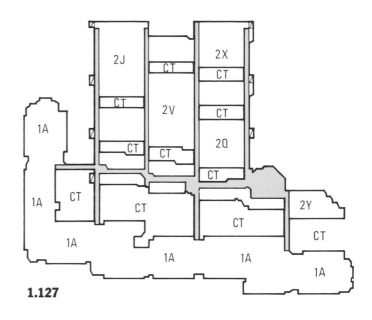

1.127

1.124–1.126   Rotherham General Hospital, UK: first phase 520 beds completed 1979. A stretched version of Best Buy plan, to accommodate over 1100 beds. Layout exploits large sloping site to obtain external access to all four levels. The support zone is located at the top level. A locomotive train system operates via a spiral ramp serving all four levels.

1.127   State Hospital, Reinickendorf, West Berlin: under construction; 620 beds in nursing zone wrapped around 2-storey clinical zone. Similar to Rotherham layout.

1.126

Horizontal monolith

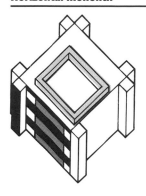

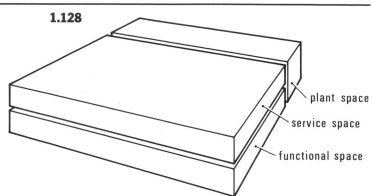

1.128

plant space

service space

functional space

Universal space strategies incorporating interstitial floors usually involve high capital costs. Overall floor areas (including sub-floors) are in the range 130 to 300m² per bed. However, it is claimed that sub-floors eliminate the need for definitive programmes and permit easy installation of engineering services and equipment. These systems were popular during the growth period (1965–75) and various examples were built in the USA and the UK.

1.128–1.130 Veterans' Administration Hospital, Loma Linda, California, USA: completed 1978; 500 beds with teaching and research facilities: 128m² per bed.

1.131–1.133 McMaster University Medical Centre, Ontario, Canada: completed 1973. 416-bed teaching hospital; 295m² per bed.

1.129

1.130

1.131

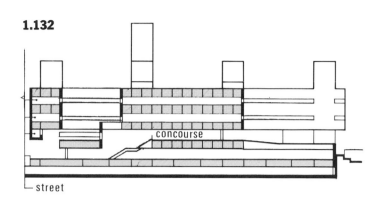

1.132

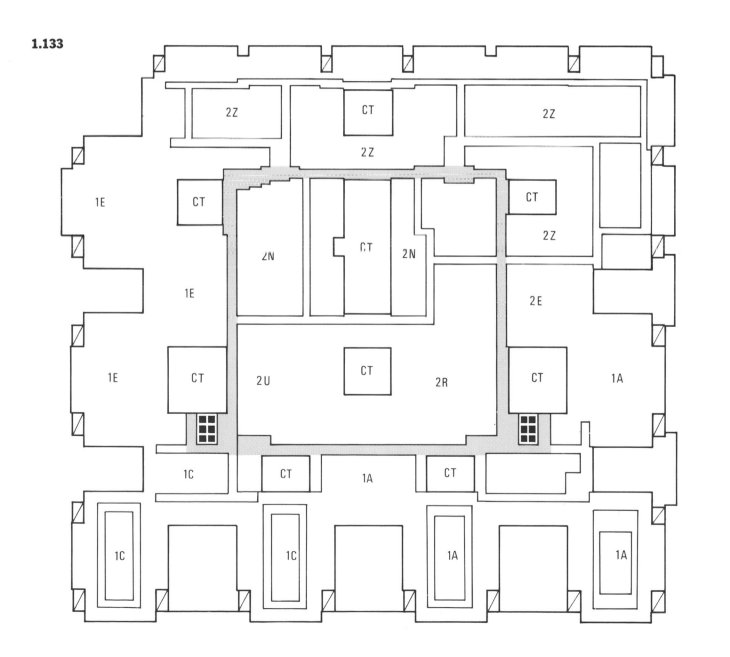

1.133

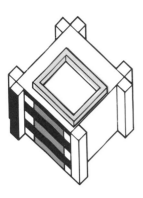

1.134–1.136   Walter Reed General Hospital, USA: a part of the US Army Medical Centre; completed 1980. Top three floors contain wards in continuous band around core of clinics. Lower floors accommodate clinical departments. Services and plant housed in interstitial floors.

1.137–1.139   Leeds General Infirmary and Medical School, Leeds, UK: teaching hospital; 1400 beds. First phase of 300 beds completed 1981. 1.137 shows typical upper floor; 1.138 is lower level.

1.134

1.135

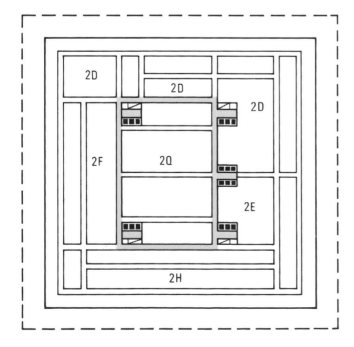

1.136

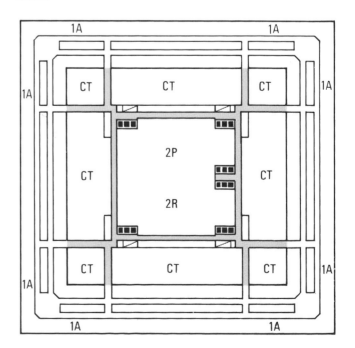

1.137

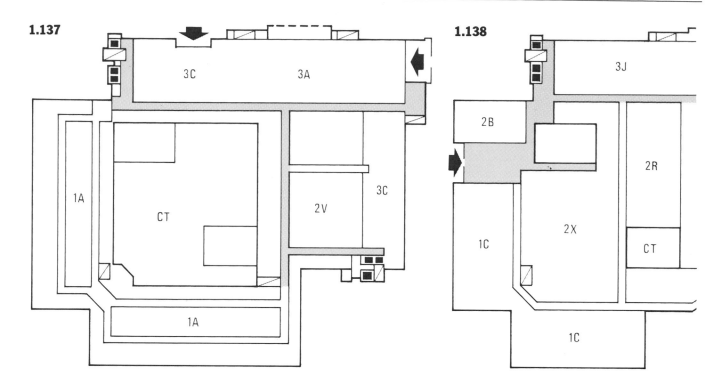

1.138

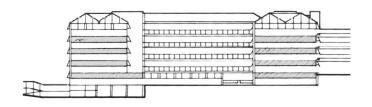

1.139

Refurbishment of existing health buildings

Recent UK policy lays emphasis on the imaginative renewal of existing buildings instead of demolition and starting from scratch.

Many of London's old hospitals have not been rebuilt as had been planned in the 1960s and the prospect of this happening in today's economic conditions is remote. Yet most of these buildings are basically sound and solid, and, given a little imagination and a willingness to compromise on the more extreme standards, can be refurbished and re-used generally at less cost than would be needed to build anew.

1.140, 1.141   Margaret Pyke Clinic, London, UK: formerly the Soho Hospital for Women, this well-known building has recently been entirely refurbished to provide medical facilities for family planning.

1.140

1.141

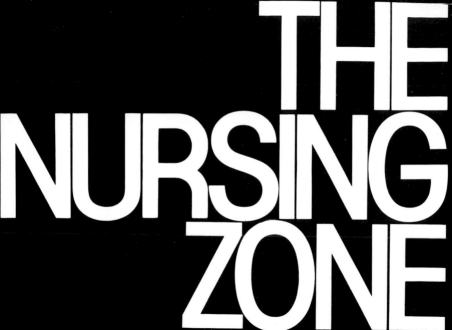

THE NURSING ZONE

Chapter 2

The nursing zone

Home care or hospital bed

Until well on into the nineteenth century it was thought that the proper place for being ill was in the home.[1]

Operations were frequently performed on the kitchen table, and day and night nurses were hired to look after the patient in his own bedroom. Only those who could not afford to pay, or whose home conditions were unsuitable, were treated in hospital.

Variety of provision

The typical hospital ward was a large room with a high ceiling, containing about 30 beds arranged at right angles to the windows, all on the lines laid down by Florence Nightingale.[2] The sister's room was at one end, the bathroom and WCs were at the other. The area per bed was about 13m[2], and the nurse complement for 30 beds was about 6. In 1910 a new arrangement was introduced at the Rigs Hospital in Copenhagen.[3] The wards were widened so that the beds could be placed parallel to the windows instead of at right angles. The sister's room was in the middle and opposite her a room for one isolated patient. Thirteen beds on either side were arranged in bays of 3 or 4, separated by 2m high partitions. The lavatories were at one end, the kitchen and linen room at the other. The Rigs arrangement had the advantage of breaking up the barrack-like appearance of the Nightingale ward and was often adopted on the continent.

In the private sector, there was a wide variety of arrangements. Those who could not afford the cost of a single room had to share with one, two or more patients. In some countries, such as Spain, rooms were designed for two beds, partly for reasons of economy and also so that members of the family could come and help nurse the patient. In the USA too, most rooms had two beds until the 1960s, when there was a gradual move towards singles.

The self-contained nursing unit

Whatever the pattern of provision, the traditional aim of the nineteenth-century hospital was to make each group of 20 to 30 beds into a self-contained unit. Each ward had its own linen, checked and counted every week; often its own cooking arrangements and its own steam kettles for sterilising instruments and dressings. All the routine work was done by student nurses

under the stern eye of the sister or charge-nurse, and supervised by matron on her daily rounds. Discipline was rigid and visiting hours restricted. Most of the medical treatment prescribed for the patients is now thought to have had little effect. Some helped; some like bleeding and purges actually did harm. By far the most important element in their recovery was the tender loving care provided by the nurses.

Privacy and early ambulation

In the USA the provision of private rooms obviously increased the overall area of the nursing zone. The addition of hotel-type accommodation and private sanitary arrangements increased it still further. But the growth of the nursing zone in the UK and in Europe has been almost as spectacular. This has been due to three factors.

The large open wards were broken up into smaller rooms or compartments containing from 2–6 beds, thus increasing the amount of circulation space needed to gain access to the beds. Second, the level of amenity offered to patients was substantially enhanced. A degree of privacy was introduced by curtains round the bed spaces, a bedside locker for personal possessions, and a comfortable chair: all helping the patient to retain some kind of personal identity. The bedside chair only found its way into the ward during World War II. Previously patients were kept in bed and only allowed up "on doctor's orders". Then it was discovered that their chances of recovery, sometimes even of survival, were improved if they sat up or better still got up and sat beside their bed. Patients often have to be encouraged to get out of bed and take a little walk on the nurse's arm. This is called early ambulation.[4] Early ambulation has led to the provision of dayrooms and additional toilets, because it is thought that a patient is more likely to be tempted to get out of bed if there is somewhere to go.

Hospital infection

The third factor which led to an increase in ancillary space within the nursing zone was the attempt to reduce infection. Infections occurring in hospitals, known as nosocomial infections, prolong the stay of between 4 and 10 per cent of patients, in all the developed countries. In 1974 the cost was estimated at $1000 million a year in the USA and $40 million in the Federal Republic of Germany in 1977.[5] The difference between the two figures is not so much an indication of relative efficiency in the two countries, as of the absence of any accepted scientific method of measurement. By any standards, it is a serious problem. Its complexity baffled and still baffles the medical profession. The origin, nature and route of transmission is still not completely understood. In lay terms, 'Do germs travel by air, or on people and things?' In the 1950s it seemed worthwhile to make an all-out attack on the airborne route. Accordingly, beds were spaced further apart, large open wards were partitioned and split up into smaller compartments, separate routes were recommended for clean and dirty traffic. Treatment rooms were recommended for every ward, each with its clean and dirty utility room on either side, and connected only by a hatch.[6] Artificial ventilation was recommended, which it was hoped (if the doors were kept shut) would prevent germs from blowing from the dirty to the clean areas. All these considerations greatly complicated the task of the hospital planner.

Physical parameters

In 1955 the Nuffield *Studies in the Functions and Design of Hospitals* was published in the UK. A multidisciplinary team under the leadership of Richard Llewelyn-Davies and John Weeks had spent five years investigating and recording almost every aspect of hospital life. It was a monumental study, bringing to light all the developments described above, and also collating and sometimes, initiating, scientific studies by outside bodies. As early as 1933, for instance, the Royal Institute of British Architects had published a report by Percy Waldrum[7] showing that the amount of sunshine falling upon a patient's bed was twice as much in a Rigs ward (with 70 per cent window area) as in the traditional Nightingale ward. The Building Research Station then measured the amount of over-heating that would result and assessed the glare[8] discomfort from different types of window. Daylight factors, standards of artificial supplementary lighting, noise levels, air-changes: everything that could be measured was measured and the results discussed with experts, sometimes far removed from the hospital scene.[9] The noise-level of 15–20 phons recommended for wards in *Post War Building Study* no 14, for instance, was once achieved at great expense; but patients only complained of 'a silence of the morgue' and eavesdropping. It was impossible for patients or staff to carry on any conversation without it being overheard by the whole ward. Nevertheless, the systematic recording of so much data was a useful exercise, and it had never before been attempted on such a scale for any other type of building. When it was also accompanied by two sets of experimental wards, at Larkfield Hospital in Scotland and Musgrove Park Hospital in Northern Ireland, demonstrating the conclusions of the team, the impact on hospital planners was considerable.

The Nuffield team discarded the traditional open ward. In its place they arranged the beds in groups of four or six in a 40-bed unit on the Rigs pattern. Eight single rooms were also provided, four of them for seriously ill or dying patients, and four on the periphery, for infectious or socially unacceptable patients. There was a treatment room with a suite of clean and dirty utility rooms, a dayroom, flower room, pantry, sister's and doctor's offices, interview room, staff's cloaks, linen, equipment and patient's clothes stores and greatly increased washing and sanitary facilities. In addition there were two nurses' stations so that 'team' nursing instead of 'task' nursing could be introduced. The nursing and ancillary staff/patient ratio was double the figure fixed by Florence Nightingale and the gross area per bed raised from the $13.4m^2$ of the Nightingale ward to $20.5m^2$.[6]

Nurses' travel distances and nursing aids

With such large increases in the area of the nursing zone, the location of the various facilities became critical. Comparative studies were therefore undertaken to determine which journeys were most frequently undertaken by staff during a typical nursing day. These were plotted in the form of string diagrams.[6] Each journey was represented by a line linking its origin and destination. The frequency of the journey could then be indicated by the density of the lines of strings on the diagram. The idea was further developed in 1960 by Pelletier and Thompson who devised a mathematical model called the Yale Traffic Index[3], which was widely used in the USA to determine the functional efficiency of layouts by computing how far staff members would have to travel in caring for their patients.

Meanwhile other changes were introduced in an attempt to ease the nurse's lot. Steam sterilisers on the ward were replaced by centrally sterilised packs and disposables. Paper sacks and plastic bags, incinerators and macerating machines took care of the waste products. Topping-up systems of supply to replenish stocks at predetermined levels were introduced. And Gordon Friesen devised an ingenious two-way cupboard, called a Nurserver, so that the nurse attending the patient could always have 'what she wanted where she wanted when she wanted,' without having to travel round the nursing unit in search of it.[10] Improved nurse-call and monitoring systems and two-way intercommunication reduced wasted journeys. But these did litle more than compensate for the increased workload. Rapid turnover and the shorter length of stay, resulting from modern methods of diagnosis and treatment, had completely transformed the nurse's life.

Progressive patient care

The Nuffield ward or continental variations of it, developed from the Rigs pattern, were enormously popular with planners. Except in the USA, where patients or their insurers demanded a private or semi-private room (the euphemism for sharing a bedroom with a total stranger), it was adopted in all the developed countries of the world. It responded well to the growing demands imposed by higher and higher standards of living. The dayrooms for instance, could be used as patients' dining rooms or to provide a choice of TV programmes. It also met some of the requirements of 'progressive patient care.' This was a concept introduced into Europe from the USA in the early 1960s. An efficient nursing unit, it was held, should be divided into three care sections; high dependency, intermediate, and self-care. Each section should have its own characteristics and the patient would 'progress' from one section to the next, as soon as he was ready for the move. After a severe operation, for instance, he would be placed in a high dependency or an intensive treatment unit. This would be designed on Nightingale principles for good observation without any sex-distinction – rather like an extension of a post-operative recovery room. 'As soon as a guy realises there is a blonde in the bed next door', it was explained, 'it is time he was moved into the intermediate care section.' This would be the traditional medium-dependency nursing unit. Finally, he would transfer to a self-care unit, designed on hotel lines, with maximum recreation facilities and minimum supervision.

Progressive patient care is sometimes compared with putting a patient on a conveyor belt. It has some of the same disadvantages. Mechanisation robs the staff of job satisfaction. The patient, too, is always

having to adjust to different nurses. And nowadays his progress is often so rapid that rather than provide a special self-care section it is easier and cheaper to send him home. But the intensive treatment and the intensive care units have come to stay, and now form a regular part of every modern hospital. If this is available, the subdivided ward can provide the continuity of nursing that a patient needs. He is first placed in a single room or in a 4 or 6 bed bay, immediately adjacent to the nurses' station, and then as his condition permits, he can move away out of sight to a distant bay, and still remain in the same nursing unit.

Cumulative effect

In retrospect, the nursing zone has come a long way from the old barrack-like basic ward tightly packed with bedridden patients. Each new development has in Europe been accommodated by adding more and more rooms or more and more square metres; while in the USA, planners tried to get back to the old nineteenth-century ideal of nursing a patient in his own home, giving him all the home comforts in a clinical setting. The problem was seen, in over-simplified terms, as 'How to make a hospital more like a hotel – home from home – the Plaza Suite, with nursing care instead of room service'.

B   Containment

The need to question all assumptions

The size of the nursing zone in Britain went up from $20.5m^2$ per bed in the 1960s to $25m^2$ and more in the 1970s. In Sweden it had risen to over $40m^2$ per bed. In the USA, where competition for patients encouraged conspicuous display, some increases were even greater. When the recession came, planners had to cut back. They looked again at the list of requirements that made for growth: precautions against airborne infection and demands for more privacy and amenity, incentives for early ambulation and so on. The first to be examined seriously was the one that had been accepted most readily – airborne infection precautions.

Controlled trials

In 1969, Whyte, Howie and Eakin of the Building Services Research Unit at the University of Glasgow reported on a four year study of Hairmyres Hospital.[11] A Nuffield type, specially air-conditioned ward had been built to compare its performance with two old Nightingale wards. One of these was subdivided on the Rigs pattern, the other was left as a control. The object of the exercise was to assess the value of air-conditioning and compartmenting. The team had some difficulty in obtaining the specified differential pressures in the new ward. They had to be certain that air would always flow from the 'clean' areas to the

'dirty' and not the reverse. But when at last they were satisfied, the installation was calibrated and clinical trials began. Patients went to the same operating theatre from all three wards and the incidence of post-operative infection and the recovery rate were recorded for twelve months. There was *no* significant difference between the three wards. This was the more remarkable because in the Nightingale wards the air change rate dropped in winter to 0.5 per hour instead of the recommended 3.0 per hour. The results were published in the *Journal of Medical Microbiology*. They were greeted with incredulity and dismissed as 'inconclusive'. It was not till 1975 when Professor Shooter's team, operating with the UK Central Public Health Laboratory, published findings of their investigation of the Department of Health's own fully air-conditioned hospital at Greenwich, that their full implication was accepted.[12] 'Reduction in direct airborne transfer of micro-organisms, from one room to another, whether by ventilation or other means, can only be of clinical advantage if transfer by other routes can be made less than by the direct air-borne route.' It was fitting that Whyte, Howie and Eakin's findings should be vindicated by Professor Shooter, because he himself had published a paper on the use of sealed paper sacks as an alternative to clean and dirty corridors in operating theatres in 1967, and it had suffered a similar fate.[13] It is now (1985) accepted that paper sacks and plastic bags, coupled with aseptic techniques, play a far more important part in reducing infection in nursing units than all the brick walls and metal ducts provided at much expense by architects and engineers.

Nurses' reaction

Another systematic comparison of old and new was carried out by Dr Beddard, Senior Administrative Medical Officer at Aberdeen. He made a careful record of levels of staffing and throughput of patients achieved in the old Nightingale ward and then moved the same nursing team into the new Nuffield ward. Although the results were better, they were still disappointing. The team took an extraordinarily long time to settle down in their new surroundings (This was subsequently found to be a common experience). More staff were required to achieve the same standard of patient care. Small rooms took longer to clean than open wards. The nurses often felt 'out of touch' and felt obliged to make special trips to make sure all was well; they found the most distant patients were now much further away. Dr Beddard was still enthusiastic, but he felt it his duty to send a report to the Department of Health in 1970.[14] It was never published because 'it was not in line with current thinking.' But every one of his doubts about the new ward have since been confirmed by later studies at other hospitals.

The importance of observation, ease of supervision and control has of course always been recognised by practical nurses. Florence Nightingale would not have any single rooms 'where patients could languish unseen.' She wanted to have all 30 patients and staff immediately visible from the entrance to the ward. Nurses also know that surgeons often arrange surreptitiously for their private patients to be put for a day or two in an open ward 'so that Sister can keep a better eye on them.' A night nurse sitting at her table in the centre of a ward can see or hear the slightest alteration in the condition of a patient. Accidents arising from falling off a chair or out of bed unobserved, are three times more common in a single room.[15] An open ward is a far safer place than a single room, unless a trained nurse is constantly in attendance in that room.

The patients' needs

It is often said that the conflict between the patients' need for privacy and nurses' need for observation presents planners with an impossible problem. At one end of the scale comes the single room, at the other the open ward. Somewhere in between comes the subdivided Rigs or Nuffield ward – neither very private nor very good for observation. The precise point selected on the scale appears to depend on tradition, cultural differences, insurance policies, and what a country can afford. But because greater privacy is obviously more expensive, it is thought to be universally desirable. It is certainly the view commonly expressed by most people faced with the prospect of becoming a patient in hospital.

The case for the single room is set out by John Burrough,[16] quoting Sir Rupert Vaughan Hudson.[17] an eminent doctor. 'The truth is that the open ward is an anachronism. It is socially undesirable and medically unsound. In 1960, the public, the doctor and the nurse should no longer be expected to put up with this scandalous impromptu.' But there is a difference between people's anticipated feelings and their actual feelings on becoming a patient. In 1974 Tatton-Brown found himself in this position. As chief architect of the UK Department of Health, he had spent eleven years advocating a policy of replacing or compartmenting open wards. To his surprise he found a public ward is much less public than he had been led to believe, and much more congenial. Sitting up in bed or in his chair he could watch the world go by or withdraw from social life, as he felt inclined. It was easy to opt out, simply by opening a book or putting on headphones and listening to the radio. Cat-naps were also possible, with the headphones acting as ear-plugs and the radio turned off. The comparatively high noise level is actually an advantage, in that it masks obtruding sounds and makes it possible to talk to visitors or staff without the embarrassment of eavesdropping experienced in the subdivided ward. Curtains can be drawn when occasion demands and all in all, the anonymity of an open ward provides more visual and audio privacy than anything but a single room. It also has another advantage, relief from boredom and loneliness. It is no accident that doors in single rooms are almost always kept open and that the Yale survey found that 30 per cent more use is made of nurse-call systems when patients are by themselves. When Professor Shooter had to place a patient for medical reasons in a single room, he confessed he often felt he was condemning him to solitary confinement. He knew that alone in his cell, he would have nothing to distract his thoughts from personal problems. In an open ward, he would have the company of other patients. Their fortitude, encouragement and good humour would set him an example. The daily improvement in their condition would be witness to the skill of the staff and enhance his own hopes of recovery. Subconsciously, every patient in an open ward is taking part in a subtle form of group therapy.

Psychological requirements

But when a patient is really in danger or finds himself tangled in drips and drains after an operation, the need for encouragement and support from the nurse becomes paramount. The sight of her moving to and fro, attending (often unasked) to the needs of other patients is incredibly reassuring. Her physical presence creates a bond which strengthens his tenuous hold on life. It is a two-way process. She needs to see him but he needs, even more, to see her. Looked at from this angle, the latest systems of closed circuit television and two-way intercom which link a private room with a nurses' station are a poor substitute. They actually hinder that most important mechanism in recovery – the intimate relationship and trust between patient and nurse. William Shee,[18] the former Secretary of the Leeds Hospital Board, understood this. After being in hospital several times on both sides of the Atlantic, he concluded 'The American nurse sitting at the end of a corridor, waiting to be summoned, is just a "bell-hop". The English girl in a Nightingale ward is a prima donna the moment she comes on duty.'

Ward evaluation

Tatton-Brown reported his experiences in a talk on the radio.[19] Over 50 correspondents wrote in – some of them normally agoraphobic characters, such as dons or elderly spinsters. All of them confirmed unexpected reactions on becoming patients themselves. But 'patients', as most investigators have remarked somewhat cynically, 'are usually happy with what they get. Though some things, notably the toilet arrangements and the nurse-call system, are particularly important to them.'[3]

Very little regard is customarily paid to what patients have to say. So it was something of an event when St Thomas' Hospital commissioned the Medical Architecture Research Unit to carry out a comparative study of three wards: the original Nightingale of the 1860s, the East wing of the 1960s and the North wing of the 1970s. All three were staffed by doctors and nurses trained at St Thomas' and handling the same cross-section of patients. The study was carried out by Ann Noble and Rodger Dixon and published in 1977.[20] Their findings were described by John Weeks as 'the most powerful book since *War and Peace!*'[21]

Of the 235 patients interviewed in the open ward, very few thought they would prefer a single room and only 27 said that at some time they would perhaps have liked more privacy. All three types of ward had their advantages and disadvantages from the points of view of patients, doctors, nurses, ancillary staff and management. But the Nightingale ward scored highest marks on the levels of 'patient satisfaction, absence of boredom, ease of supervision and job satisfaction.'

The study upset almost all the ideas on which up-to-date planning of the nursing zone has been based. On nurses' journeys, for instance, it shows that string diagrams are meaningless unless they distinguish between journeys where a nurse can see and be seen by patients, and journeys out of sight down a corridor. It is not the length of journey, but the difference between a springy timber floor and hard tiles which matters to a nurse's feet. Anxiety about patients out of sight robs sisters of job satisfaction in the infinitely superior working conditions on a modern ward. But some patients' reactions are even more surprising. They like their food better in open wards, where meals are often brought round by ambulant patients, than in four-bed wards, where one patient may be eating alone while the ambulant patients are fed in a dayroom (the food of course is identical, served in the same way and cooked in the same kitchen). There are more complaints about the inadequacies of toilets in the new wards, where there

are 8, than in the old wards where there are only 2, simply because in an open ward it is possible to see (as in an aeroplane) whether a toilet is free before embarking on the journey. Similarly, patients are more understanding and tolerant of delay when summoning a nurse, if they can see that there is an emergency at the other end of a ward and other patients are in greater need.

Effectiveness and efficiency

What is interesting in the St Thomas' study is not that it shows the superiority of one type of ward over another, but the importance of psychological factors and the limitations of scientific measurement. The physical parameters of temperature, air change, noise level etc., are found to be largely irrelevant. Patients get well just as quickly in wards almost half the size and requiring a fraction of the energy to heat and cool and clean.

An important conclusion is that patients are less concerned with their material surroundings than with seeing and hearing the people who are caring for them. This was something of a shock to those who for years had been busy putting up physical barriers between patient and nurse in the interests of patient privacy. The overriding considerations are highly subjective. They have much more to do with human relationships and the bond between nurse and patient than with physical surroundings. The irreconcilable conflict between privacy and observation recedes as the planner devises new ways of helping them get together. Already the use of radial plans in the USA and on the continent and cluster layouts such as those now being evolved in the UK (see p. 89) are bringing the nurse into much closer contact with the patient.[22] The area has come down to $18m^2$ per bed. It is a recognition of the fact that what the patient wants above all is to get well and get back home as quickly as possible. If that can be done better in new ways, in unfamiliar surroundings which are different from his own home, he will put up with them for a few days, even for a few weeks. The key figure is the nurse. The key measurements are the number of bed-heads that can be seen from the nurse's base and the distance from the base to the farthest bed.[23] And the heart of the planning problem is the enhancement of the nurse-patient relationship.

If this is accepted, then there is a case for a wide variety of experiments. We are not suggesting a return to the old Nightingale open ward, though there are good reasons for retaining it for the time being, where it is giving good service, as at St Thomas' hospital in London. Every country, every society will have to work out what suits its patients and its nurses best. So much depends on climate, culture and tradition. What is clear is that there is a great deal to criticise in what has been provided up to now. The most expensive developments, both in terms of space and electronics, are neither the most effective nor the most efficient.

Already in the USA it is recognised that the average

figure of 4–5 hours nursing per patient day is likely to go up in an acute nursing unit. As patients requiring less nursing are removed (under utilisation review machinery), the remaining patients will require more. They will have to be given similar care to that provided in an intensive care unit. Their insurance cover may stipulate a private room. But unless they can be given their own day and night nurse in constant attendance, a private room will not allow a higher standard of care. Once this is recognised and the value of increased nurse-patient contact is more generally appreciated, the need to take a fresh look at the nursing unit becomes paramount, especially in the private sector. In this respect the public sector is leading the way. The planning solutions which we illustrate in the following pages may provide some of the answers.

C   The planners' response 1900–1985

Nursing zone: key to drawings in chapter 2C only

Patient space

1	Single-bed room		7	WC and wash basin
2	Multi-bed room		8	Clothes store
3	Day/dining room or space		9	Flower room
4	Balcony/veranda		10	Relative's room
5	Bathroom		11	Visitors' room or space
6	Shower		12	Visitors' toilet

Staff space

13	Staff/nurse base or station		22	Kitchen/pantry
14	Treatment room		23	Laboratory
15	Assisted bathrooms		24	Specimen/test room
16	Clean utility/supplies		25	Clinical teaching room
17	Dirty utility/disposal		26	Seminar room
18	Sluice room		27	Doctors' office
19	Cleaners' room		28	Nurses' office
20	Linen store		29	Staff toilet/cloaks
21	Equipment store		30	Overnight/duty room

Circulation space

C	Ward corridor	▮▮	Lifts
L	Lobby	◺	Staircase
D	Duct		

Size, type and content of nursing zone

The nursing zone includes all those areas used for fostering patients during their stay in hospital. Unlike the other zones, it is in full occupation 24 hours per day. It makes the heaviest demands on numbers of staff employed, materials and energy. Although it now constitutes less than half the total area of the hospital, its size and shape will often dictate the overall design of the whole complex.

There is a wide disparity in the gross area per bed in nursing zones currently being planned in different countries (2.1). The figures stretch from 18m² in the UK to 43m² in Sweden. In Scandinavia the preference for single bedrooms, and in USA for two-bed rooms and in UK for 4 to 6-bed bays in open wards, partly accounts for this difference. But as with the numbers of beds provided by each country per 1000 population the differences go deeper than variations in climate or standard of living. Cultural factors and nursing traditions are equally important.

2.1   Gross area, m² per bed 1980.

In the UK the dominant influence has been Florence Nightingale. She specified four goals: generous bed spacing; good natural light and ventilation; economy of attendance (30–32 beds per ward); and ease of supervision (all patients visible from the nurse's station). The goals were obtainable in the traditional mediaeval open ward. Accordingly she recommended

an adaptation of Lavoisier's spine and pavilion plan designed in Paris in 1788. Many of her hospitals are still in use today.

The nursing zone comprises one or more nursing units. A nursing unit consists of three elements: patient space (beds, toilets and day space); nursing space (staff base, utility rooms, offices) and corridors.

2.2   The different ways in which these elements are arranged can be classified into a number of different types. Starting with the simple open or Nightingale form, changes have been introduced in the pursuit of more privacy (corridor or continental); greater amenity for patients and staff (duplex or Nuffield); compactness (racetrack or double corridor); economy (courtyard, a naturally ventilated version of the above); better observation of all patients (cruciform or cluster); shorter distance between patient and nurse (radial).

Each type represents some compromise between privacy for the patient and good nursing supervision. Some like the single room plans, score high marks on one count, others like the open ward, on another. But each new development seeks to capitalise on what has gone before. Collectively, they represent a monument to the dedication of the nurses, who stated the requirements, and the inventiveness of the architects, who arrived at the solutions.

2.1

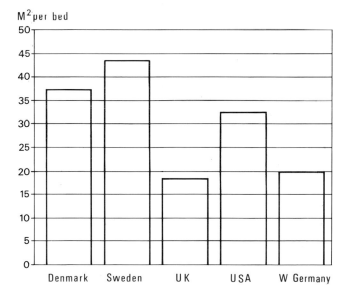

M² per bed

2.2 Comparative ward layouts

Type	Simple forms	Complex forms	
Open or Nightingale			
Corridor or continental			
Duplex or Nuffield			
Racetrack or double corridor			
Courtyard			
Cruciform or cluster			
Radial			

▢ Patient space   ★ Nurses' base   ▨ Staff space

Open or Nightingale

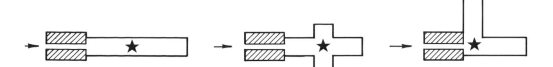

2.3 One of the most famous examples of the Nightingale ward: St Thomas' Hospital, London, UK, designed in 1867 and still in use today.

2.4 St Thomas' about 1900. Note fireplaces and flues in centre aisle between two rows of beds.

2.5 Bed curtains were introduced to St Thomas' after World War II; when drawn they form individual cubicles and give a degree of visual privacy.

2.6 University College Hospital, London, UK: to cut down on the overall length of the open ward a cruciform plan was adopted. This hospital was designed in 1903 and is still is use.

2.7 Guy's Hospital, London, UK (1956): the open ward is broken down with two wings in the form of an L. One of the earliest and most successful plans built after World War II.

2.8, 2.9 Tembisa Hospital, Transvaal, South Africa (1960); three parallel open ward sections planned in a single storey deep-plan form with clerestory day lighting.

2.10 Grantham Hospital, UK: a recent plan (1982) reflects the return to Nightingale principles of ease of supervision, with open ward sections on either side of a central nurses' base.

2.3

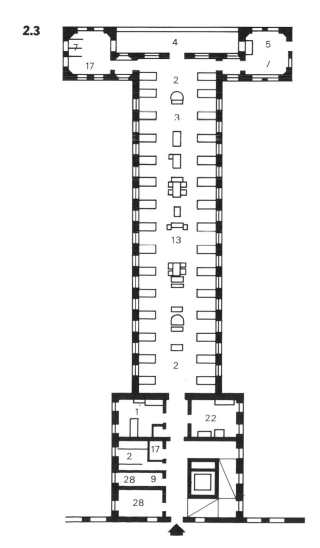

2.4

2.5

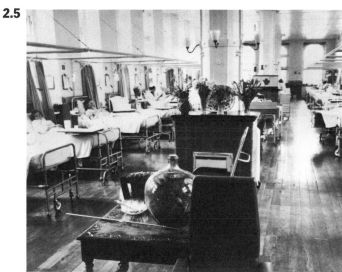

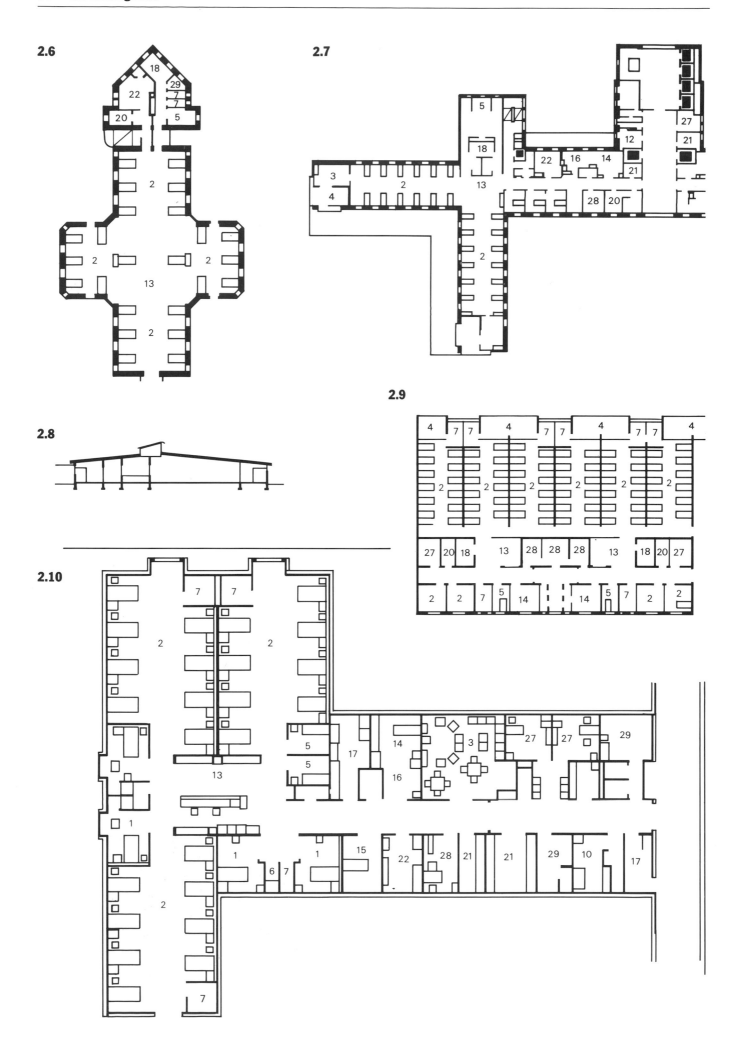

2.6

2.7

2.8

2.9

2.10

Corridor or continental

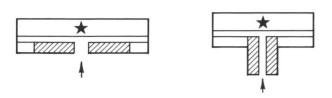

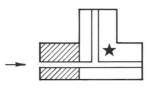

The move away from the open or Nightingale layout started in Europe in the early 1900s. Beds were moved from the external walls and arranged in bays, usually of up to 4 beds, separated by crosswalls or screens. A corridor was needed to gain access to the bays.

2.11   Varburg Hospital, Sweden (1973): during and after World War II, Scandinavian hospital wards became fully compartmented, with beds arranged in rooms each with their own toilet facilities and day space. These patient suites of 1, 2 and 4 beds with nursing ancillaries were placed on both sides of a spine corridor (2.12).

2.13, 2.14   St Thomas' Hospital, London, UK: typical ward floor in east wing, designed in early 1960s. Reluctant to give up Nightingale principles, UK planners sought compromises between privacy and ease of supervision.

2.15, 2.16   Airedale Hospital, UK: designed in 1963, this layout did achieve good supervision from a carefully sited nurses' base by means of part-glazed screens between bed bays.

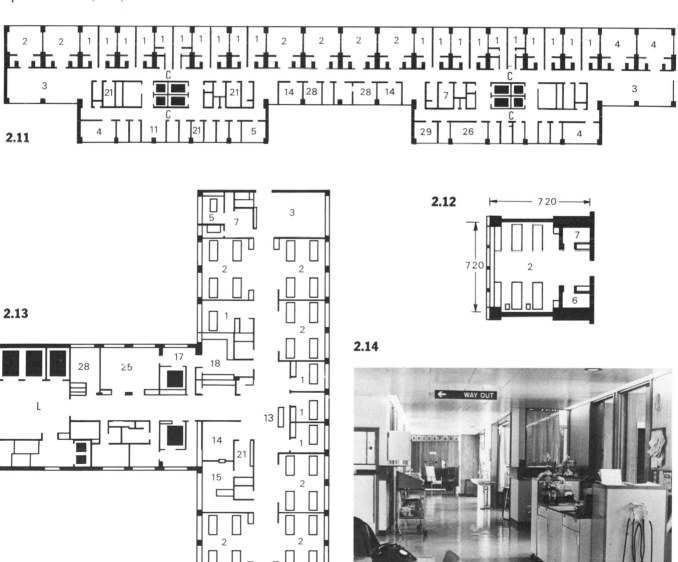

2.11

2.13

2.12

2.14

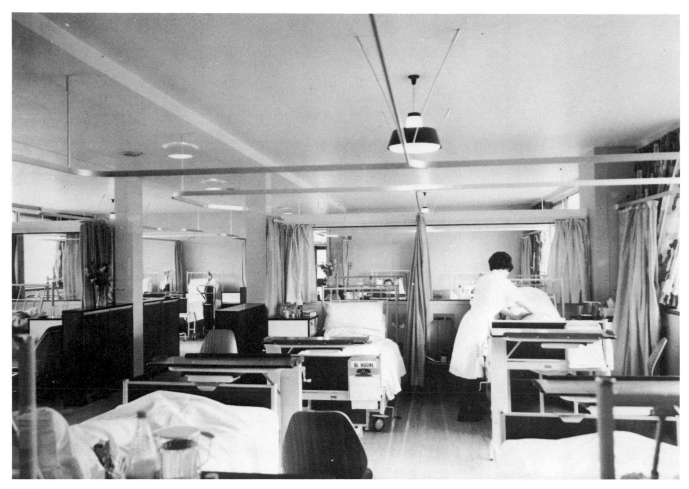

2.15

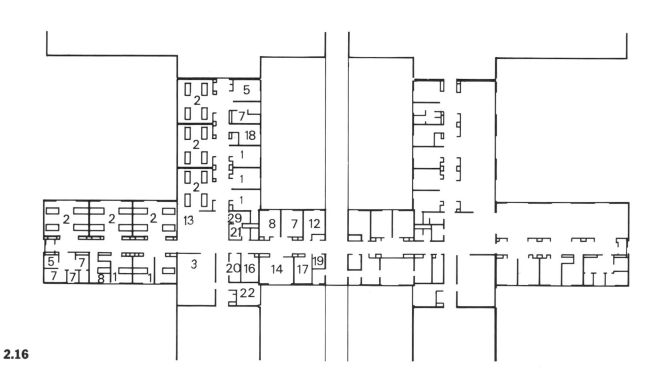

2.16

Duplex or Nuffield

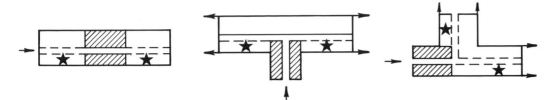

The Nuffield *Studies in the Function and Design of Hospitals*, published in 1955, broke with the Nightingale tradition in the UK. In addition to adopting the continental or corridor type layout the report questioned the economy of attendance principle (30 beds to one sister) and instead proposed a new concept of team nursing which would enable more patients to be nursed on one unit. This gave rise to the duplex layout which splits the ward into two equal sections of up to 20 beds, each with its own nurses' base. Nursing ancillary space is shared between the two sections.

2.17 Larkfield Hospital, UK: one of the two experimental wards built by the Nuffield team. A total of 32 beds in two equal sections.

2.18 Swindon Hospital, UK: 40-bed unit using a mix of 6-bed and 4-bed bays in order to reduce the length of the corridors.

2.19 Huddersfield Hospital, UK: 2 duplex wards per floor, one linear in form, the other L-shaped. Note open wards with informal grouping of beds, using glazed screens. Reflects conflict between Nightingale principles and the demand for privacy.

2.20, 2.21 Ninewells Teaching Hospital and Medical School, Dundee, UK: here the two halves each become self-contained nursing sections of 25 beds. Day space, administrative and teaching facilities are shared between 50 beds.

2.22–2.24 Wexham Park Hospital, UK: ingenious duplex plan with each section of 16 beds arranged in each arm of an L.

2.17

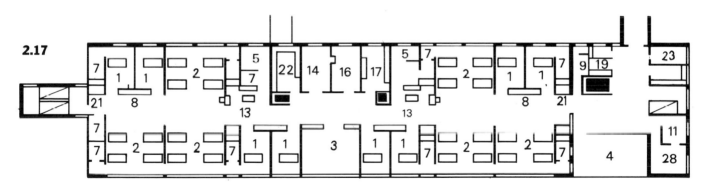

2.18

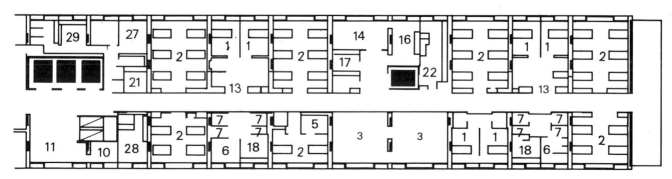

2.19

2.21

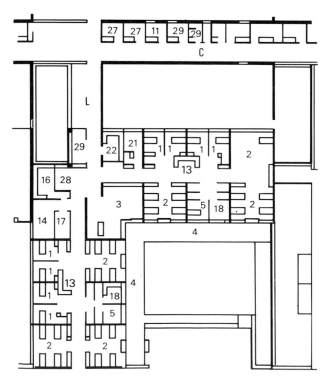

2.20

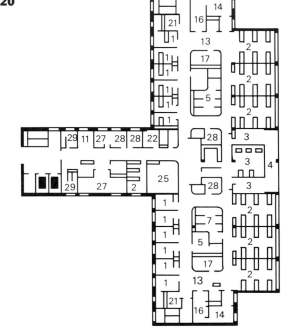

2.23

2.24

2.22

Racetrack or double corridor

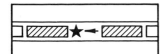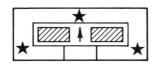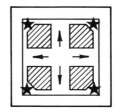

In the 1950s modern frame structures, air-conditioning and mechanical conveyor systems contributed to the development of the racetrack or double corridor ward layouts which soon became the norm in the USA and on the continent of Europe.

2.25 Typical racetrack plan pioneered by Gordon Friesen: 50 to 60 beds per floor in single and two-bed rooms, each with *en suite* toilet facilities. Vertical conveyors deliver supplies direct from central storage and processing departments into the central staff core on each floor.

2.26 Gelsenkirchen Hospital, West Germany: plan of 78-bed ward floor. The continental version of the racetrack plan. Note the 3-bed rooms with beds placed closer together, giving a substantial reduction in area per bed when compared with North American examples.

2.25

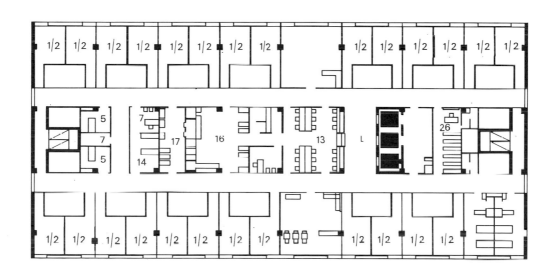

2.26

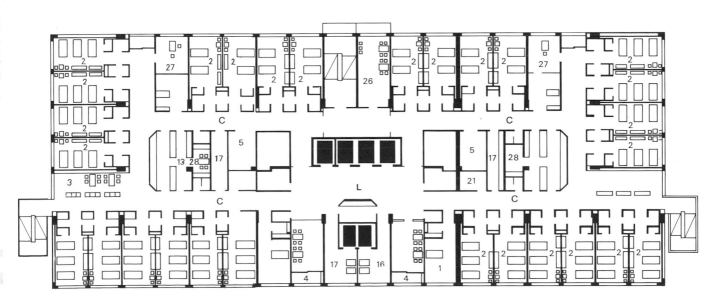

Cruciform or cluster

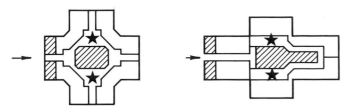

By the 1970s it was generally accepted that modern corridor ward plans did provide the patient with greater privacy and amenity than the old open layouts. However nurses soon realised that these 'improvements' had been largely bought at the expense of the Nightingale goal of ease of supervision. They found that not only were they having to travel greater distances but that more and more barriers – walls, doors, toilets – were being erected between them and their patients. Designers responded by manipulating the shape of the plan in order to group as many patients as possible around the nurses' base; at the same time toilets were moved away from the entrances to the patient rooms.

2.34, 2.35   Southlands Hospital, Shoreham, UK: typical harness cruciform ward layout. Nursing ancillaries are grouped into a central core with patient rooms on the outside.

2.36   Central Emergency Hospital, Abu Dhabi: plan of typical ward unit of 52 beds.

2.37   Nucleus ward plan, UK: standard 56-bed ward unit.

2.38, 2.39   Weston-super-Mare, UK: 28-bed acute ward unit designed by South Western Regional Health Authority, UK.

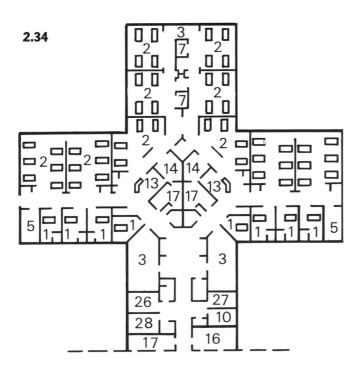

2.34

2.35

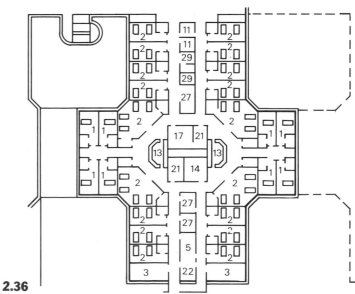

2.36

2.37

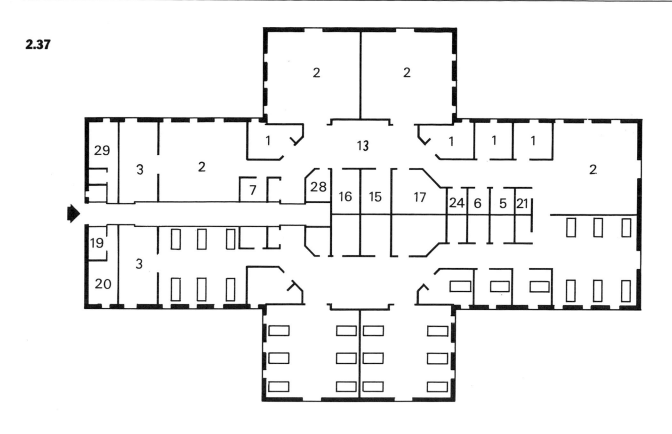

2.38

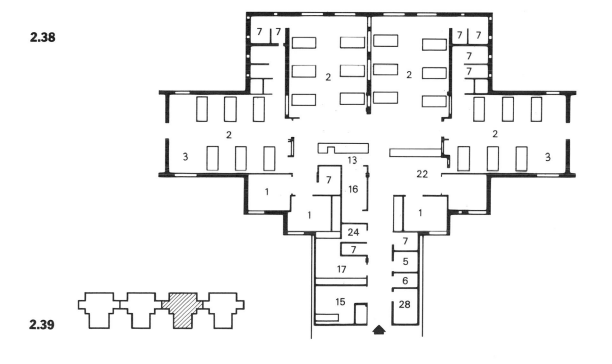

2.39

Radial

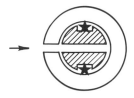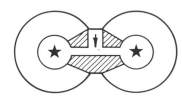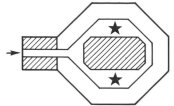

Radial forms – circles, squares, polygons – have been used for ward plans for many years. Early examples were built at the City Hospital, Antwerp (1878) and at Johns Hopkins Hospital, USA (1885). These were open layouts. However in recent years designers have adopted these forms for modern corridor layouts.

2.40   Fraubrunnen Hospital, Switzerland: part plan of first floor showing 26-bed section. Notice the short distances between nurses and all their patients. However, observation from nurses' base is obstructed by toilets and ancillary rooms.

2.41

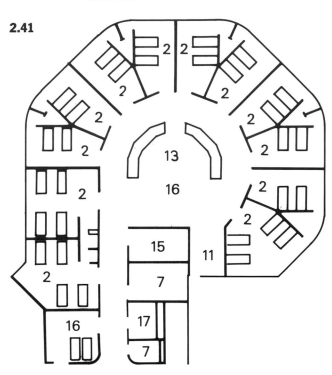

2.40

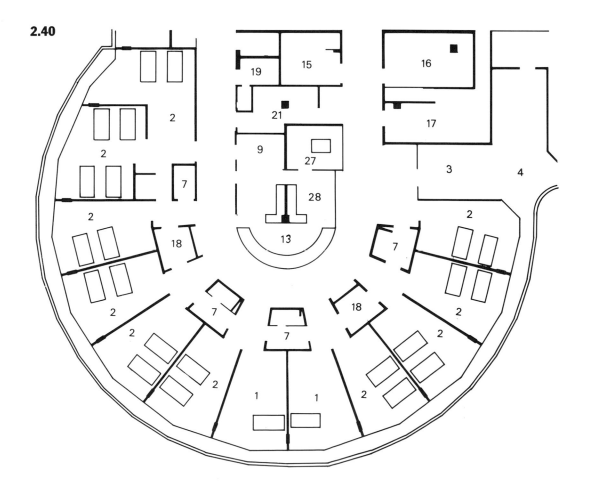

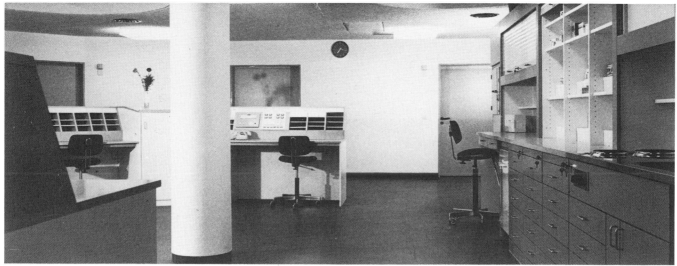

2.42

2.41, 2.42 Nordenham Hospital, West Germany: part plan of second floor, showing 30-bed section. Here toilets are placed on outside wall, leaving unobstructed view of patients from nurses' base.

2.43, 2.44 Chesterfield Hospital, UK: typical 28-bed ward unit. Observation of 24-beds is unobstructed by partitions, doors, etc. Patients' privacy and amenities are somewhat reduced when compared with 2.40 and 2.41.

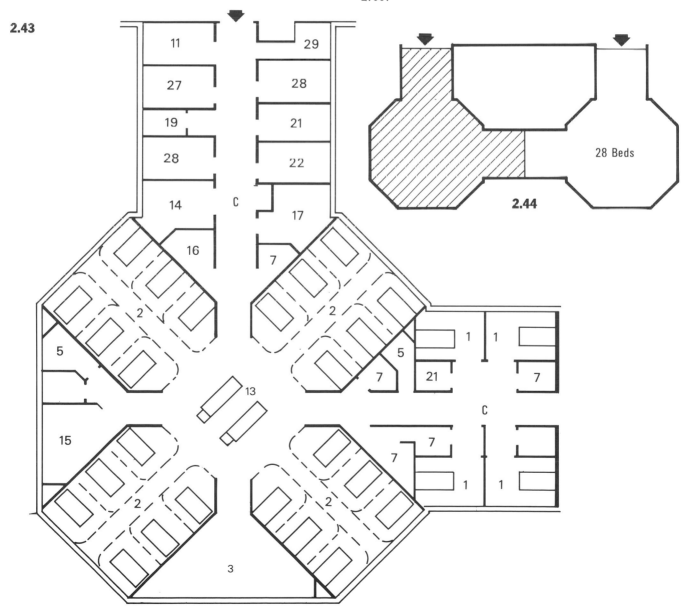

2.45 Staff–patient contact

Example	Type	Form	Average distance nurse–bed (m)
St Thomas' UK 1870	Open		9·3
Grantham UK 1982	Open		9·8
Varburg Sweden 1978	Corridor		22·4
Airedale UK 1963	Corridor		18·4
Holy Cross USA 1963	Racetrack		16·5
Gelsenkirchen W. Germany 1977	Racetrack		15·3
Hvidovre Denmark 1978	Courtyard		26·5
West Suffolk UK 1972	Courtyard		19·3
Newham UK 1982	Cruciform		11·5
S. Western RHA UK 1983	Cruciform		9·8
Jegensdorf Switzerland 1978	Radial		10·4
Nordenham W. Germany 1974	Radial		9·3

Efficiency and economy of design

2.45 The main preoccupation of ward planners is the search for an acceptable compromise between the conflicting requirements for providing privacy and a high level of amenity and at the same time allowing ease of supervision. The problem is the impossibility of simultaneously achieving perfect privacy and perfect nursing supervision.

Although different countries attach importance to different factors in ward design, some objective yardsticks are useful. One of these is staff-patient contact (2.45). A crude measure of this is the average distance in a ward between the bed and the nurses' base. The closer the nurse (particularly the night nurse) is to the patient, the better. It was very good in the open wards of the 1870s in the UK, and has become very good in the radial wards of the 1970s in

Germany. The very long distances in racetrack and courtyard plans are mitigated by two-way intercom and, sometimes, closed-circuit television. But nurses, and sometimes patients, complain that they feel out of touch.

2.46 Economy is another factor which cannot be ignored. An efficient plan is one in which every square metre of space is in use for the maximum number of hours per day. A corridor is of course necessary, but it is only used intermittently. If doors are kept closed, a nurse in a corridor is out of sight and out of touch. The numbers of beds per 3m run of corridor is therefore a useful indicator (2.46). The higher the number, the more compact the plan and the more efficient the arrangement.

2.46 Number of beds to corridor length

Example	Room type	Built form and corridor type	Total length of corridor (m)	No of beds in unit	No of beds 3m run of corridor
Newham, UK 1981 (Nucleus)	Mainly 6-bed rooms	Cruciform Part double Part single corridor	72.0	56	2.33
Frimley Park, UK 1974 (Best Buy)	Mainly 6-bed rooms	Courtyard Single corridor	99.0	68	2.06
Nordenham, West Germany 1974	Mainly 2-bed rooms	Radial Part circular corridor	99.0	60	1.82
Gelsenkirchen, West Germany 1977	Mainly 3-bed rooms	Racetrack Double corridor	134.0	78	1.74
High Wycombe, UK 1966	Mainly 4-bed and 6-bed rooms	Racetrack Double corridor	78.0	40	1.54
Centinela Valley USA, 1969	All single rooms, beds at right angles to corridor	Racetrack Double corridor	70.0	34	1.47
Valley Presbyterian USA, 1971	All single rooms, beds at right angles to corridor	Radial Circular corridor	66.0	32	1.45
St Marks USA, 1974	All single rooms, beds at right angles to corridor	Radial Triangular corridor	87.0	35	1.21

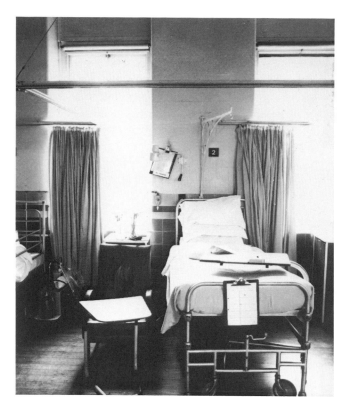

2.47

2.48

2.50

2.49

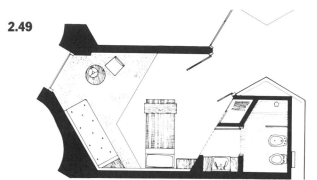

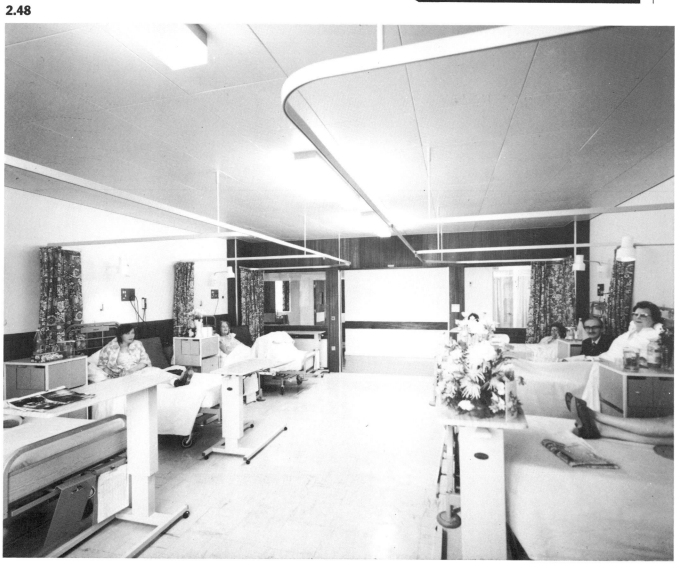

Patient space

The amount of space in a nursing unit which is allocated to accommodate the patient varies widely from country to country: (see p. 98). Space allocations are influenced by several factors: open or corridor layouts, number of beds in a room, bed spacing, ratio of toilet accommodation, provision of sitting-up space, etc.

2.47 St Thomas' Hospital, London, UK: view of one of the beds in an open ward which is still in use today. The beds are spaced at 2.4m centre to centre. However, due to the open plan the total area required for the bed, for the people and furniture around it and to gain access to the beds, is much less than for corridor type wards (2.51).

2.48 Rotherham Hospital, UK; typical 6-bed bay, which has become the standard layout in Britain. The bed spacing is similar to the open ward at St. Thomas'. However, extra space is provided at the entrance to each bay for a washbasin and sometimes for sitting-up space. Additional space is also required between the ends of the beds to allow for mobile beds or for trolleys to pass when the bed curtains are drawn. In addition more lavish toilet provision results in an overall increase of patient space when compared with the open layout.

2.49 King Faisal Specialist Hospital, Saudi Arabia: plan and view (2.50) of one of the 240 single-bed rooms, each with toilet facilities *en suite* and space for visitors. Wards based on this lavish standard require more than twice the patient space in an open ward.

2.51 Table comparing different standards of patient accommodation and illustrating the effect on the allocation of patient space, nursing space and corridor space.

2.51

Room type	Source	Size and Form	Area per bed m²
1-bed rooms with toilet	Average USA	32 35 beds Racetrack	30·2
2-bed rooms with toilet	Holy Cross USA	66 beds Racetrack	24·1
2-bed rooms shared toilets	Nordenham W. Germany	60 beds Radial	17·7
3-bed rooms shared toilets	Gelsenkirchen W. Germeany	78 beds Racetrack	23·8
4-bed bays shared toilets	Airedale UK	30 beds Corridor	24·1
6-bed bays shared toilets	Newham UK (Nucleus)	56 beds Cruciform	18·5
30-bed room shared toilets	St Thomas' UK (Nightingale)	31 beds Open	13·5

Patient space   Nursing space   Corridor

2.52 Gelsenkirchen Hospital, West Germany: layout of typical 3-bed room. Net space per bed is 7.8m², little more than in an open ward. However bed centres are only 1.68m. The space saved around the bed is put into a high ratio of toilet provision: a shower, wc and 2 washbasins for every 3 beds.

2.53 St Josef's Hospital, Wiesbaden, West Germany: alternative bed arrangements and bay windows to make the most of the limited space available.

2.54 City Hospital, Velbert, West Germany: reduced toilet accommodation shared between two rooms.

2.55, 2.56 Hvidovre Hospital, Denmark: in Scandinavia generally, bed spacings are more generous than in central and southern Europe. Toilet provision and sitting-up space is ample both for patients and visitors.

2.57, 2.58 Sundsvall Hospital, Sweden: bay dimensions are generous allowing ample space for sitting-up.

2.52

2.54   **2.53**

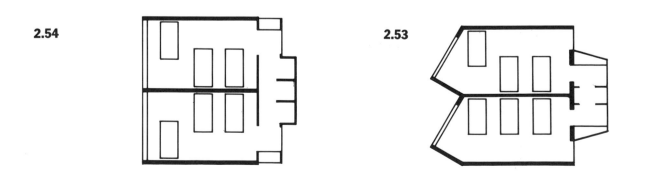

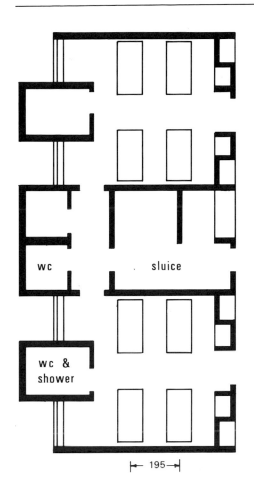

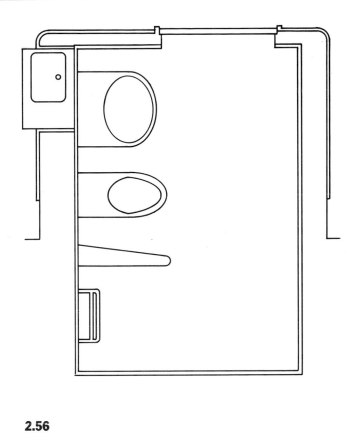

2.55

2.56

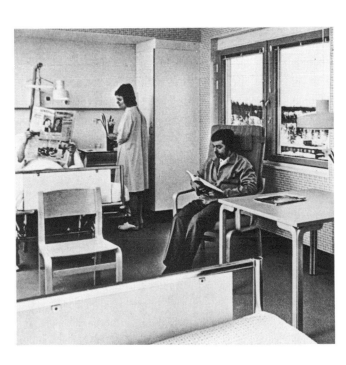

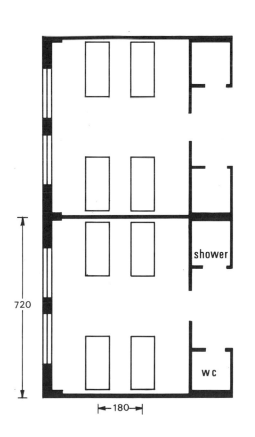

2.57

2.58

In England larger rooms, each with 5–6 beds and integral day space are preferred. Generous bed spacing (2.4m) permits the use of cubicle curtains, giving a degree of privacy to each patient.

The spacing of beds has been determined after intensive research initiated by Nuffield and continued by the Department of Health. (2.59, 2.60) It is governed by nursing procedures requiring the circulation of treatment trolleys, drip-stands, wheel-chairs, etc; 2.5m also allows room for a locker and a chair.

2.61   Northwick Park Hospital, Harrow, UK: detail of typical 5-bed rooms, twinned to provide a shared day space.

2.62   Falkirk Hospital, Scotland: an experimental ward which became the standard layout for new Scottish hospitals, 4-bed rooms with day space, shower, wc and 3 washbasins *en suite*.

2.63–2.65   Bromsgrove General Hospital, UK: based on the standard Nucleus ward but with bay window to provide additional sitting-up space. Note use of rooflights to give increased natural daylight along inside wall.

2.66–2.68   Frimley Park Hospital, UK: one of the Best Buy hospitals. The ward design is much liked by both patients and staff and became the basis of the Nucleus plan. Note lower ratio of toilet accommodation in British ward layouts compared with USA and Continental examples.

2.59

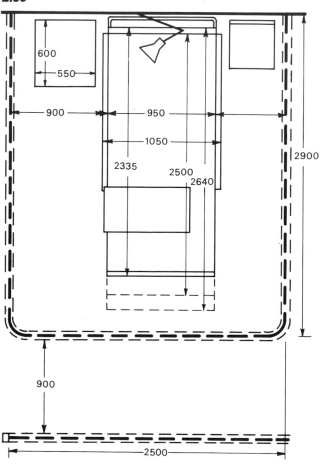

2.61

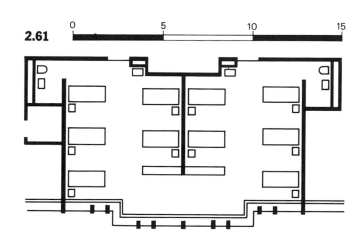

2.60

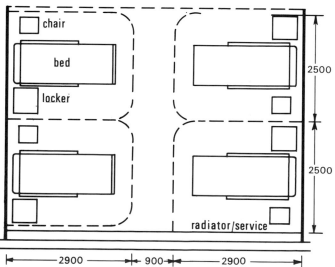

2.62

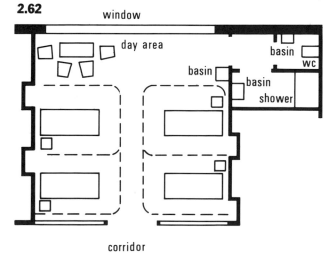

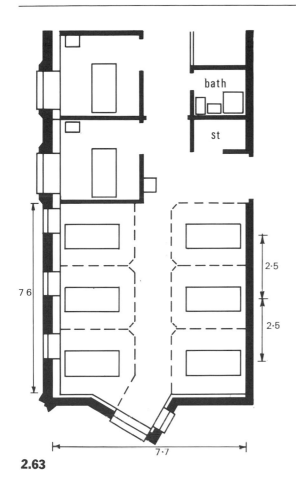

2.63

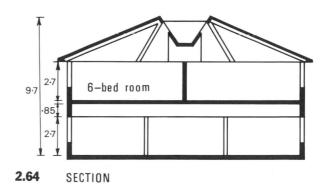

2.64   SECTION

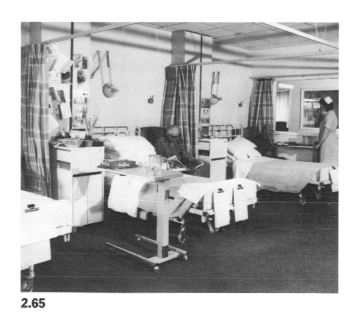

2.65

2.68

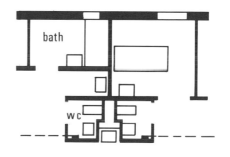

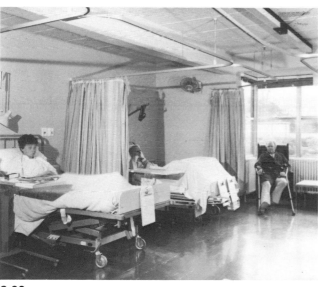

2.66

2.67

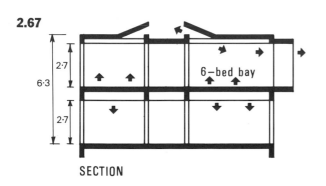

SECTION

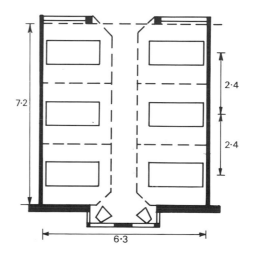

In the USA, where hospital care is dominated by a private sector based on insurance, the demand is for private or semi-private suites.

2.69 Holy Cross Hospital, Maryland, USA: typical patient suite comprising a bedroom sized to accommodate one or two beds together with shower, wc, basin and wardrobe. Note 'nurse server' on corridor wall. The total floor area is substantially in excess of European standards.

2.70 Mercy Hospital, San Juan, USA: alternate layout with beds placed at right angles to external wall. This arrangement gives improved privacy when the room is occupied by two patients.

2.72 Bath Clinic, UK: private suite in a recently completed private hospital. Space standards are similar to those in USA.

2.73 Bath Clinic, UK: patient room.

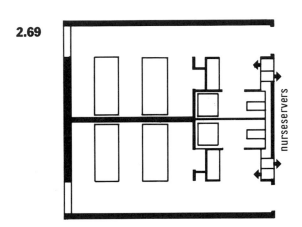

2.69

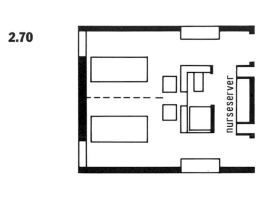

2.70

2.71 Patient room: comparative standards in various countries

National examples	Beds in room	Bed spacing	Ratio of fittings to beds					Net area of bedroom (m²/bed)
UK St Thomas'	30	2.40	1:15	1:15	1:15	1:6	✓	7.00
UK Newham	6	2.50	1:14	1:28	1:6	1:6	✓	10.20
USA Holy Cross	2	1.98	1:28	1:2	1:2	1:2	✓	8.25
Sweden Sundsvall	4	1.85	1:30	1:4	1:4	1:4	✓	9.72
Denmark Hvdovre	4	1.83	1:28	1:4	1:2	1:2	✓	8.89
West Germany Gelsenkirchen	3	1.68	1:39	1:3	1:3	1:3	✓	7.85
West Germany Nordenham	2	1.68	1:30	1:30	1:2	1:2	✓	8.75
Switzerland Jegensdorf	2	1.68	1:26	1:26	1:5	1:2	✓	11.79

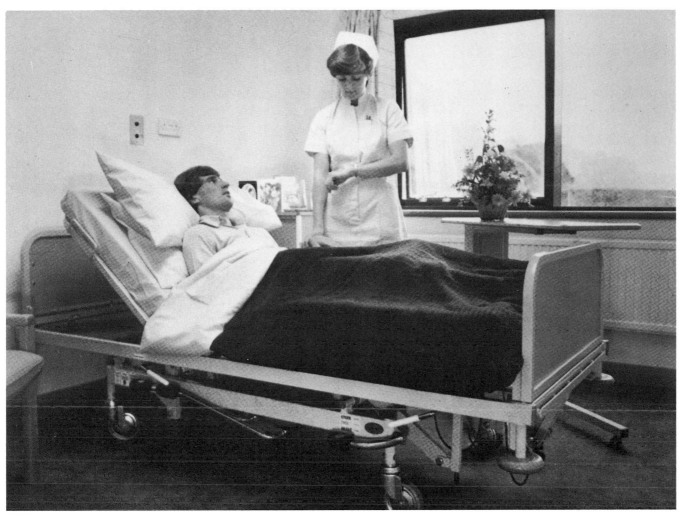

2.73

2.72

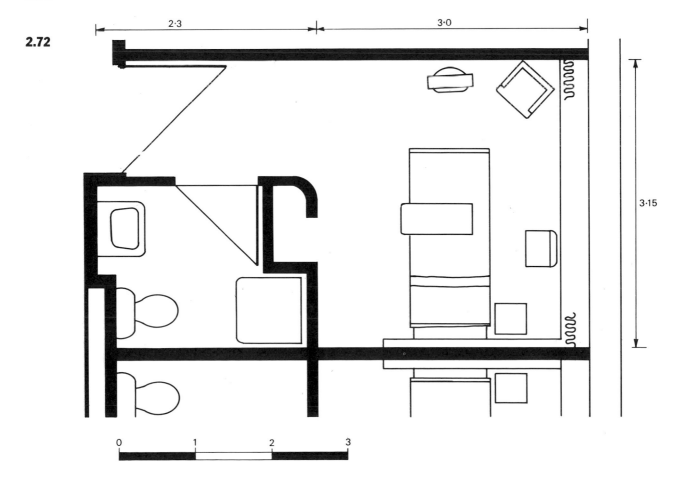

Staff space

The location of space for nursing ancillaries – staff base, utility rooms, stores, treatment room, etc. – will depend on the type of organisation employed. Basically there are two systems:

2.74, 2.75 Central system: diagrams show the nurse's tasks and movement pattern and the back-up facilities she needs.

2.76 Plan of nursing floor at Frimley Park Hospital, UK: staff space is centralised near the entrances to each nursing section (34 beds).

2.77 Decentralised system: typical floor plan of Mercy Hospital, USA. Here there is no central nurses' base. The nurse goes direct to the patient's room where a nurse server provides her with all she needs to lay up her trolley and attend to the patient. Nurse servers are kept stocked up from central utility rooms provided on each floor.

2.78 Nordenham Hospital, West Germany: staff base and clean utility planned centrally (see also 2.42).

2.79, 2.80 Southlands Hospital, UK: central staff facilities.

2.74
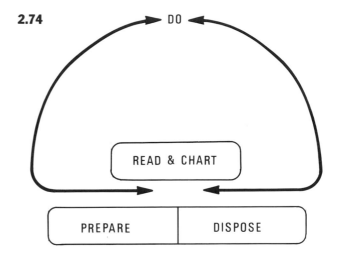

2.75
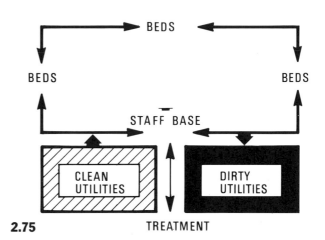

2.76
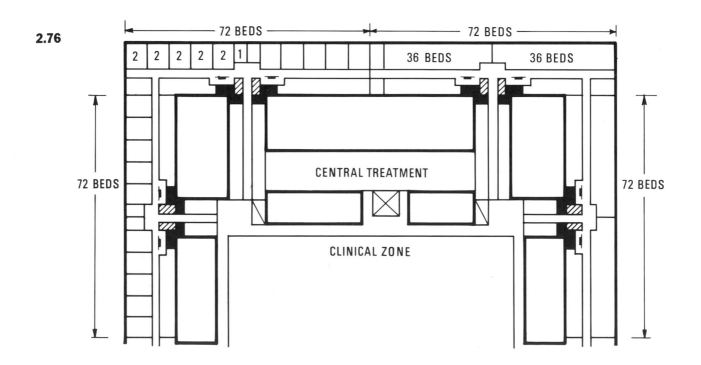

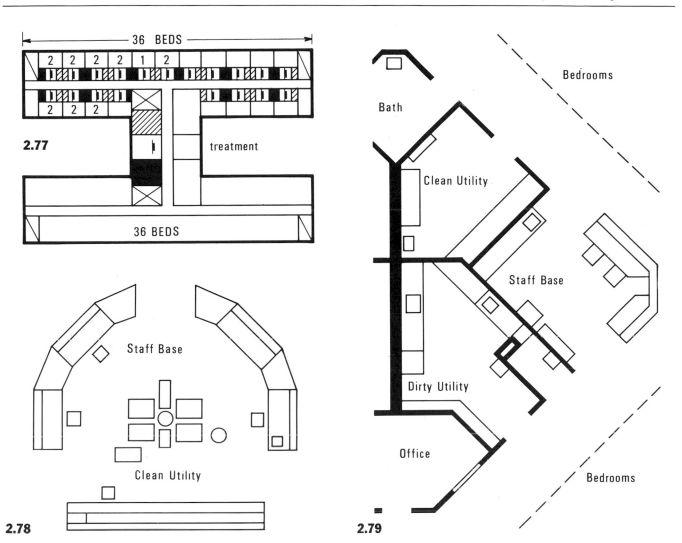

2.77

2.78

2.79

2.80

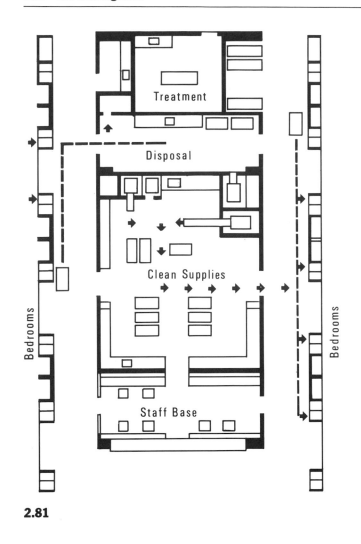

2.81

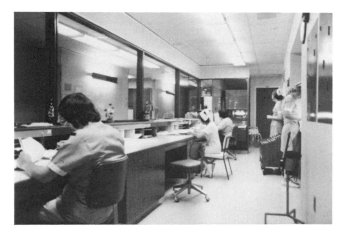

2.83

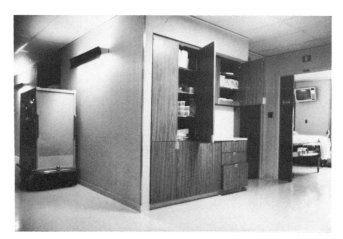

2.84

2.82

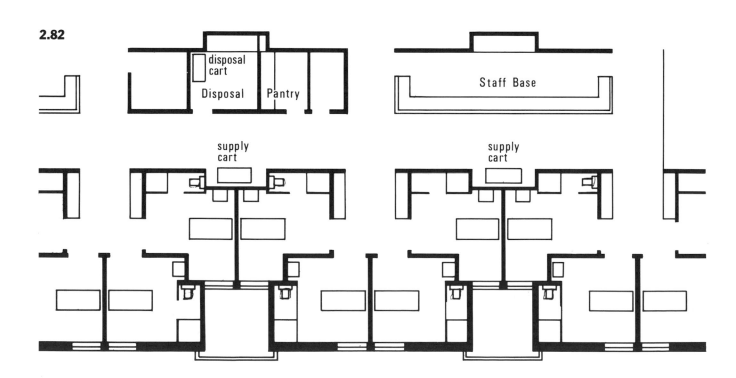

2.81 Holy Cross Hospital, USA: plan of staff space in central core of typical racetrack ward. Clean supplies and meals are received from central stores and processing departments in the basement.

2.82 Greater Baltimore Medical Centre, USA: part plan of typical nursing unit (2.83). Supplies are received on mobile carts which are parked in recesses off the corridors. Cupboards serving groups of patient rooms are topped-up regularly with clean supplies (2.84).

2.85 Central staff base: equipment layout and recommended dimensions.

2.86 Dirty utility/disposal room: equipment layout and recommended dimensions.

2.87 Clean utility/supplies room: equipment layout and recommended dimensions.

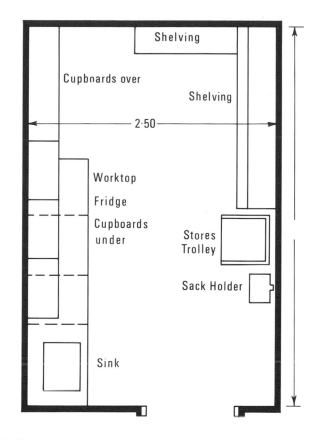

2.87

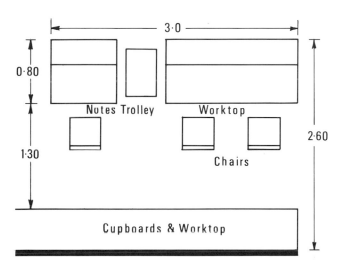

2.85

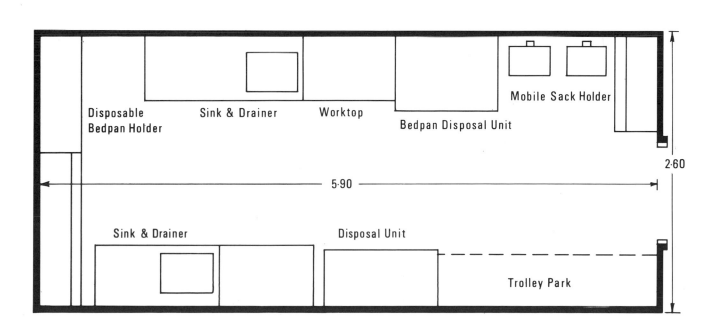

2.86

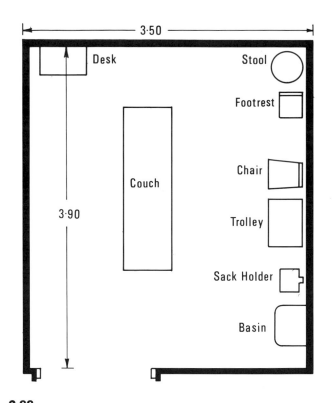

2.88

Where treatment cannot be carried out at the bedside, the patient may be wheeled to a treatment room. Originally one was provided in every ward. Recent research has indicated that in some wards treatment rooms are under-used. In the UK treatment rooms have been centralised in groups on a floor basis.

2.88 Treatment room: equipment layout and recommended dimensions.

2.89 Frimley Park Hospital, UK: centralised treatment suite of 5 rooms serving 8 wards (280 beds) as well as day treatment centre.

2.90 Charing Cross Hospital, UK: treatment room.

2.91 Treatment bathroom: equipment layout and recommended dimensions.

2.92 Southlands Hospital, UK: treatment bathroom.

2.89

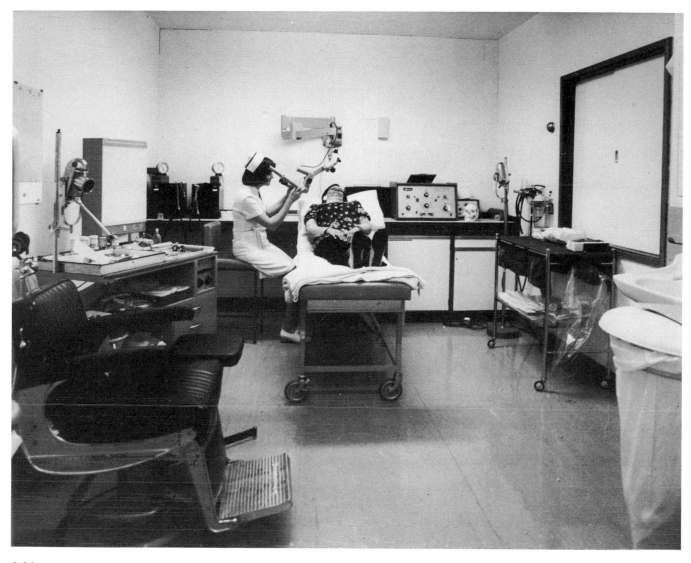

2.90

2.91

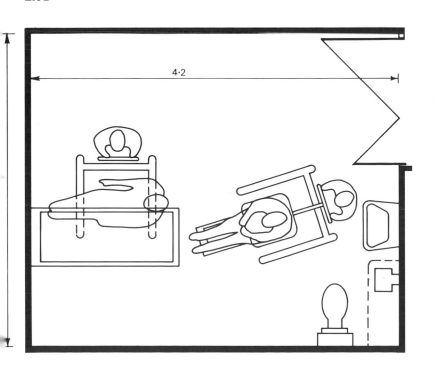

2.92

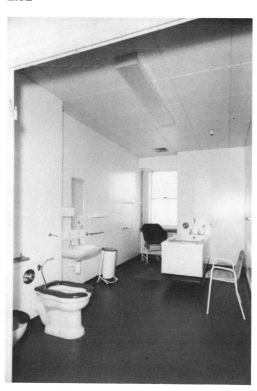

Corridor space

The most important decisions in planning the nursing zone are the number of beds per nursing unit and the way these beds are arranged; whether in open wards or multi-bed bays or rooms, or in single rooms. Such decisions will influence the amount of space required for corridors.

2.93   King Faisal Specialist Hospital, Saudi Arabia: ward corridor. Its great length is due to the fact that all beds are in single rooms.

2.94   Table illustrating four alternative ways of arranging 24 beds in a ward and the effect on the length of corridor needed to gain access to these beds. Because ward corridors need to be wide enough to allow movement and turning of beds, the width has to be a constant 2.1m.

2.93

2.94   Alternative arrangements for 24-bed ward

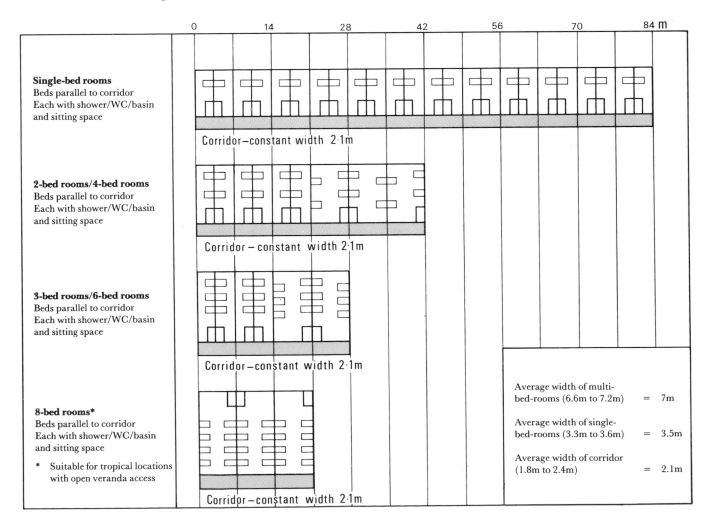

Single-bed rooms
Beds parallel to corridor
Each with shower/WC/basin
and sitting space

Corridor—constant width 2·1m

2-bed rooms/4-bed rooms
Beds parallel to corridor
Each with shower/WC/basin
and sitting space

Corridor—constant width 2·1m

3-bed rooms/6-bed rooms
Beds parallel to corridor
Each with shower/WC/basin
and sitting space

Corridor—constant width 2·1m

8-bed rooms*
Beds parallel to corridor
Each with shower/WC/basin
and sitting space

*   Suitable for tropical locations with open veranda access

Corridor—constant width 2·1m

Average width of multi-bed-rooms (6.6m to 7.2m)   = 7m

Average width of single-bed-rooms (3.3m to 3.6m)   = 3.5m

Average width of corridor (1.8m to 2.4m)   = 2.1m

2.95 Greater Baltimore Medical Centre, USA: typical 36 bed ward unit. By overlapping the single rooms along the external wall the length of the corridor is substantially reduced.

2.96 Filderclinik, West Germany: part plan of ward unit. The width of the corridor is varied by providing offsets to give the required width opposite the entrance to rooms.

2.97 St Mark's Hospital, USA: typical single-bed room. Ingenious design reduces width of room which in turn reduces length of corridor by 30 per cent. Good visibility of patient from corridor.

2.95

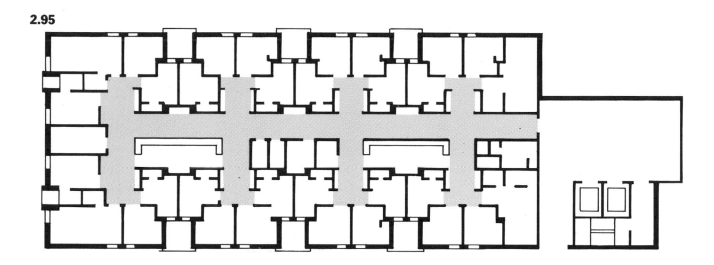

2.96

2.97

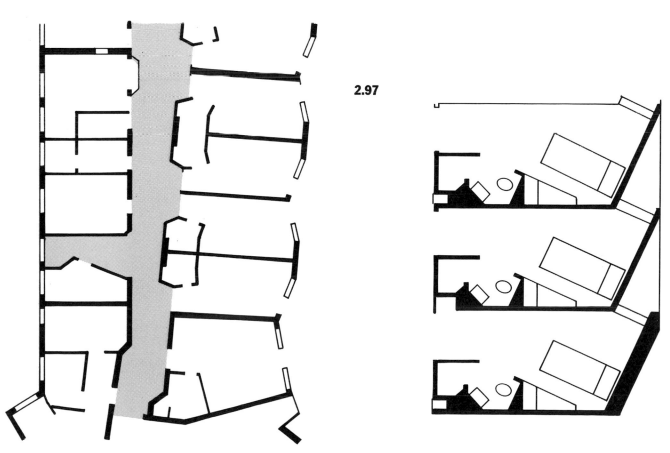

2.98

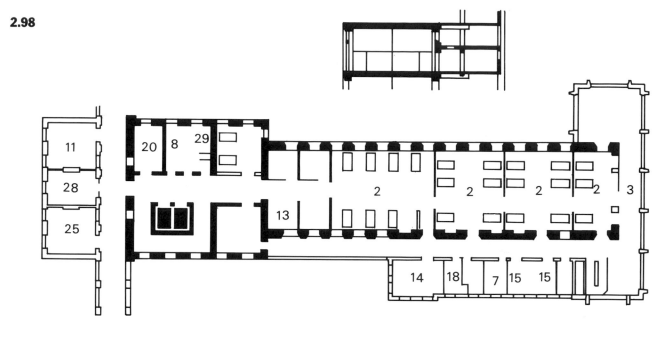

2.99

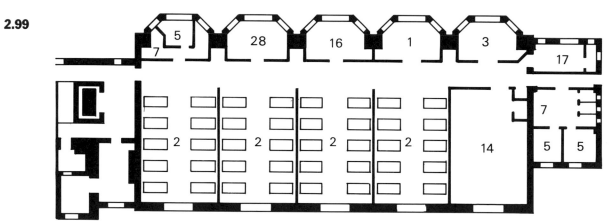

2.100

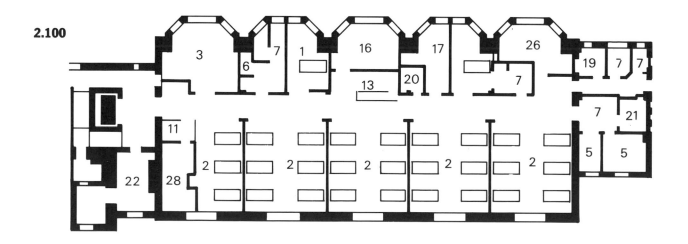

Conversion and refurbishment

Recent surveys in the UK have shown that about half the existing stock of hospital wards are capable of rehabilitation. Many of the later nineteenth-century buildings have sound structures and some require less maintenance than buildings of this century.

Refurbishment can require considerable skill. Crude additions to old buildings to make them conform to predetermined standards such as fire regulations can destroy their character (eg. an early proposal for the conversion of the wards at St. Thomas' Hospital, 2.98).

2.99, 2.100 Sensitively handled, with some give-and-take on standards, rearranging the accommodation within the existing envelope can often be done at less cost than building anew.

2.101, 2.102 St Mary's Hospital, UK. Recent internal and external refurbishment of this famous London teaching hospital has provided ward accommodation to modern standards.

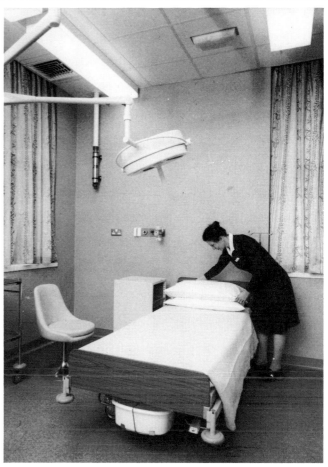

2.101

2.102

2.103

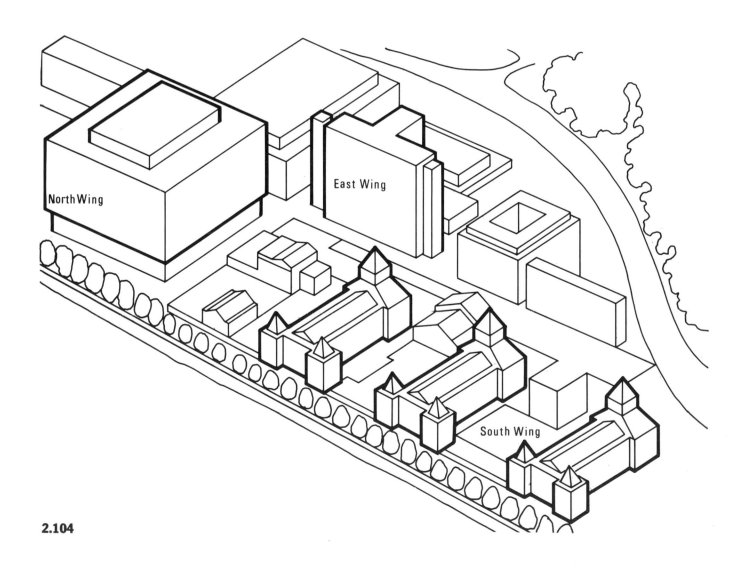

2.104

Evaluation of wards in use

The final stage in the planning of the nursing zone is evaluation and feed-back. An opportunity arose at St. Thomas' Hospital to do this on a systematic basis in 1976. Three different types of ward were completed over a span of 100 years. North (1970s), east (1960s) and south (1870s) were selected for study.

They were used by the same doctors and nurses, trained and working within the same constraints, in a single hospital. Patients were admitted to the three types of ward indiscriminately. They recovered at the same rate. The only variable factors were the age and design of the wards.

The study was carried out over a period of eighteen months. Two investigators used the classic methods of consumer research. After a pilot survey working with the hospital steering group, they compiled questionnaires for use in interviewing staff, management and patients. Answers obtained in four different wards in north, east and south blocks were then analysed and tabulated. In this way they were able to build up a profile of the things that did and did not matter to staff and patients. An entirely new light was thrown on such things as privacy, anxiety, boredom, communication, job-satisfaction and so on.

A number of strongly held preconceived convictions on patient's preferences and staff priorities were upset.

When the enormous differences in capital, maintenance and staffing costs of different ward types is taken into consideration, and the wide variety of ways of satisfying staff and patients' needs, the importance of evaluation can hardly be exaggerated. It also suggests the need for fresh experiments in producing more efficient and more cost-effective ward designs in the future.

2.103 St. Thomas' Hospital, showing north, east and south wings.

2.104 Axonometric of St Thomas' Hospital.

2.105 St Thomas' Hospital: plan of typical pavilion south wing.

2.106 St Thomas' Hospital: plan of east wing ward.

2.107 St Thomas' Hospital: part plan of north wing ward.

2.106

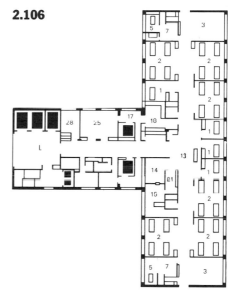

2.105

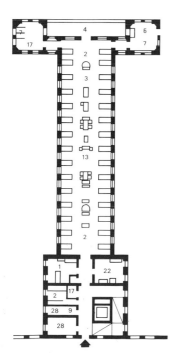

2.107

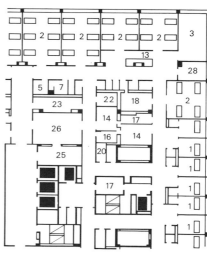

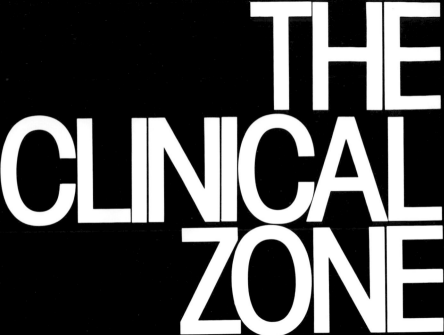

THE CLINICAL ZONE

Chapter 3

The clinical zone

A   Growth

Origins

The prototype of the clinical zone is the Anatomy Theatre of Padua.[1] Built in 1594, attended by Harvey, the first to propound the theory of the circulation of the blood, it was the birthplace of modern medicine.[2] The wealth of Venice provided the money for the building, and insatiable curiosity the incentive. It housed a clandestine, complex, and entirely illicit organisation. The corpses used for dissection were those of executed criminals. They were cut down from the gallows at night and brought secretly by underground waterway to the cellars of the building. The investigators had to work quickly before putrefaction set in. Five tiers of steps around the dissecting table accommodated the 'cognoscenti', who stood for hours watching the demonstrators, while artists made notes and drew hurriedly by candlelight. Their drawings preserved the discoveries that were made, long after the incriminating evidence of bones and tissues had been gathered up and incinerated. The practice of cremation was of course forbidden by the church.

The building, which still exists, functioned so well that it became a centre for medical developments for over two centuries. Leading doctors and scientists from all over Europe attended demonstrations, returning to work on similar lines in their own countries. An associate of Harvey's, Doctor Charles Scarborough, employed Wren (later Sir Christopher) at the age of sixteen, to make pasteboard models demonstrating the working of muscles. These were used in his lectures at Surgeon's Hall.[3] And the link with Padua is still preserved in the word operating 'theatre'.

But the real significance of this building was the change in people's attitude to the human body. Instead of regarding it as a temple for an immortal soul, it became a vehicle for investigation and study. A mechanism which could be manipulated and repaired. It paved the way for the 'staggering success of modern technological medicine with its transplants and its dialysis machines, its potent drugs and radiation therapies, its surgical precision and its confident, almost arrogant assumption of ultimate success in the battle against disease'.[4] At Padua one can see the inspiration, if not the origin, of whole disciplines and departments such as morbid anatomy, pathology, medical art and photography, and records. It is not too fanciful also to see in it the prototype of the modern medical centre, the place where doctors from many disciplines can come together to watch experts demonstrate their skills and discuss their work.

Specialisation

The growth of the clinical zone was slow at first. In the nineteenth century it gained impetus from the foundation of specialist hospitals; eye hospitals, ear, nose and throat hospitals, skin diseases, diseases of women and so on. In England there were no fewer than 230 by 1940.[5] They were mostly founded by philanthropists and relied for finances on voluntary contributions. The queues outside waiting admission for treatment were an important element in fundraising. Large waiting halls had to be built to accommodate them. They were lined with wooden benches, well polished by the bottoms of patients as they slid to the head of the queue. There they would be examined by medical students and then taken before the great man in his consulting room. If they were lucky enough to suffer from an interesting condition (that is if they were useful teaching material) and a bed was available, they would be admitted. Many were sent away with a few words of advice and a bottle of medicine. The accommodation was specifically designed by each specialist for his own needs. As he was giving his services voluntarily, it was often highly idiosyncratic and no expense was spared. It was natural that each specialist should regard his place of work as his own personal territory over which he exercised authority and his writ held the force of law.

Bailiwicks or self-contained kingdoms

In Europe this bailiwick concept was even more pronounced. In the new teaching hospitals, each head professor thought himself entitled to 90 beds, two operating theatres and his own laboratories, waiting room and consulting suite.[6] The Beaujon Hospital at Clichy in Paris, built in 1935, was one of the first examples of this, followed by the great Scandinavian hospitals such as Carolinski in Stockholm and the Glostrup in Copenhagen. The proliferation of specialities (Tucson Medical Centre in USA has 32)[7] enormously complicated the planner's task. The provision of separate bailiwicks is also extremely expensive to run; at the Ramon y Cajal Hospital in Madrid, for instance, 1600 beds have been provided, with over 50 designated operating theatres and X-ray suites. It was opened in 1975, but by 1983 some 30 of these had had to be closed for lack of funds.[8]

Each department as it develops naturally requires more space. Pathology for instance requires fume cupboards and animal houses. Radiology needs dark rooms, undressing cubicles, fluoroscopy, ultrasonic and computerised tomography scanners and an ever-expanding film store.[9] Physical medicine requires a hydrotherapy pool, a gymnasium, facilities for occupational therapy, rehabilitation and appliance fitting and so on.

There is a natural tendency for the importance of a department to be judged by the area of accommodation alotted. This has affected the oldest department of all, surgery. Thus at University College Hospital in London, built in 1903, the surgical department was placed right at the very core of the complex. But it consisted only of three rooms on each floor – an operating theatre with an anaesthetic room on one side and recovery on the other. Surgical patients were wheeled across a corridor from and to the wards.

A modern surgical department has between a third and a quarter of its area actually occupied by theatres. More than two-thirds are taken up by the changing area, scrub-up, gowning, preparation, anaesthesia, stores, sterilisation, instrument repairs and disposal, reception, bed-exchange and holding area as well as offices, on-call room, staff lounge, refreshment and pantry. Separate corridors for clean and dirty traffic are also often specified (pages 137–39). The recovery room where patients used only to spend 45 minutes now has an intensive care unit added, where they may spend days. This in turn has to have its own service arrangement for staff and even for relatives. In Spain, for instance, special viewing galleries in the form of an external balcony are provided at Santa Fe Hospital in Valencia, so that anxious relatives can see that their nearest and dearest has safely emerged from an operation alive, albeit still unconscious.

Day care reduces need for beds

Advances in medical practice which affect hospital design come about often as a result of a breakdown in the service. In chapter 2 we saw how wartime conditions led to early ambulation. This profoundly altered the character of the nursing zone. A similar departure from traditional practice has taken place in the clinical zone, not by accident but by design.

In the 1950s, two Scottish surgeons faced with an ever-growing waiting list due to a shortage of beds, offered the alternative of day surgery. Specially selected patients with suitable facilities for home care were admitted in the morning, prepared and treated, and after recovery sent home the same evening. In 1961 Stephens and Dudley published the results of their operations for hernia repair and varicose veins.[10] Special arrangements were made with general practitioners for supervision at home and for visits from the district nurse. Additional beds and recovery facilities, planned as an extension of the emergency department,

were provided in the hospital. This experiment proved so successful it has been taken up all over the world. The US Defence Department published a study showing that as many as 20 per cent of current surgical patients are suitable for day-surgery.[11] The saving in costs is enormous. Tucson Medical Centre, USA, for instance, reckoned that 1000 surgical operations were carried out on day patients in 1974 at one-eighth of the corresponding in-patient cost.[12]

Similar breakthroughs came about in the psychiatric field. Owing to shortage of beds, out-patients were admitted during the day to make use of ECT, consulting and occupational therapy facilities, returning home at night, while in-patients often shared the same transport arrangements on a shuttle basis, going out to sheltered workshops in the community during the day. This arrangement, originally carried out as an emergency measure after World War II at hospitals in Canada and UK, has now become a regular part of psychiatric treatment.[13] The success of all these day care developments has led to the rapid growth of the clinical zone in Europe.

Emergency department expansion

The expansion of the clinical zone in USA took place later than in Europe. The pattern of insurance delayed the introduction of out-patients' departments and day care. Physicians often arranged for the admission of patients for procedures that could have been carried out in the out-patients' department, simply to enable them to claim a larger share of expenses from their insurance company.[14] This led of course to expansion of the nursing as opposed to the clinical zone, which remained comparatively small. But the uninsured could not benefit from this practice; their only access to the health-care system was the emergency department. A study made at the University of California Hospital, Los Angeles showed that it was being used essentially only as a primary care clinic. Only 1 per cent of patients really needed immediate treatment; 18 per cent could wait for two hours. The remainder were there simply because there was nowhere else to go for the medical attention they required at the price they could afford to pay.[14]

The expansion of the emergency department, which had grown by 500 per cent between 1945–70, was expected to increase by a further 500 per cent in the following five years. The advent of medi-care and the introduction of universal insurance seem likely to lead to ever greater demands for space. A backlog of patients awaiting treatment will be released. The number of operations for common conditions such as hernias and varicose veins is double that in Britain.[15]

Preventive medicine and health maintenance

The character of the clinical zone, so long a private precinct reserved for the professional, is threatened by the arrival of preventive medicine. The trickle of patients from cold admission from the nursing zone or hot from casualty may become a flood. The healthy as well as the sick take part in the invasion and here the USA takes the lead. The craze for health checks has doubled the pressures on the accommodation. A further boost comes from the transfer of many doctors' offices onto the hospital campus. The increasing cost of medical equipment makes it necessary for them to rely more and more on what can only be provided in a general hospital. The multiphasic scanning techniques invented in the 1960s brought in thousands of people in the 1970s who had never been near a hospital before. Between 1975 and 1978 Tucson Medical Centre for instance carried out 11,823 brain scans. The average number of laboratory tests per patient was 20.[12] Under the Kaiser Plan (where patients pay doctors to keep them well) routine tests were developed to provide a dynamic record of health over a number of annual examinations. It looked as though there would be a vital change in the role of the hospital, 'a shift in structure from crisis intervention to health maintenance', and with it the size of the clinical zone would exceed the nursing and support zones added together.[11]

Complex organisation

Planners in 1970 thus saw the mainstream of health care facilities flowing outside the nursing zone, through the greatly enlarged clinical zone, equally accessible to out-patients as well as in-patients. The consultants' suites and waiting areas would act then as a diaphragm, providing 'comforting and hospitable spaces that enhance a warm and co-operative relationship with the community'.[16] It was an exhilarating prospect.

John Weeks, writing in 1979, in his brilliant introduction to Pütsep's *Modern Hospital* saw the planner 'designing a highly complex structure for a very complex organisation . . .' It must be capable of allowing each bailiwick almost unlimited expansion. 'In addition he has to design territories – the departments – for each of the groups whose successful interaction is the basis of the work of the hospital. Two different scales of perception are present throughout the building; the intimate, group-based department environments, and the less intimate but no less important image of the whole'.

'The architect must design a street system, locate the front doors and allow the inhabitants of each of the departments to effect the changes required to serve changing functions without distorting the image of the whole'.[17]

B   Containment

A problem of management

The clinical zone is of course the most expensive area to build and equip. Because of its central position, its expansion and contraction has a vital effect on the size of the rest of the hospital. Containment is largely an organisational and management problem. It is a question of deciding what tasks will be carried out and how to make the maximum use of the staff and available equipment. The strategies, as we have seen, are already well established – concentration and consolidation of resources; versatility of accommodation; mechanistion and miniaturisation and finally more consideration for the patient's convenience by relocating some services nearer his own home and so freeing more space for procedures that can only be carried out in hospital.

Concentration and consolidation

In temperate climates the cost of engineering services can be reduced if rooms requiring air-conditioning are concentrated in one zone. In chapter two we described how a central treatment area can take the place of dispersed treatment rooms previously attached to each nursing unit. Surgery and emergency and more recently obstetrics, can also be placed side by side. This department can not of course be merged with surgery because operations are planned, whereas babies are born at all hours of the day and night. But it may be cheaper and often more convenient if facilities for a caesarian can be provided across a corridor, rather than in a separate theatre suite located in an isolated maternity department.[18]

Versatility of spaces and time sharing

Consolidation means, if not the abandonment, at least the modification of the bailiwick concept. As early as 1961 Dr Bridgman coined the word banalisation from the French word *banal*, meaning ordinary.[19] He suggested that planners should study the peculiar requirements of each speciality to see how far they could be met by repetitive units of ordinary accommodation. This highest common factor, or lowest common multiple, approach was first applied to the out-patients department.

After several experiments in British hospitals the Scottish Home and Health Department published a definitive study of the *Organisation and Design of Out-Patients' Department* in 1967.[20] A doctor and an architect (wearing a white coat) sat in on all the clinics over a period of several weeks, timing the consultations and noting the arrangements made for dressing and undressing, examination and note-taking etc. They showed that consulting suites consisting of standard rooms (instead of offices, examination rooms and undressing cubicles) could meet the needs of most specialities such as dermatology, ear nose and throat, eye, gynaecology, and orthopaedics, as well as general medicine and surgery. By planning the rooms *en suite*, different clinics could use a combination of 2, 4 or 6 rooms as appropriate on different days of the week, simply by changing the name on the door and bringing out of store the equipment required. The team thus invented time sharing, long before estate agents coined the phrase for holiday accommodation and second homes. They also made a study of waiting times, using mathematical models. They found that an acceptable appointment system could be devised by which a doctor never had to wait more than 5 minutes and a patient 13 to 18 minutes. These studies greatly reduced the area of waiting space required, while at the same time of course increasing the convenience of patients and their escorts.

Another example of versatility can be seen in the laboratory. In 1961 Musgrove showed that the peculiar requirements of bacteriology, serology, histology, bio-chemistry, urinalysis and haematology can nearly all be met using a set of standard serviced bench tops laid out at right angles to the window wall.[21] Interchangeable trolleys carrying special equipment can then be plugged in as under-bench units. The technicians of the various disciplines can thus be fitted out with the appropriate trolley without redesigning the laboratory. This has been taken a stage further in the sub-servo lab system developed by Zeidler for the McMaster Health Science Centre in Canada. Here completely serviced prefabricated standard demountable units can be assembled and attached to the energy harness of the building at strategic points in the clinical zone.[22] Each one is a kind of mini-lab on wheels.

Making more use of facilities provided

Many specialised departments of a hospital are seldom fully occupied. Although this is inevitable, it is clearly undesirable for them to stand idle for the greater part of the day. Raymond Moss and his Medical Architecture Research Unit team in the UK have developed a technique of recording the amount of time different areas of a hospital are occupied.[23] Starting with fairly humble studies of staff changing rooms (in which they discovered that the showers were never used) they have extended their studies to the clinical zone. Their survey of operating theatres in the National Health Service in Britain confirmed an earlier survey carried out by USA consultants on 55 general hospitals in the Philadelphia–South Jersey Metropolitan Area in 1969.[24] There are very wide differences in the intensity of use. The average utilisation is little over half the theoretically possible figure and very much below the figure previously used for planning purposes.[25]

A survey made in 1980 by the Oxford Regional Health Authority in UK lists the most important factors such as extending the use of theatres outside prime time (daytime weekday periods), the effect of bed allocation, admission policies and length of stay, treatment facilities (anaesthetic rooms, recovery rooms), the efficiency of schedules, and so on.[26]

Progress towards the better use of operating theatres can only be made if and when those directly concerned in running these units are prepared to analyse and discuss the problems. Improvements in levels of efficiency cannot be achieved without the effort and co-operation of all levels of staff in all the professions directly involved. This is one of the areas which the new managers at present being appointed in the National Health Service will wish to study closely.

Today the average cost of building and equipping a single theatre suite is over £250,000. The estimated running costs are over £1 a minute or £100,000 a year. There is an ever-growing waiting list for surgery. Have the planners, architects or engineers also got anything to contribute?

Planning and design of operating theatres

At the beginning of this century the operating theatre department was a small and simple affair. In 1903 the surgical department at University College Hospital, London, had a total area of about $60m^2$. A modern twin-theatre department has about 25 separate rooms and spaces and requires a total floor area equivalent to nearly $300m^2$ per theatre.

The main reason for the complexity and compartmentation of modern surgical departments is of course the demand for more and more measures to combat infection. The air-conditioning system of every department is designed to provide a range of pressures which will permit air movement from clean to dirty areas, and not the reverse. Enormous sums have been invested in complex engineering. But they have not resulted in the anticipated reduction in the infection rate. W. Whyte, the Bacteriologist Research Fellow of the Building Services Research Unit of the University of Glasgow sums up the present position:
'It is highly likely that all these "improvements" have brought little change to wound sepsis because they have not caused a substantial reduction in the critical factors that cause bacterial contamination in the wound. It is clear that elaborate designs can do little to reduce the important route of endogenous infection, i.e. infection of the patients by their own bacteria, and can only be expected to influence infection from the room environment. The main means of environmental spread to "clean" operations is by the air and it is clear that the elaborate designs of ventilation and air movement control have given a comparatively small reduction in airborne bacteria . . . However, this airborne risk can now be reduced enormously, if not eliminated, by the use of ultra clean air Systems.'[27]

Ultra clean air systems (UCA) are a development of the laminar flow principle used in industry. Air is blown from the ceiling downwards at 20m a minute in a uni-directional manner over an area 3m square. An ultra clean area is formed immediately around the operating table. This effectively isolates the table and the instruments from the rest of the theatre suite. The surgical team can be equipped with special gowns and masks fitted to the suction outlet.

The rest of the theatre staff are therefore outside the ultra clean 'enclosure', and their cleanliness is of comparatively little importance.

Controlled trials of UCA systems were conducted by the British Medical Research Council in 19 hospitals in UK and Sweden between 1974 and 1979. These showed that UCA systems and the wearing of whole-body exhaust suits can quarter the incidence of sepsis in joint replacements (as compared with conventional clothing in conventional operating theatres)[28]. Not only that; it can be calculated that these systems are cost-effective, in that their cost is quickly paid back from the savings in extra hospital costs through reduced patient stay.[29]

The use of UCA systems and their development may well have a profound effect on theatre planning and design, leading to a reduction in compartmentation. Already open plan multi-table operating theatres using laminar-flow enclosures have been built in Switzerland and South Africa. Cowan has suggested a four enclosure department with screens between the tables (pages 145–47) and claims the following advantages:

Little or no possibility of infection entering the wound via the airborne route.

Ease of supervision, and control of staff, which could encourage better discipline.

No doors between corridors and operating zone.

Teaching of medical and nursing students could be easier and safer.

Finally, he states that a new multi-enclosure department need cost no more than a conventionally planned department. 'Cost savings can be achieved by installing a number of enclosures manufactured as integrated items of surgical equipment within one space. This would enable the architect to plan the department purely from the functional point of view without the constraints of designing complicated physical arrangements to combat airborne wound infection.'[30]

The way may now be clear for the wheel to come full circle; for a return to the efficient economical open plan layout similar to the wartime St Thomas' Hospital (page 132). The use of UCA enclosures will result in better space utilisation and more efficient deployment of staff. Alternative layouts can be worked out (using movable screens) to suit surgeons' individual preferences. Some would offer more ease of supervision and communication; others more privacy. There would be no diminution in the need to preserve the highest standard of discipline and concentration. But these things will be made that much easier to provide in an operating department planned from first principles on a rational basis. It may well be that such a department will offer more patients more surgery in safer surroundings built in a smaller space, for less money.

Mechanisation and miniaturisation

The enormous increase in X-ray examinations and laboratory tests already described has led to the mechanisation of some processes previously carried out by hand. Film processors eliminate the need for dark rooms. Auto-analysers process 3 man-weeks worth of tests in 8 hours.[30] The unit dose system, enabling the pharmacy to supply a nurse with a specific dosage of a particular drug, to be taken at a particular time by a particular patient, means that all the work of preparation and measurement can be done more accurately in advance.

Clibbon has pointed out that these developments ease the pressure on the clinical zone. She draws a distinction between procedures which involve the patient directly, such as taking specimens, and what is done with the specimens in the absence of the patient. Processing of specimens can be carried out in the industrial or support zones. She sees a progressive increase of these zones as more and more mechanisation is introduced.[16]

Patients' convenience

Space research has enabled heart monitoring to take place on the far side of the moon. Similar less dramatic developments are taking place on earth. X-ray images can be transmitted by wire, so that hospitals can have the benefit of an interpretation by a radiologist sitting at a central point.[31] His diagnosis can be given immediately, without waiting for films to be developed and despatched; and, more important for the patient, without a special journey to a District General Hospital. Closer links with the centre enable general practitioners to give a higher standard of medicine on the spot. Relocation of as many services as possible in residential areas will greatly add to patients' convenience and reduce the pressures on the clinical zone. Professor Chester calculates that in the UK some 50 million people call on the National Health Service an average of 4 times a year. Of these calls, 5 million are addressed to hospitals. The remaining 195 million or 97.5 per cent are satisfied at community level.[32] Doctor Bridgman sees the concept of the hospital changing all over the world. It is no longer so much a place where patients *come*, as a base from which staff *go* to organise community care, and to which they return to learn the latest methods of prevention, diagnosis and treatment.[33]

The invasion of the clinical zone by the healthy can only be checked by a change in attitude. People must accept more responsibility for the health of their own bodies. They must stop blaming their doctors for anything that goes wrong. Otherwise there is a risk that the art of physical diagnosis will be overtaken by the practice of defensive medicine, which all too often leads to crippling hospital costs and the bankruptcy of health care systems.

The last word must lie with Professor Stolte of Holland.[34] He describes our present dilemma as "a kind of defensive medicine, characterised by superfluous diagnostic and even therapeutic procedures without any real use and perhaps even doing harm to the patient." One may observe similar behaviour with trainees in response to too-demanding chiefs of departments. Every day spent in hospital that could just as well have been spent at home is wrong. The hospital is a dangerous place to be in, both from the physical as from the psychosocial point of view. Many kinds of costly screening are deplorable because they lead to thrusting the sick role upon people who will not benefit from it and will certainly not become happier by it.

The modern hospital is a very young institution. As an organisation it is still learning how to cope with its mission and how to behave rationally. This is where the task of hospital management lies. It asks for much specific knowledge and skills, for perseverance and patience and above all for courage.'

C   The planners' response

Clinical zone: key to drawings in chapter 3C only

Accident and emergency
1   Resuscitation
2   Examination cubicles
3   Nurses' work space
4   Cleansing
5   Relative's overnight stay
6   Plaster suite

Administration and records
7   General office
8   Office
9   Records store
10   Diagnostic index
11   Plaster suite

Day centre
12   Treatment/endoscopy
13   Day ward/space

Intensive therapy unit and coronary care
14   Multi-bed space
15   Single-bed room
16   Staff overnight stay
17   Equipment

Laboratory (service and teaching)
18   Haematology
19   Chemical pathology
20   Microbiology
21   (Not allocated)
22   Histology
23   Blood bank
24   Specimen, reception, etc
25   Automated section

Mortuary
26   Body store
27   Viewing room
28   Post mortem

Teaching and training
29   Classroom
30   Seminar
31   Lecture theatre
32   Demonstration
33   Library

Operating theatres
34   Anaesthetic room
35   Exit bay/recovery
36   Scrub-up
37   Preparation
38   Disposal
39   Transfer, reception, bed park
40   Operating room/bay
41   Sterilising
42   Post-operation recovery

Out-patients
43   Consulting/examination rooms
44   Dental surgery
45   Snack bar/pantry
46   Sub-waiting
47   Dispensary

Obstetric delivery and premature baby
48   Delivery suite
49   Labour rooms
50   Cots and incubators

X-Ray and radiotherapy
51   Radiodiagnostic room
52   Dark room/processing
53   Undressing cubicles
54   X-ray records/reception
55   Radiotherapy room

Rehabilitation and day hospital
56   Physiotherapy
57   Hydrotherapy
58   Occupational therapy
59   Gymnasium/exercise space
60   Day/dining space

Common areas
61   Waiting space
62   Patients' toilets
63   Reception/records
64   Staff base
65   Clean utility/supplies
66   Dirty utility/sluice
67   Stores
68   Trolleys/wheelchairs
69   Cleaner
70   Staff changing/toilets/rest

Content of clinical zone

The growth of the clinical zone reflects the advances in diagnostic and treatment techniques that have taken place this century. A general hospital today will require about three times the area to house its clinical zone that it did at the turn of the century. This is the most highly serviced and most expensive part of the hospital. It is also the fastest-growing.

Functions forming the clinical zone of a typical general hospital include:

3.1 Operating theatre (King Faisal Specialist Hospital, Saudi Arabia).

3.2 X-ray (King Faisal Specialist Hospital, Saudi Arabia).

3.3 Rehabilitation (Rotherham District General Hospital, UK).

3.4 Laboratories (Frimley Park Hospital UK).

3.1

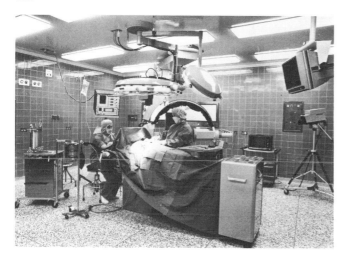

3.3

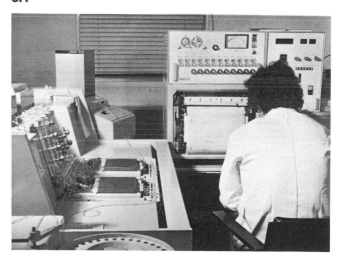

3.2

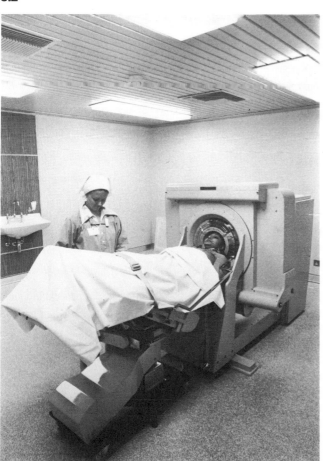

3.4

Relationships between departments

As new specialities developed in the nineteenth century they were given their own specialist hospitals: eye, ear, nose and throat, children's etc. Later, when they were incorporated in a single General Hospital, they retained their identity and independence. Each consultant built up separate bailiwicks. Rigid boundaries between departments and a grid system of by-pass corridors inhibited the possibilities of sharing space and equipment and made expansion difficult.

3.5, 3.6   Ground floor layout and view of corridor, Varburg Hospital, Sweden.

In recent years planners have sought to break down departmental boundaries so that one department can flow into another. Open-ended sections permit future extensions.

3.7   Ground floor plan (part) Central Emergency Hospital, Abu Dhabi, UAE.

3.5

3.6

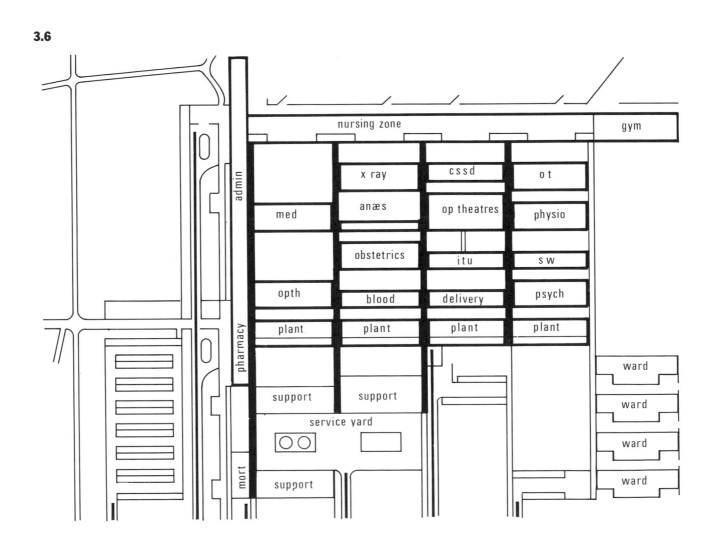

3.7

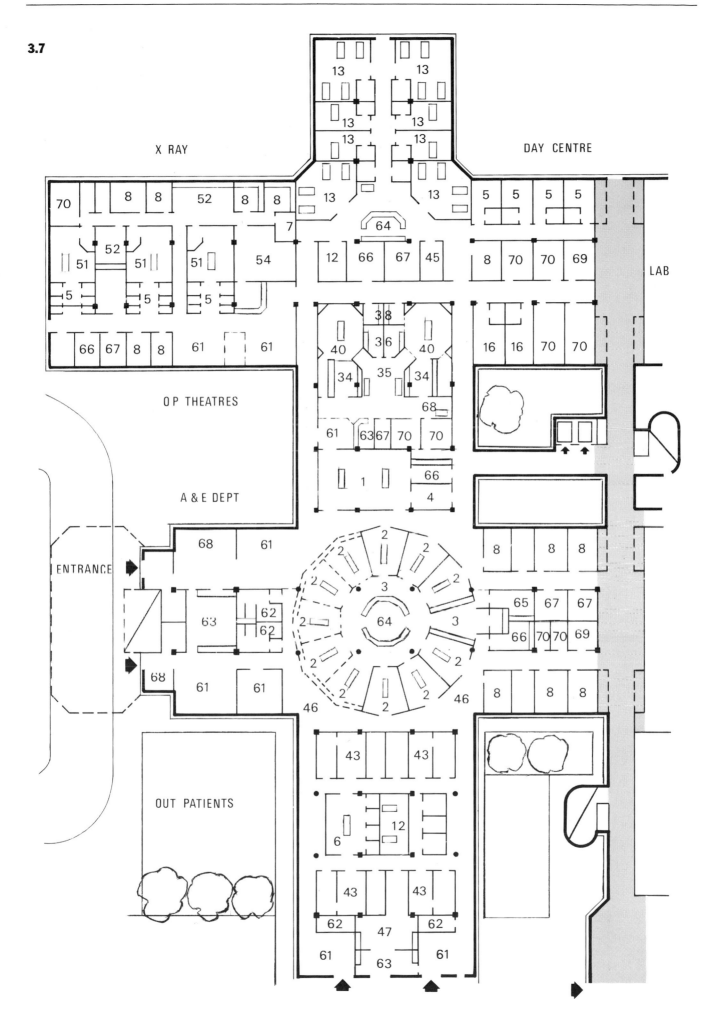

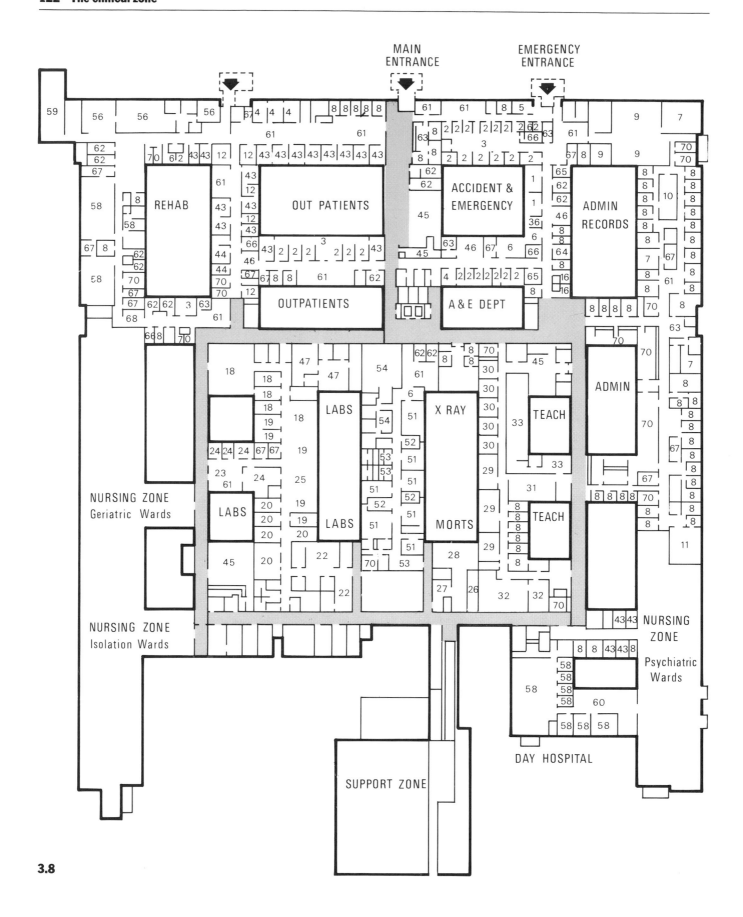

3.8

3.8 Ground floor plan, Bury St Edmunds, UK. Here planning policics were adopted to exploit the possibilities of sharing spaces such as treatment rooms, utility rooms, waiting space, and toilets, between departments. To facilitate this, the clinical zone was planned on two levels in a continuous horizontal form. Boundaries were not defined, so that one department merges with another e.g. postgraduate medical teaching with nurse training, rehabilitation with geriatric day centre.

3.9 Bury St Edmunds, UK. Main out-patient waiting area with view into one of the seventeen landscaped courtyards.

3.10 Bury St Edmunds, UK: dental surgery.

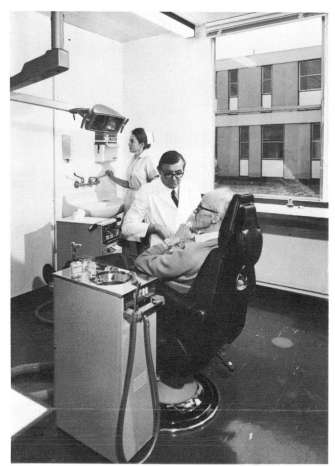

3.10

3.9

3.11 Bury St Edmunds, UK. Intensive therapy unit on the first floor, planned immediately adjacent to the post-operative recovery unit so that supporting ancillary rooms can be shared.

3.12 Bury St Edmunds, UK. One of five central treatment rooms on the first floor used by both in-patients from the adjacent nursing zone and by out-patients.

3.13 Bury St Edmunds, UK: first floor plan. The same principles of sharing and multi-use of space are applied. The combined observation and day ward is in use throughout 24 hours, for emergency admissions at night and for out-patient treatment and recovery during the day.
Numerous design-in-use studies have been carried out for the UK Department of Health by the Medical Architectural Research Unit of London, using Bury St Edmunds hospital as a test bed. Those studies confirm the validity of policies aimed at achieving more intensive use of expensive clinical facilities. They have formed the basis of recent UK guidance on space utilisation.

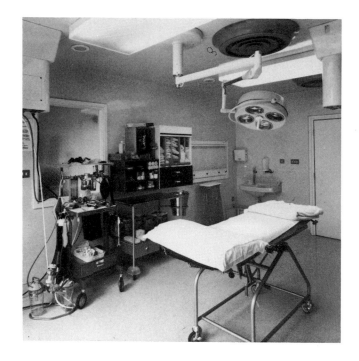

3.12

3.11

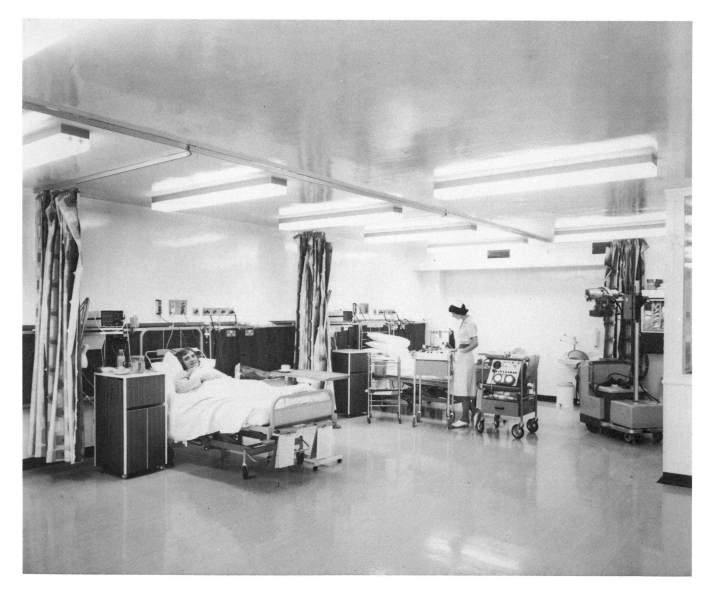

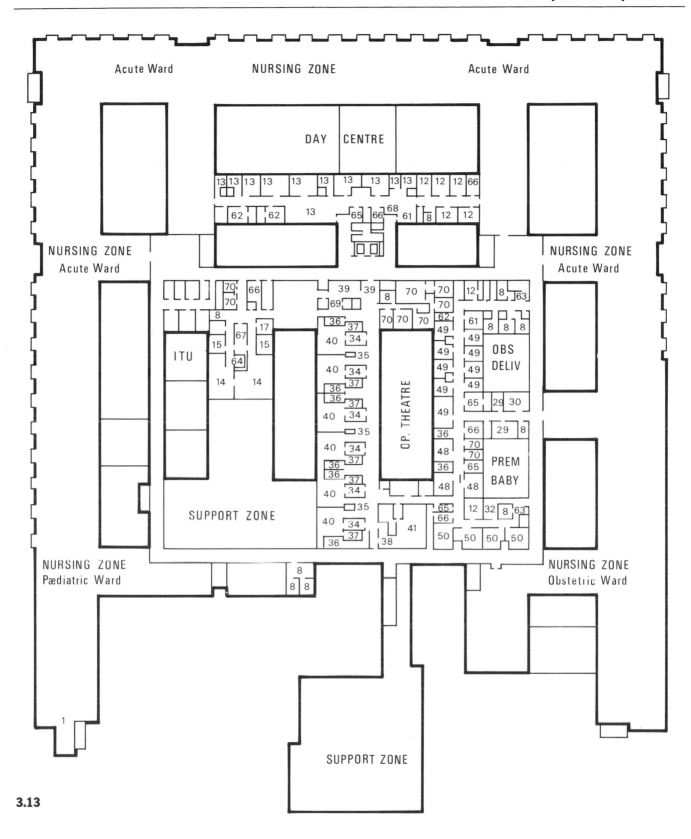

3.13

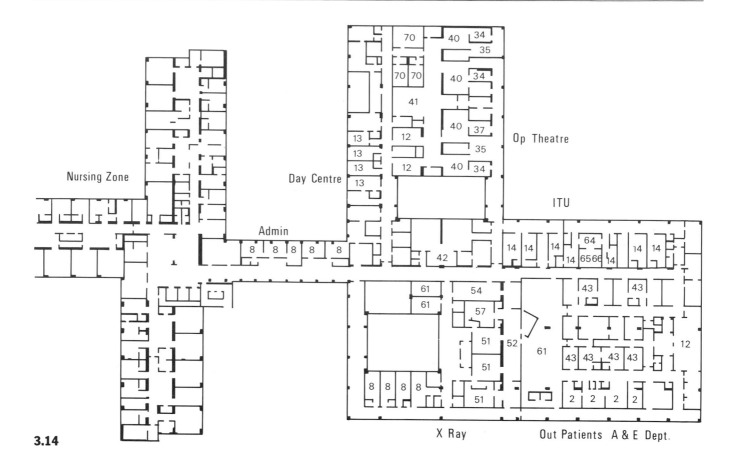

3.14

3.15

Recent continental examples make use of deep-planned floors to accommodate clinical zones with compact horizontal relationships between departments.

3.14 Frederiksborg Hospital, Denmark: plan at level 3. Note contiguous relationships of ITU to operating theatres and out-patient department to X-ray.

3.15 Frederiksborg Hospital, Denmark: block housing the clinical zone on two levels.

3.16 Nordenham Hospital, West Germany: first floor plan. Cruciform plan provides independent access for in-patients and out-patients from a central point. Note contiguous relationships of out-patients, emergency, operating theatres and ITU.

3.17 Nordenham Hospital, West Germany: view of intensive therapy unit.

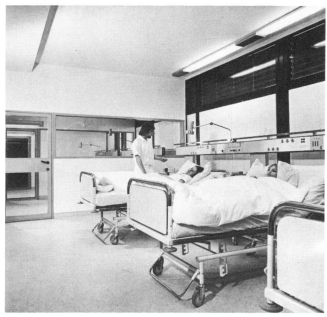

3.17

3.16

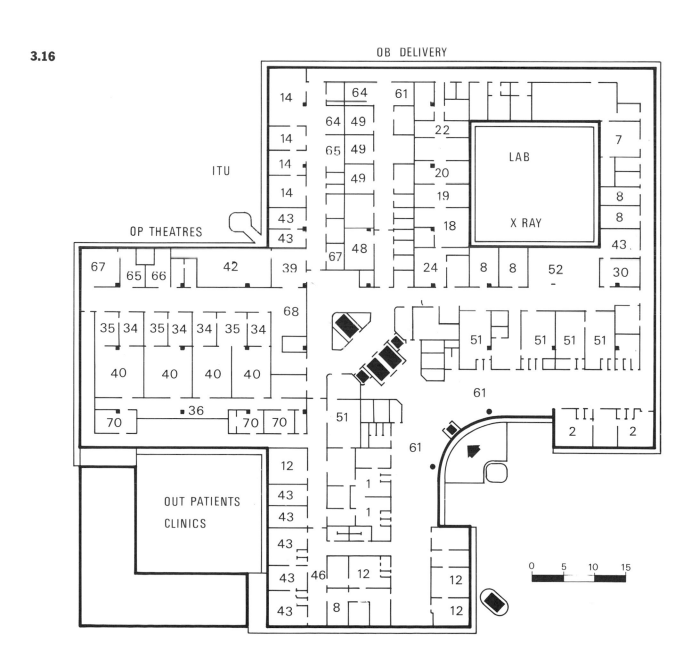

The plans of the clinical zones of two large (800–1000 beds) general hospitals reflect different planning policies.

3.18 Rotherham Hospital, UK. Plan at level B. All the emergency diagnostic and treatment departments – operating theatres, intensive therapy, X-ray and accident and emergency – are arranged on one level, together with the acute surgical wards. Thus all patient movement is independent of lifts. Patients are moved directly between accident and emergency and X-ray and between operating theatres and intensive therapy without having to use the main hospital corridor (shown hatched).

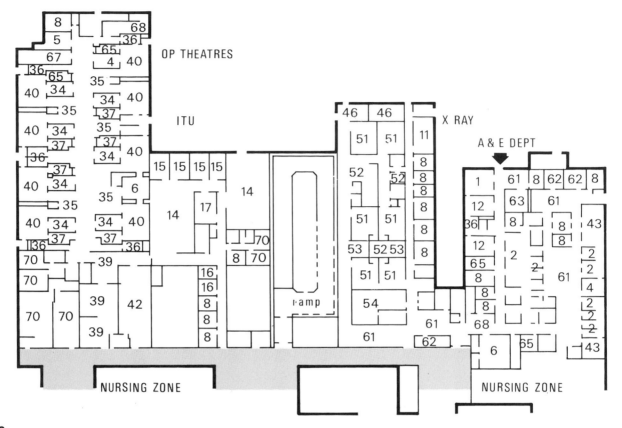

3.18

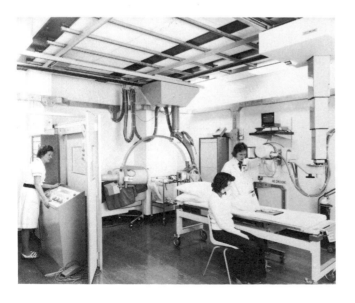

3.19

3.20

3.19 Rotherham Hospital, UK: view of X-ray room.

3.20 Rotherham Hospital, UK: accident and emergency.

3.21   York Hospital, UK: ground floor plan. Here treatment and diagnostic departments are planned in separated pavilions on two levels. There is no direct link between accident and emergency and X-ray; hence the need for a separate X-ray section within the accident and emergency department. Operating theatres are on the floor above intensive therapy.

3.22 York Hospital, UK: intensive therapy unit.

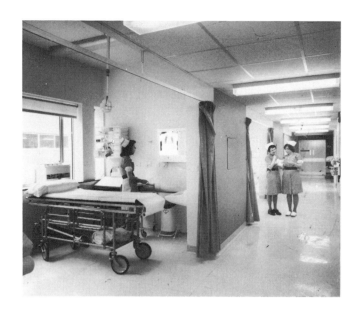

3.22

3.21

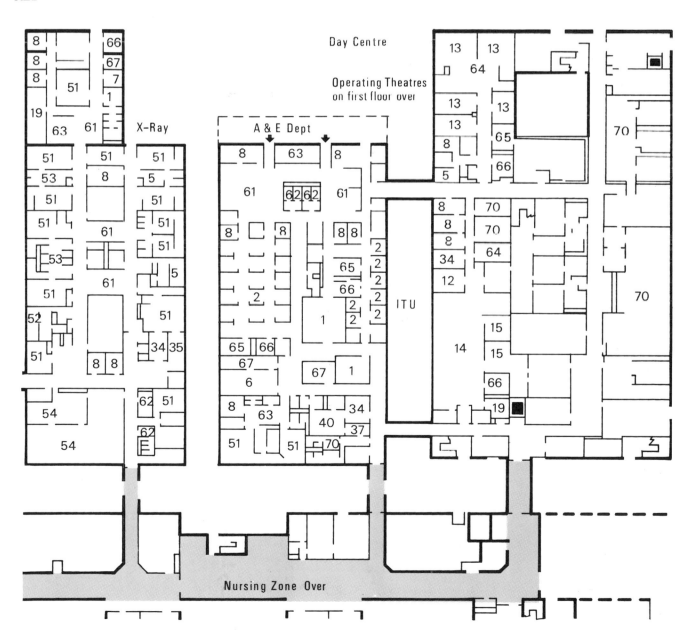

Three examples in which the clinical zone is conceived as one continuous deep-planned space, rather like a department store. The spaces are unrelieved by boundaries, light wells or courtyards and are wholly dependent on artificial light and ventilation.

3.23 Gelsenkirchen Hospital, West Germany: ground floor plan.

3.24 Etobicoke Hospital, Canada: ground floor. Access corridor and waiting spaces for patients and visitors are arranged around the perimeter of a vast rectangular space, housing all the departments of the

clinical zone. Note the combined operating theatres and obstetric delivery suites. This type of layout fully exploits the possibilities of sharing and multi-use of space.

3.25 Bath Clinic, UK: the clinical zone of a small 50-bed private hospital. One open-plan space with movable screens provides highly flexible facilities for the combined functions of post-operative recovery, intensive therapy and day care.

3.26 Bath Clinic, UK: operating theatre.

3.23

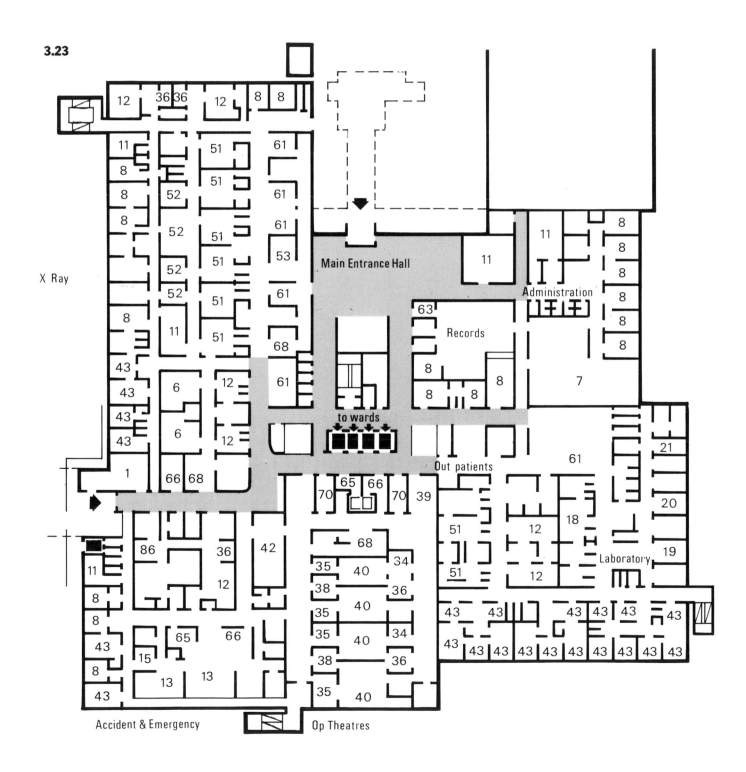

3.24

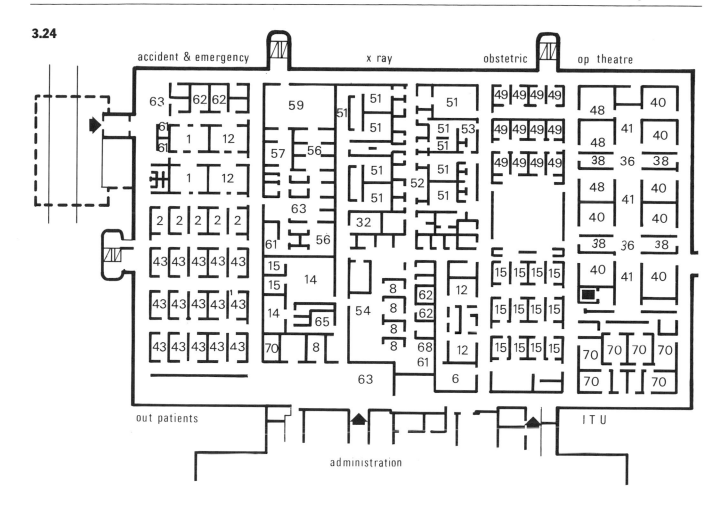

accident & emergency   x ray   obstetric   op theatre

out patients

administration

ITU

3.26

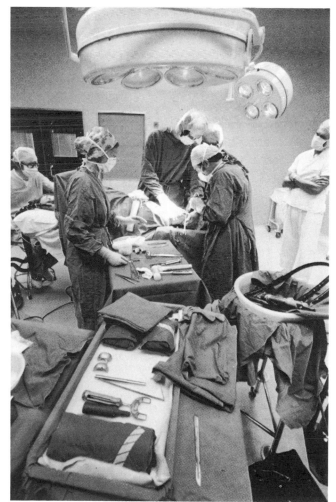

3.25

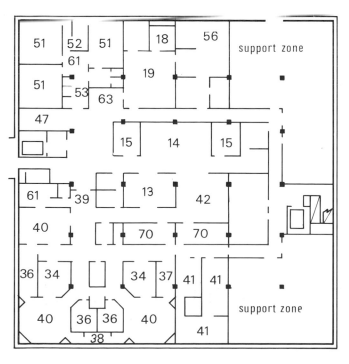

Operating theatres

Since World War II there has been an enormous expansion in the number and size of operating theatres. At St Thomas' Hospital, London, a series of operating theatre departments, using different layouts, have been brought into use at intervals over the past 40 years. Figures 3.27–3.30 inclusive illustrate the plans of four of these.

3.27 St Thomas' Hospital, UK: basement theatre suite, 1945. Soon after the outbreak of war all surgery was transferred to an emergency four-table theatre in the basement. After the installation of a new ventilation system this efficient and well-used facility continued in use for some years after the end of the war. Despite the open plan, wound sepsis rates were within the national average.

3.28 St Thomas' Hospital, UK: block VIIA, 1955. A new twin theatre suite based on early Ministry of Health guidance was completed as part of the rebuilding of the bomb-damaged south wing.

3.29 St Thomas' Hospital, UK: east wing. Second floor of major new extension added in 1965; contains a four-theatre department. The plan was based on the draft *Hospital Building Note* then in preparation.

3.30 St Thomas' Hospital, UK: north wing, 1975. Large department containing 8 theatre suites on the third floor of the most recently completed section of the hospital. Planning was based on the latest Department of Health guidance.

3.27

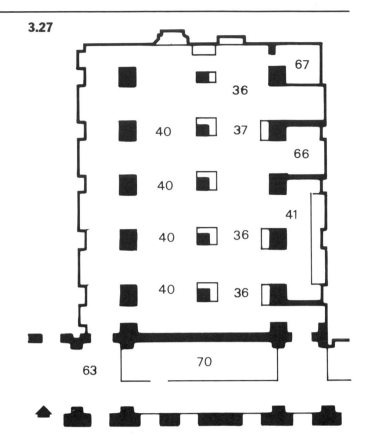

3.28

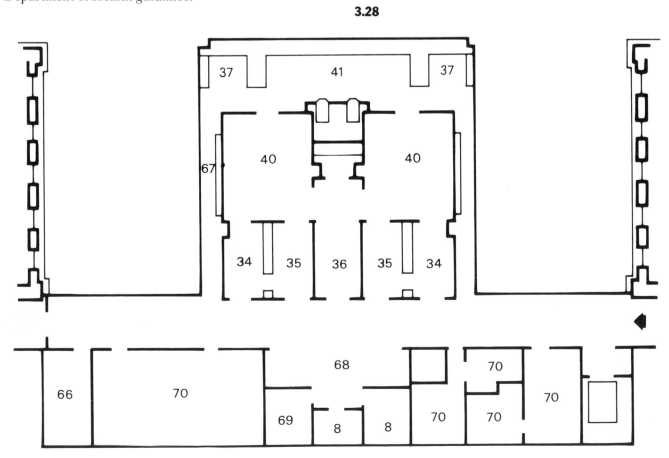

3.29

3.30

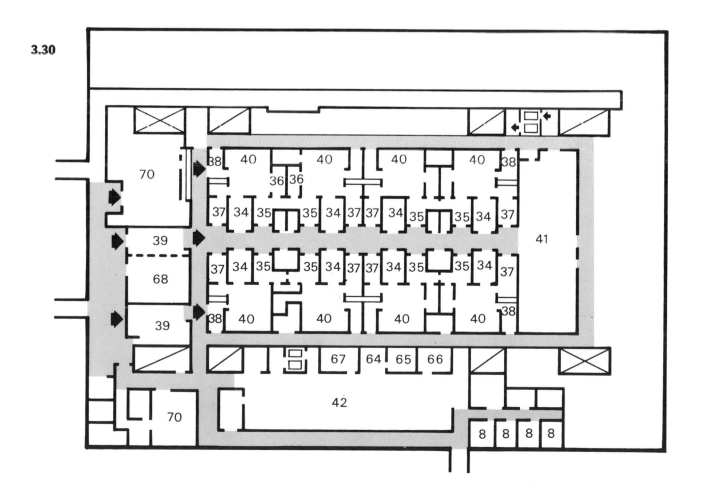

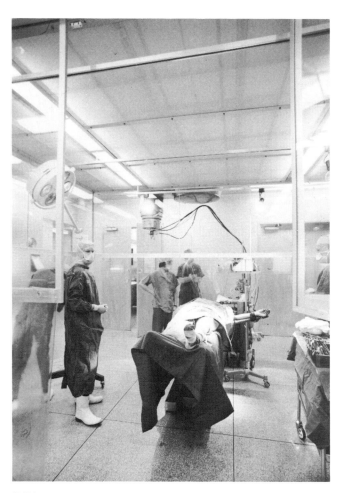

3.31

3.31 St Thomas' Hospital, UK: one of the new operating theatres in the north wing.

3.32 Comparison of floor areas per theatre table and analysis of the use of space. The huge increases in area of the examples built since the war are partly due to the compartmentation of the operating functions into separate rooms for anaesthetics, scrub-up and gowning and instrument trolley lay-up, in addition to the operating room itself. In the north wing department approximately 40 per cent of the total net area is allocated to operating space, 30 per cent to ancillaries and the remaining 30 per cent to the corridors and lobbies needed to service the multiplicity of separate rooms. Excessive compartmentation can inhibit the efficient utilisation of space. Supervision is more difficult and cleaning more expensive. The possibilities of multi-use and sharing of space are diminished. Corridors cannot be used for other functions, unlike circulation space within a room. Theatre corridors are very wide – up to 3m – to accommodate the movement of beds and trolleys. In some recent examples corridor space equals the total amount of operating space.

3.32

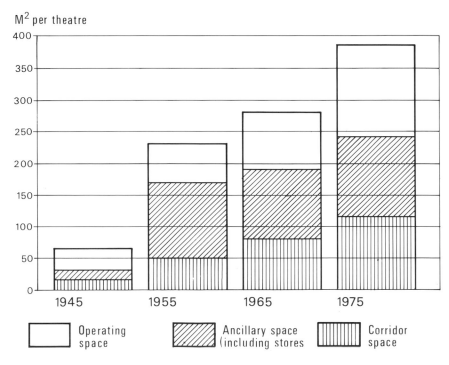

M^2 per theatre

3.33 Classification of types of operating theatre layouts. Space in the operating theatre department can be classified into three main areas: the operating suite, comprising the theatre, anaesthetic room, scrub-up, preparation space and exit/recovery lobby; the stores and processing section, including theatre sterilising unit, sterile store. The third area comprises reception, transfer, post-operative recovery, staff changing and staff rest rooms, together with administrative offices. These three areas are linked by a complex system of corridors.

3.34 The way in which these three areas are put together, and the corridor system employed, will determine the type of layout. Diagrams A to F identify six layouts which have formed the basis of recent examples in the USA, Europe and the Middle East, and are illustrated on the following pages.

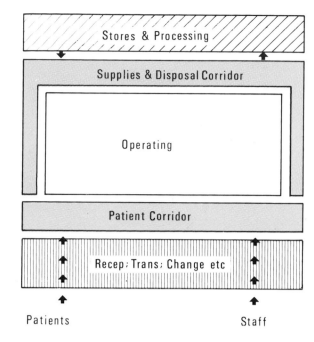

3.33

3.34

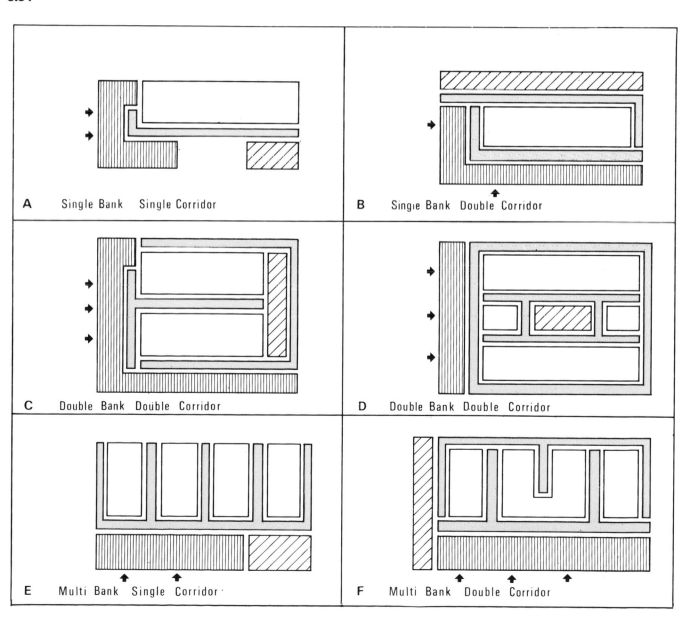

A   Single Bank   Single Corridor

B   Single Bank   Double Corridor

C   Double Bank   Double Corridor

D   Double Bank   Double Corridor

E   Multi Bank   Single Corridor

F   Multi Bank   Double Corridor

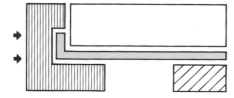

A   Single Bank   Single Corridor

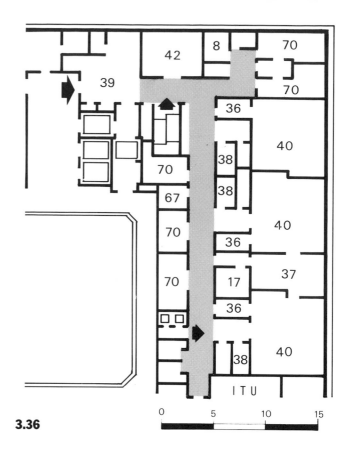

Operating suites are arranged in line on one side of a single corridor. The stores and processing section is placed at the opposite end of the corridor to the reception, transfer, change section; this helps to separate patient traffic from supplies and disposal. One corridor greatly facilitates the supervision and control of the whole department. This type of layout is suitable for up to six theatre suites.

3.35 Frimley Park Hospital, UK: six operating suites on one side of a single corridor. Note external maintenance access doors to each suite from courtyard.

3.36 Alexander Onassis Memorial Cardiac Surgery Centre, Greece: single corridor serving three operating suites.

3.36

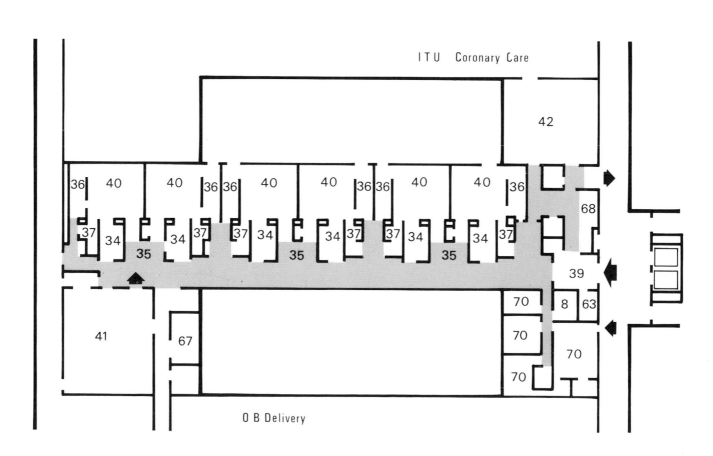

3.35

3.37

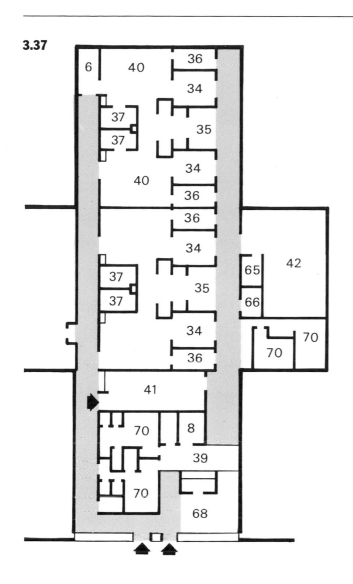

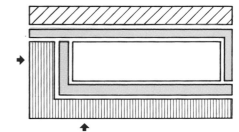

B   Single Bank Double Corridor

Operating suites are planned in line flanked, by two corridors, one for the movement of patients, the other for supplies and disposal traffic.

3.37 Standard Nucleus Hospital, UK: plan of four-theatre department. Both patients and staff enter the right-hand corridor via the transfer bay. Clean supplies use the right-hand corridor. All items for reprocessing and disposal use the left-hand corridor.

3.38 Nordenham Hospital, West Germany: four-theatre department.

3.38

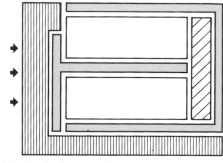

C Double Bank Double Corridor

In larger departments the operating suites are arranged in two banks in order to reduce the lengths of the patient and supplies corridors.

3.39 Central Emergency Hospital, Abu Dhabi: six-theatre department.

3.40 Ostersunds Hospital, Sweden: large eight-theatre department. Central patient corridor with twin supplies corridors.

3.39

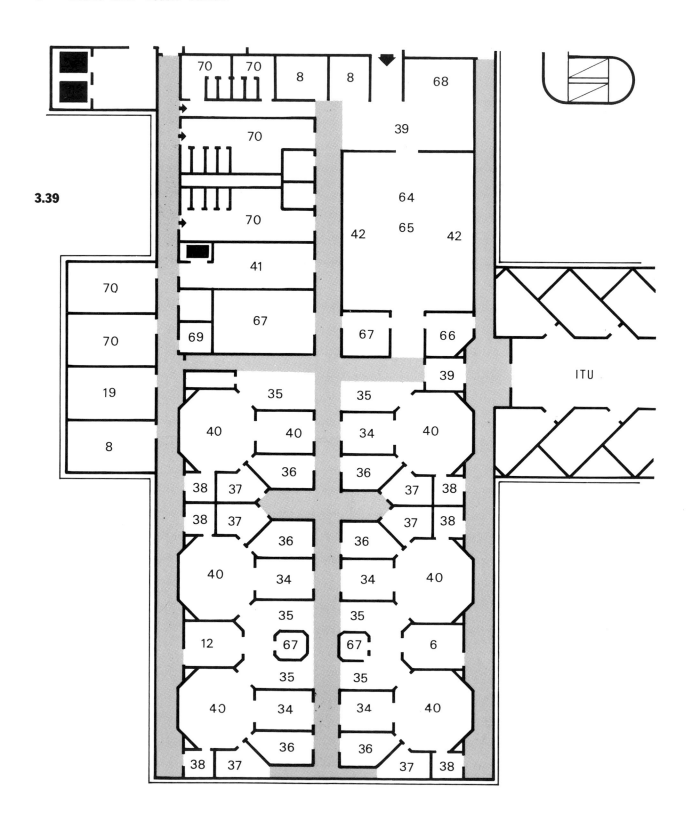

3.40

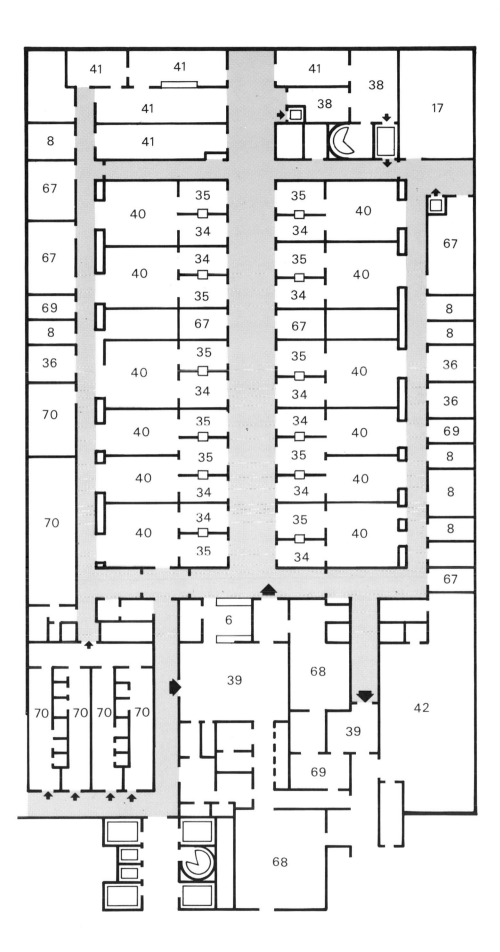

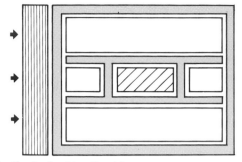

D   Double Bank Double Corridor

The stores and processing section is planned between two banks of operating suites. Supplies arrive by lift direct into this section. A separate perimeter corridor provides access for patients to all operating suites.

3.41   Beth Israel Hospital, USA: typical American plan. Note absence of anaesthetic rooms and exit bays.

3.42, 3.43   Hvidovre Hospital, Denmark: huge sixteen-theatre department.

3.41

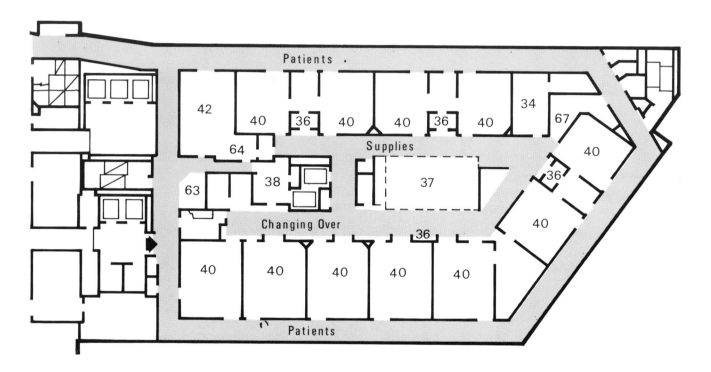

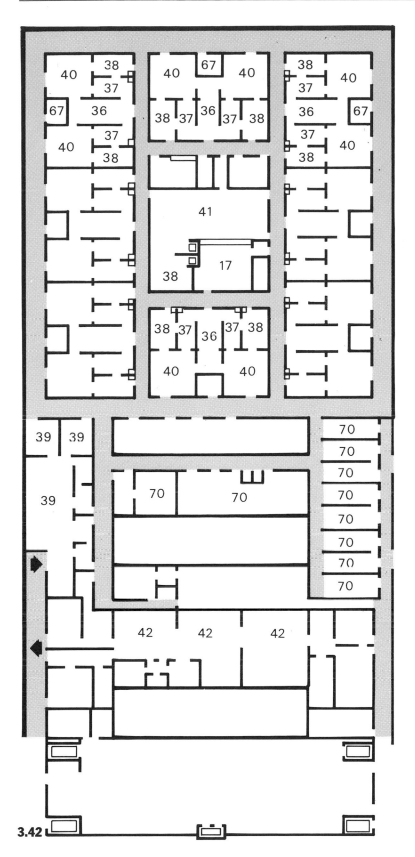

3.42

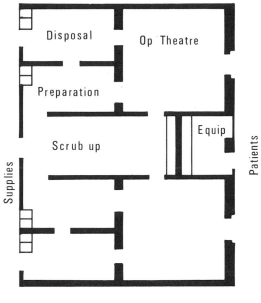

3.43

3.44

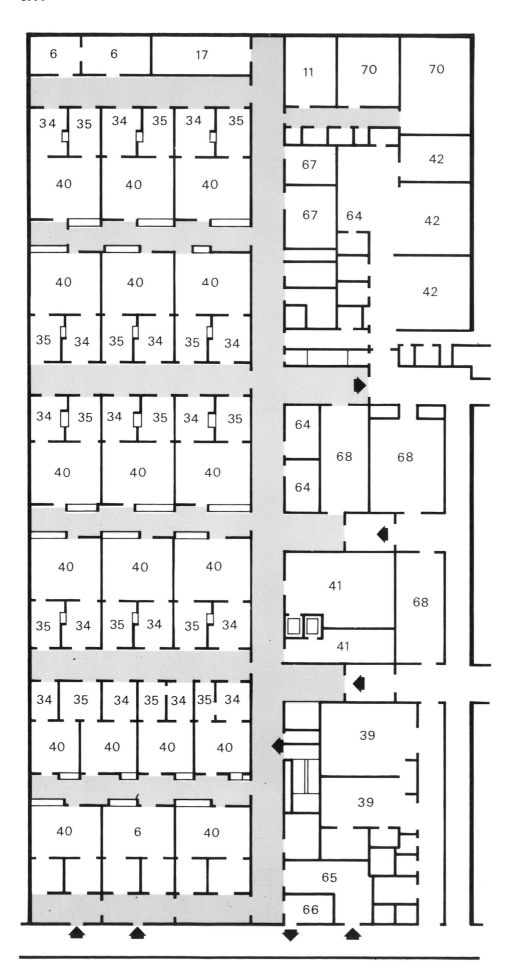

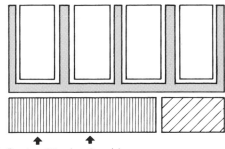

E   Multi Bank Single Corridor

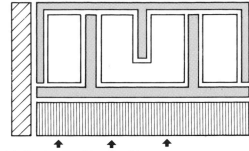

F   Multi Bank Double Corridor

Multiple banks of operating suites are used in an attempt to reduce the spread of very large departments, resulting in a complex network of corridors.

3.44 Sundsvall Hospital, Sweden: a total of 19 operating suites arranged in 6 banks served by a single corridor system.

3.45 Royal Free Hospital, UK: separate corridor system for all items for disposal and reprocessing.

3.45

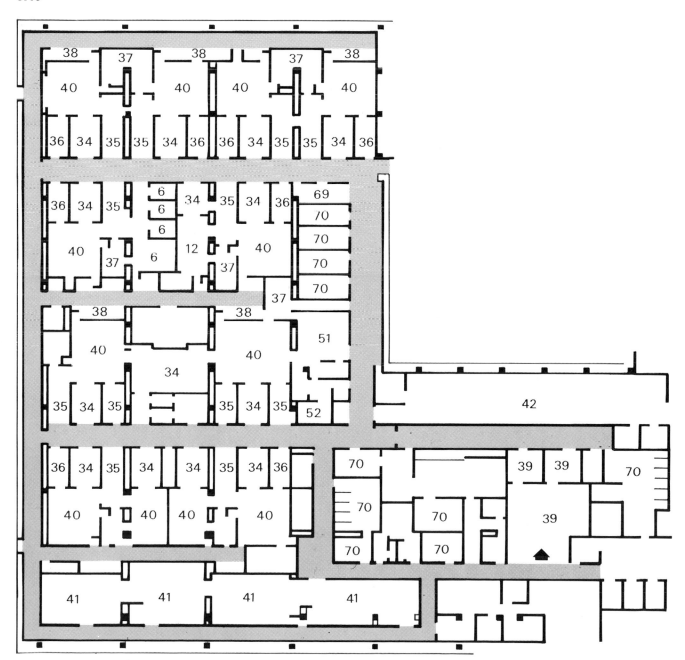

3.46 Nucleus Hospital, UK: standard plan of typical twin operating suite showing layout of equipment. Each suite comprises four compartments: operating theatre, anaesthetic room, scrub-up and preparation room. Most other countries in Western Europe follow this general arrangement. In recent years many theatres are being equipped with ultra clean air (UCA) enclosures. The use of UCA systems brings into question the need for multi-compartment layouts.

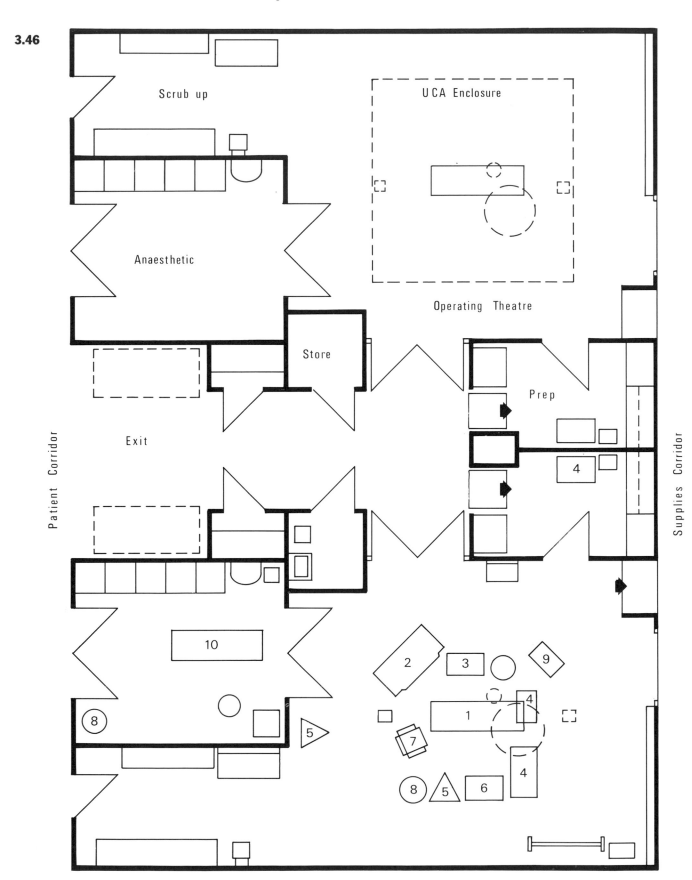

3.46

3.47 The area per theatre of the operating suites (operating, anaesthetic, scrub-up and preparation space) of a number of recent international examples of conventionally planned operating departments compared with the new multi-enclosure layouts. Reductions in area of up to 50 per cent are possible. In addition there will be a substantial reduction in under-utilised corridor space.

3.47

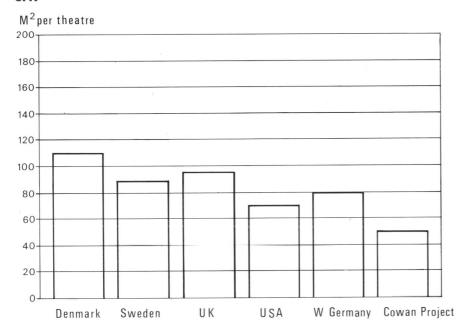

M^2 per theatre

3.48 Charnley-Howarth Exflo UCA system. A continuous flow of clean air is directed over the target area: a space 3×3m which includes the patient, operating table drapes, instruments and the surgical team.

3.50

3.49

3.49, 3.50 Charnley-Howarth body exhaust and protective clothing system: consists of a mask and gown made of an impermeable material. Air is exhausted from the gown, thereby inhibiting the passage of organisms from the wearer's body to the outside of the gown. Replacement clean-air from the enclosure enters at the lower edge of the gown and sweeps upwards to the face mask exhaust outlet.

3.51 Eugene Marais Hospital, South Africa: open plan operating suite using five UCA enclosures.

3.52 Plan of four-enclosure operating suite proposed by Cowan. Movable screens give privacy for patients being anaesthetised. The area of the operating suite is halved when compared with a conventional layout.

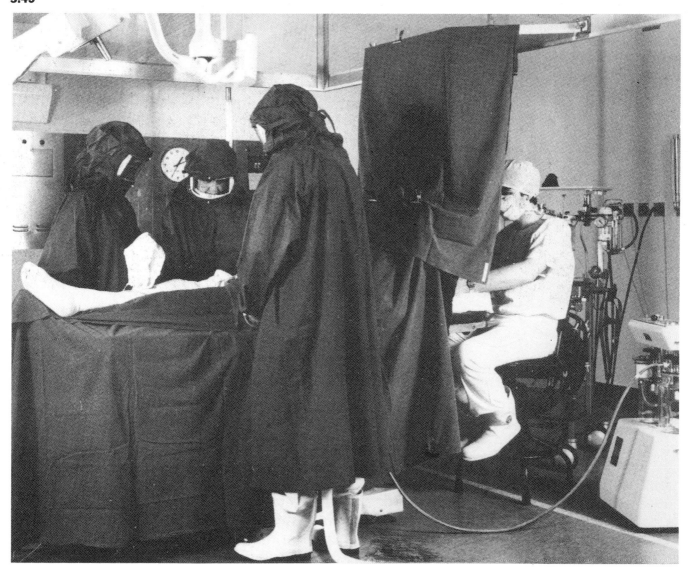

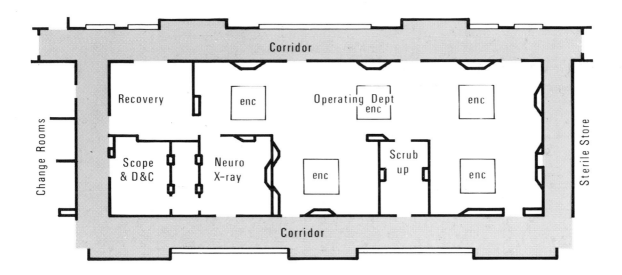

3.51

3.52

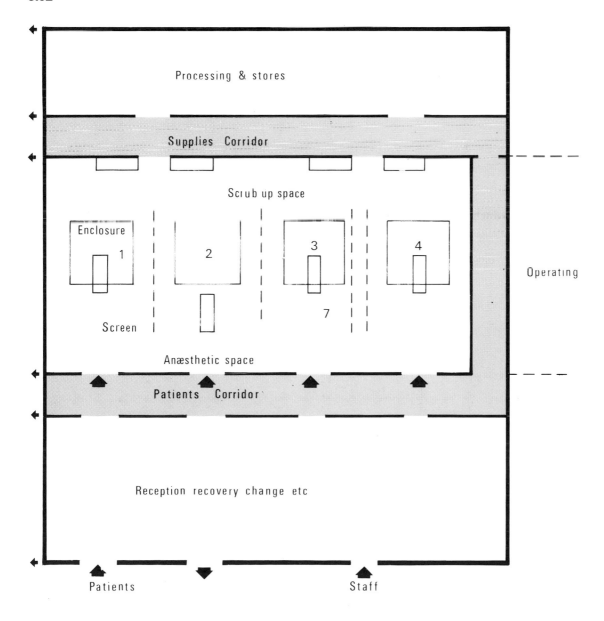

THE
SUPPORT
ZONE

Chapter 4

The support zone

A   Growth

Function

The support zone is the third main section of the hospital: it includes those areas not already allocated to the nursing or clinical zones. Its purpose is to satisfy all their physical and material needs: food, energy, goods and services. It has to provide for the reception, handling, distribution, storage, and disposal of everything that comes into or goes out of the hospital.

At first glance, the basic needs of a patient arriving in hospital may not seem to have altered much over the years. He has to be provided with a bed, clean sheets and towels, pills and dressings, toilet facilities, fresh air, food, light and warmth (or coolth). But while he lies in bed or sits idly unaware, everything else in a modern hospital is on the move. Behind the scenes there is a hive of activity. Air is blown, water is pumped, drains flow, energy courses along pipes and wires, messages are received and dispatched, staff arrive, change, proceed to their work stations, patients are accompanied from one zone to another and so on. And all this takes place almost uninterruptedly with greater or lesser intensity, twenty-four hours a day, three hundred and sixty-five days a year.

History: self-sufficiency

The growth of the support zone is comparatively recent. Just over a hundred and fifty years ago, all these basic needs could be satisfied anywhere in the world by a cookhouse, a sanitary block, and a shed for stores. When Brunel produced his design for a prefabricated hospital for export in 1856, the layout differed little from that of an army barracks. The changes that have occurred reflect the changes that have taken place in our way of life. The goals may be summarised as follows: reliability, satisfaction (of the expectations of the patients), convenience (of staff) and economy.

Reliability is of course the first consideration when dealing with sick people. At first this was thought to be best obtained if everything supplied was under the strict control of those nearest to the patient. In chapter 2 we saw how, traditionally, a sister in charge of a nursing unit liked to keep a strict eye on everything. She would have her own linen counted on the ward floor, prepare her own dosages, sterilise her own instruments and in some countries even have meals cooked on the premises. Gradually these functions were relinquished. The hospital boiler provided central heating instead of open fires in every room, the hospital washed the sheets, the hospital kitchen provided the meals. Everything that was required was provided on the hospital's own land.

The precedent for this development was of course the traditional country house.[1] In the eighteenth century, each establishment had to be self-sufficient. The home farm produced the vegetables; the house cow the milk. Butter was churned in the dairy. The stables provided horses which formed the links with the outside world now supplied by the telephone, mail and radio. Workshops kept the place in good repair. The laundry and sewing room took care of the washing and mending. The kitchens, scullery, pantry and servants' hall supplied the catering and housekeeping. The area of buildings required for the sum total of all these functions was often much greater than that of the mansion whose needs they served.

Piecemeal development

Hospitals naturally followed the same pattern. As new developments took place extra buildings were added: workshops to maintain furniture and equipment, garages for ambulances and lorries, a transformer station, a telephone exchange, changing rooms, cafeteria and crèches for non-resident staff, educational and recreational facilities, shops and a bank. Dominating the whole complex might be a huge factory chimney, a water tower, and boiler house supplying central heating and steam for the laundry and kitchens and the sterilisers located all over the hospital. All the buildings on the site would be linked by a complex infrastructure of walkway ducts housing engineering services requiring constant maintenance and attention, while above ground, more and more of the landscape was taken over by an ever-growing car park.

Concentration

The enormous area required to house these activities prompted postwar planners to take a fresh look at what was going on. Instead of providing for them on an additive basis, could they not be grouped together into one zone with a more orderly system of distribution and disposal? The pioneer in this field was Gordon Friesen in USA. In the 1950s he introduced the concept of supply centres in the mine workers' hospitals on which he was consultant. The supply centre groups together bulk stores, kitchen, pharmacy, laundry, decontamination, preparation, sterilisation and processing of everything for the nursing and clinical zones. The object is to relieve medical and nursing staff of the need to hoard and spend time on work that could be done elsewhere. The supply centre can be located in a basement or in a separate factory-like structure, built at much lower cost. Friesen also pioneered the introduction of industrial methods of handling goods. Conveyor belts were used for the preparation of meals and pneumatic tubes for passing messages and prescriptions to and from pharmacy and administration.

Automation

The culmination of this concept was his projected SPD (supply, processing and distribution) building for Cologne University Medical Centre designed in the early 1970s. Here a six storey SPD building provides all the physical and material needs of a 1000-bed nursing tower and all the teaching and research facilities of the clinical zone. Supplies are conveyed in carts suspended from overhead rails through tunnels and shafts connecting the different buildings. The whole process is fully automated.[2]

Air-conditioning

The next development to hit hospitals was air-conditioning. In the USA it spread rapidly from houses to offices and its introduction into health-care buildings presented no particular problems. But in more temperate climates, it was at first confined to surgery, X-ray and the treatment rooms scattered throughout the building. American precedents and the hope of reducing nosocomial infection (chapter 2) eventually stimulated the demand throughout the world for fully air-conditioned hospitals.

Enormous extra burdens were thus thrust onto the supply zone. Fresh air previously available simply by opening windows had now to be pumped all over the building. It had also to be cooled in summer, and cooling (with conventional systems) consumes much more energy than heating and requires more space. At Greenwich hospital, UK, for instance, three out of the four vertical shafts contain air-handling plant dealing with some $100m^3$ of air per second. The heating, cooling and humidification of the air is carried out at each air-handling unit. A hot and cold dual duct system provides air at high velocity to air mixing boxes, from which it is distributed at low velocity to

the rooms below. Refrigeration for the air-conditioning is by three absorption type units situated centrally on the roof with three cooling towers above. The plants supply a total of nearly 8,500 kW of refrigeration. Cold water storage of 386,000 litres is provided in tanks at the top of the engineering shafts.[3]

Interstitial space

Greenwich, as we have seen, was the first hospital to provide complete floors entirely dedicated to the maintenance and distribution of engineering services. Howard Goodman was able to do this at very little extra cost because these floors are housed in the depth of the beams, which span nearly 20m. The pipes and ducts are threaded through the webs of the lattice girders, hence the name interstitial space. Interstitial space not only enables routine maintenance to be carried out with less disturbance, it accommodates change of use on the clinical or nursing floor above or below. It postpones obsolescence and makes possible plant replacement with less disruption when the time comes to introduce more up-to-date equipment. But what is more important is that it opens up a new dimension for the supply zone. Instead of having to choose between horizontal extensions or vertical stacking, planners began to see interstitial space (in some hospitals occupying some 40 per cent of the total volume) as a new way to accommodate unknown future requirements. As Clibbon pointed out in 1971 (page 117) these areas need not be restricted to pipes and wires and air handling plant. Slightly enlarged, they can house any service not requiring the presence of a patient. They can be used equally by white-clad and blue-collar workers. The support zone might then be renamed the 'support and industrial techniques zone'.[4]

A Canadian research team after investigating 13 recently completed hospitals recorded its conviction of the potential advantages of the adoption of interstitial space for all future hospitals of over 400 beds. 'Progress' they said, 'will lead to change, and that change will lead to further progress'.[5]

Total energy

All these extensions of the supply function led to higher and higher energy consumption. This in turn stimulated the concept of total energy: the idea that the hospital should generate its own electricity. Fuelled partly by burning waste products, it would make use of surplus energy to boost the grid or provide district heating to surrounding communities. Prototypes have been built in Britain, New Zealand and elsewhere. These and other exciting prospects occupied the minds of planners in the 1960s and 70s.

B   Containment

Shedding the load

While some planners were thinking in these expansionist terms, others were concerned with contraction. Using electrical analogies, they believed this could be achieved by a reduction in peak demand and load-shedding. By load-shedding they meant ceasing to make every hospital self-sufficient; hiving off as many supply functions as possible, either to other hospital sites or to industry.

As we saw in the clinical zone, reduction in peak demand is largely an organisational and management problem. The abolition of fixed visiting hours, for instance, reduces pressure on car parking and eliminates the need for holding areas for visitors before they are admitted to the nursing units. Appointment systems cut down on the space required for waiting rooms. Spreading the lunch hour from 12 to 2:30 increases the number of sittings. Staggered shift-starting and finishing times reduce the requirements for staff changing and so on. All these arrangements help to flatten peak demand and so reduce space required for energy distribution and the circulation of goods and people.

Still greater reductions come where hospitals cease to try to cater for all their own requirements. Few householders now produce any of the goods, services or energy they consume. Hospitals have been reluctant to follow their example. There is a feeling that they will lose control, that they will be more exposed to power failures or industrial action. But it is a different matter when one hospital undertakes to supply another. In this section we look at ways in which their autonomy has been slowly relinquished. It has a surprisingly long history and often came about through individual initiative after a breakdown in the service.

Off-siting the laundry

The first building to disappear from the hospital complex was the laundry. The breakthrough was organisational rather than physical and came about almost accidentally. The Royal Melbourne Hospital in Australia had a large laundry. S. Morris, its manager, found he had spare capacity. If he took in other hospitals' washing he could afford to buy modern machinery. He was allowed to go ahead in 1953. The idea was so successful that more and more hospitals joined in the scheme and by 1967 some 240 tons of laundry for 73 institutions were handled each week. But Morris found that the sorting and dispatch of each particular hospital's linen was more troublesome than washing and ironing. By introducing a linen exchange system, and a reasonable degree of standardisation, the whole business of counting sheets, time-consuming and possibly hazardous, could be eliminated. Laundry need only be weighed.[6] Linen exchange systems followed all over the world. Centralised laundries located off site, sometimes in adapted buildings in old hospitals, are now able to compete with commercial laundries and free valuable space within the hospitals they serve.

Sterile supplies

The next to go was the sterilisation of supplies. During the period 1955–59 there was an increasing awareness of the inadequacy of sterilising facilities in hospitals. In the 1960s Dr Cameron Weymes, Medical Superintendant of the Victoria Infirmary at Glasgow, expanded his syringe service to a central sterile supply department for a number of hospitals in the area.[7] Adapting a disused casualty department and six old wartime huts, he rapidly met the needs of some 50,000 beds for ward packs. The service now has a total storage and 'factory' area of 3,000m^2 providing packs and serving some 300 theatres in the region. A similar regional development took place in the south of England. The widespread use of materials sterilised off site and commercially produced disposables sometimes increases the area required for storage and the stocks of instruments that have to be carried. But it reduces the complexity of the support zone. And the overriding advantage is that it completely eliminates the need for steam to be pumped all over the hospital. Any local demand for sterilisation can be met by small electric autoclaves installed at far less cost.

Catering

The next department to be affected may be catering. Two problems have always concerned catering planners. The first is how to get food from the hot plate to the patient within half an hour (food values as well as palatability, deteriorate rapidly, if this period is exceeded). The second is how to get a better return from costly equipment in the kitchens, unused at weekends and lying idle for long periods during the week. Now both problems appear to be nearer solution. Recent developments in convenience foods and cook-and-chill techniques combine more intensive use of equipment with better service to the consumer.[8] It is now possible for staff and patients to get as palatable meals as they would have in their own home. Food prepared centrally is subjected to initial cooking, blast chilled and stored for up to five days. It is then distributed in insulated vehicles and further portioning can take place. Reheating is by infra-red or microwave units and takes only 15 minutes. The special trolleys containing both hot and cold dishes are plugged in at the nursing zone, the moment patients are ready for their meal. The quality of the food is greatly enhanced, but what is more important is that food preparation and cooking can be spread over a much longer period. Cooking equipment can be used more economically. Space is saved, and in the smaller satellite hospitals kitchens can be eliminated altogether.

All-electric hospital

The most obtrusive and hygienically perhaps the most inappropriate elements of the support zone are the boiler house, chimney and fuel store. Can they be eliminated too? The obvious solution is the all-electric hospital. But engineers have always claimed that running costs would be some 30 per cent higher, and this appeared to rule it out from any further consideration.

In 1970 the British Department of Health, in association with the Elecricity Council, commissioned a study by P. Ferguson, an independent consulting engineer.[9] He took a conventional hospital, the Lister Hospital at Stevenage, and redesigned the heating and hot water system using electrical alternatives. He showed that the running costs would indeed be some 30 per cent higher. But when the savings on capital cost of the buildings and installation, cleaning and decoration, plant replacement and maintenance – the life-cycle costs – are considered, the electrical solution would be competitive. His conclusions have since been vindicated by an all-electric hospital opened in 1980 at Peterborough in England, and others in Norway, France, USA and elsewhere.[10]

An interesting fact that comes to light in Ferguson's analysis of the Lister Hospital is the very high cost of heating air. About 40 per cent of the fuel bill is accounted for by this factor. In order to warm the coldest patient, all the other occupants have to be heated to the same temperature and suffer considerable inconvenience. Not surprisingly the working staff throw open windows and are too busy to close them. While the hot air escapes, thermostatically controlled convectors and pumps work all the harder to replace the lost heat. The Department of Health Low Energy Hospital in the Isle of Wight aims to combat this. Energy consumption will be cut by half, using solar gain, high insulation and heat-recovery methods. It is a brilliant concept. But it relies on conventional boilers and artificial ventilation and a costly investment in sophisticated engineering.[11]

Personal choice of climate

There is always a danger when one particular objective (such as energy-saving) is pursued too far. Most people would agree that patients entering hospital should be given as far as possible the sort of ventilation system they are accustomed to in their own homes. If they have air-conditioning, then the hospital should be air-conditioned. But if they are used to open windows and fresh air, fixed windows and artificial ventilation may add to their anxieties. There is nothing like opening a window for a few minutes to cool down or remove unpleasant smells! The important thing is that temperature and ventilation should be controllable on the spot and not by some remote robot.

Electricity provides an opportunity for each patient to create his own environment. When off-peak radiant heating is employed to warm the whole fabric – walls, floors and ceilings – it is possible to open a window for a short spell without cooling down the whole building. Nurses on the move require lower temperatures than sedentary patients. The difference should be made up by boosting local sources of heat. At the turn of a switch each patient should be able to control his own climate, just as he can choose his own menu and his own radio programme. This concept of 'task-heating,' just like task-lighting, or task ultra-clean air systems for operating theatres, opens up new possibilities for greater personal choice at no additional expense. Electrical systems are far more economical in space. The virtual elimination of ducts and false ceilings speeds up construction and provides a prospect of much simpler, cleaner, maintenance-free methods of heating for hospitals in the future.

Logistics of materials handling

A classic example of the benefits of design research is the study of the way supplies are moved about in hospitals, carried out for the Greater Baltimore Medical Center in 1966. It showed that reductions in handling costs resulting from automation were hard to realise. The expected economies proved elusive. The team looked at conveyors, automatic ejection devices, dumb-waiters, paternosters, (a lift system consisting of containers attached to a continuous belt), elevators and so on.

They concluded that the basic difference between hospital and industrial systems is that in the former, deliveries are intermittent, in the latter continuous. They adopted the slogan KISS ('keep it simple and stupid') and decided on an electric tug towing trolleys round a hospital street, (pages 168–171). At either end a 1:12 ramp connects one floor to another. There are no maintenance problems. The only thing that has to be changed is the battery on the tug.[12]

Paul James adopted this system for the Best Buy hospitals in Britain. He placed the central supply, disposal and workshop building at intermediate level. All goods entering or leaving the hospital are loaded onto trolley trains and tugged up or down a short ramp to the 'street' systems serving all departments on the ground and first floors. Deliveries are planned when pedestrian traffic is minimal. The streets are used by public and patients and all categories of staff. There are no problems of infection and the simplicity of the scheme makes it universally applicable when sites allow horizontal development. Two further benefits have resulted. Ramps double up as means of escape; bedfast patients can be evacuated in a fraction of the time required to move them in lifts or by stairs. Secondly, ramps reduce construction and commissioning time. Contractors and equipment manufacturers use them extensively for delivering materials and plant.

Finding the appropriate location

The support zone is a good place to end this brief survey of the growth and containment of the different hospital zones. Planners do not know and cannot tell whether hospitals will get bigger or smaller, more or less self-contained in the future. But at least they can show that it is possible to move in whatever direction that is required of them. It is the zone where Cochrane's two criteria of effectiveness and efficiency can be most easily applied.[13] But there are occasions when the simple test of reducing running costs (a 1 per cent improvement in productivity justifies at least a 20 per cent increase in first cost) is not the only consideration. There may be times when land is limited or extra initial capital is just not available. Any increase in the size or cost of the support zone is likely to be at the expense of the other two zones. It is then that containment becomes the primary objective, and the strategies of load-shedding described above come into their own. The more functions that can be handled off site, the better. It is a question of choosing, in each particular situation, methods which are most appropriate to the climate, customs and economy of the community to be served. It is largely a matter of balance and common sense. In the case of the supply zone as in the rest of the hospital 'tail must not be allowed to wag dog.'

C   The planners' response

Support zone: key to drawings in chapter 4C only

1	Central kitchen	26	Processed stores
2	Meat preparation	27	Trolley make-up
3	Fish preparation	28	Despatch centre
4	Pastry preparation	29	Loading bank
5	Larder preparation	30	Disposal centre/incinerator
6	Diet preparation	31	Maintenance
7	Refrigerated store	32	Workshops
8	Provision store	33	Works stores
9	Tray make-up	34	Main plant
10	Trolley park	35	Switchgear
11	Laundry	36	Housekeeping
12	Clean linen store	37	Bed clean/store
13	Soiled linen store	38	Central staff change
14	Decontamination	39	Staff cafeteria
15	Pharmacy	40	Central wash-up
16	Bulk preparation	41	Goods entrance
17	Wash-up	42	Staff entrance
18	Issue lobby	43	Garage/parking
19	Dressings	44	Goods lifts
20	Central sterilising	45	Ramp
21	Workroom	46	Conveyor
22	Sorting and washing	47	Animal house
23	Sterile store	48	Records store
24	Autoclaves	49	Automated carts
25	Central stores	50	Goods receiving

Content of the support zone

Unlike the other zones the support zone comprises several departments which can be found in other building types. There is little about hospital kitchens, laundries, bulk stores and energy centres which distinguishes them from similar functions in universities, hotels or large commercial and industrial buildings. There are only two areas which are unique to hospitals: central sterilising and disinfecting departments and manufacturing pharmacies.

The main difference between hospital support functions and those in other building types is centred on the need for most materials to be moved to a static consumer, mainly on a routine basis but sometimes in a hurry. It is this problem of materials handling with the logistics of supply and disposal, which has produced solutions which are unique to hospitals. On the following pages we describe some of the materials/ handling systems which have been developed in recent years.

4.1   Royal Free Hospital, London, UK: support zone for 800-bed hospital. Basement plan of podium showing relationships of the main processing and storage departments. All materials are moved by trolleys to the nursing and clinical zones via a central bank of service lifts.

4.2   Rotherham Hospital, UK: view of central pharmacy.

4.1

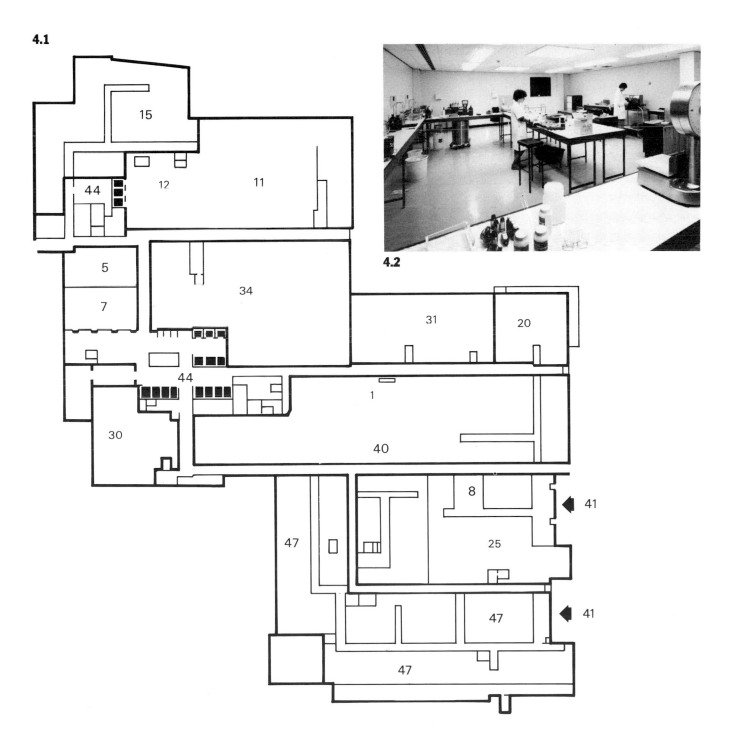

4.2

Location of the support zone

Until recently most hospitals have been planned with comprehensive support zones within the building, either in the basement (vertical schemes) or in a separate but linked block (horizontal schemes). The demand for palatable meals at the bedside and for no delay in the supply of sterile items to the doctor and nurse meant that each hospital had to have a complete support zone. Today, due mainly to technological developments in catering, sterilising and laundry equipment, it is more efficient to provide these services on an area or regional basis.

This, with the increasing use of commercially supplied disposables, has resulted in the reduction of the support zone within the hospital. Indeed there are examples in the USA and in West Germany which feature separately sited industrial complexes housing most of the support functions.

4.3

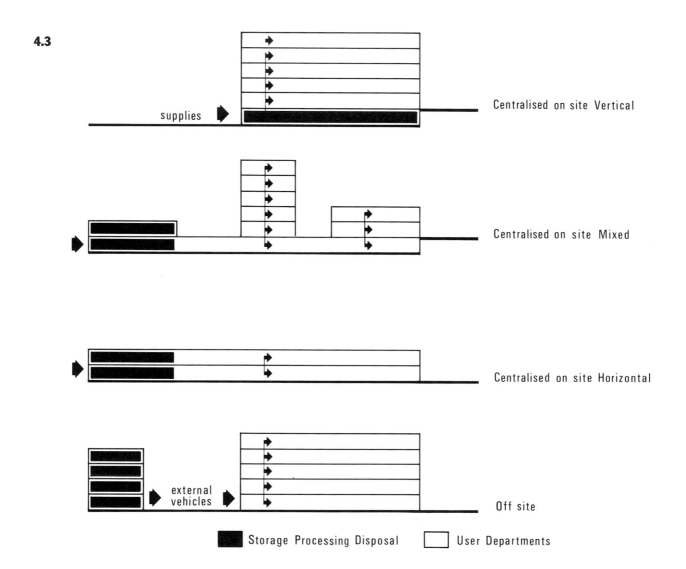

supplies

Centralised on site Vertical

Centralised on site Mixed

Centralised on site Horizontal

external vehicles

Off site

Storage Processing Disposal   User Departments

Distribution systems

4.4 The method of distributing supplies requires careful integration with the overall design of the building. In North America, following World War II, the use of automatic vertical systems employing mechanical conveyors and chutes tended to force planners into straightjacket design solutions such as the tower-on-podium.
More recently various systems have been developed in the USA and in West Germany, offering more flexibility in use and taking account of future growth and change. In addition to manually operated trolleys or carts, these include automated carts and locomotive train systems.

4.5 St Luke's Hospital, Huddersfield, UK: view of typical locomotive train. The use of trolley trains pulled by man-rider tugs has become popular in the UK.

4.4

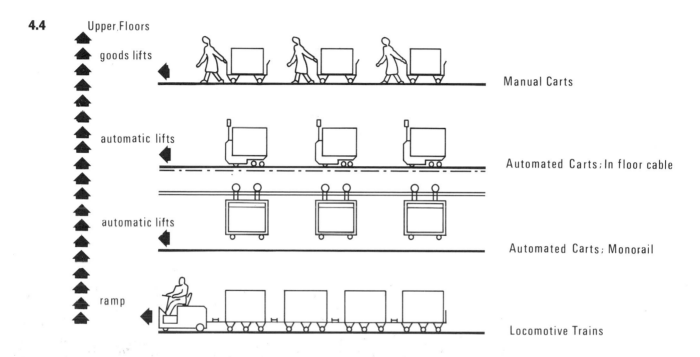

Upper Floors
goods lifts — Manual Carts
automatic lifts — Automated Carts; In floor cable
automatic lifts — Automated Carts; Monorail
ramp — Locomotive Trains

4.5

St. Luke's Hospital, Huddersfield

4.6

4.7

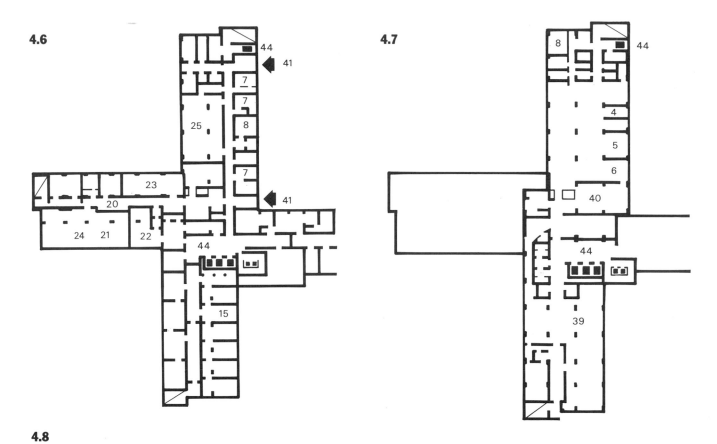

4.8

4.6, 4.7   Fredriksborg Hospital, Denmark: plans of support zone. Main reception storage and processing departments are in the basement. The catering service is on the top floor of the nursing zone.

4.8   Fredriksborg Hospital, Denmark: view of central kitchen.

4.9   Gelsenkirchen Hospital, West Germany: plan of basement. All support departments except the laundry are located here. Note the dispatch centre (28), where mobile carts are parked before being loaded with supplies and then moved to the user zones via the central bank of lifts. Separate lifts deliver meals direct to the nursing floors.

4.9

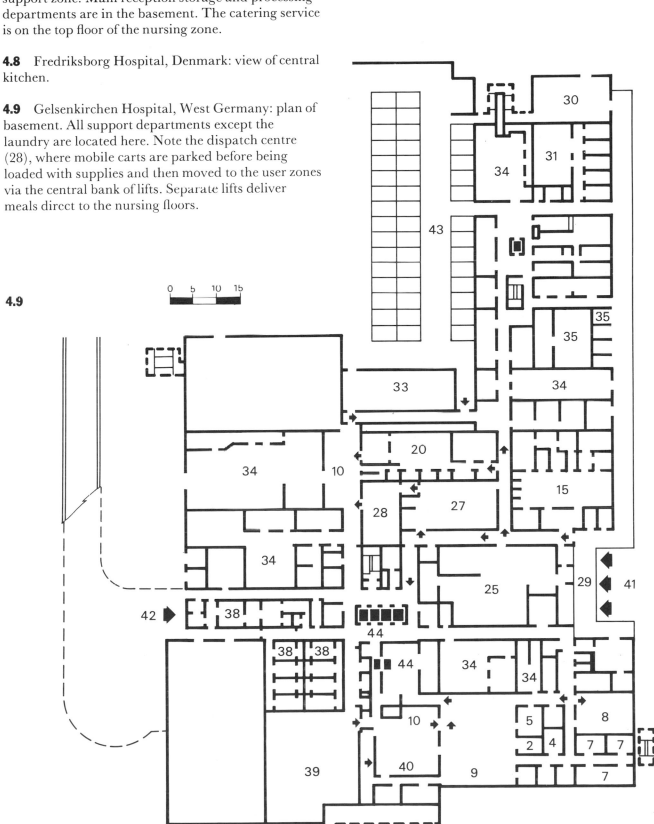

4.10

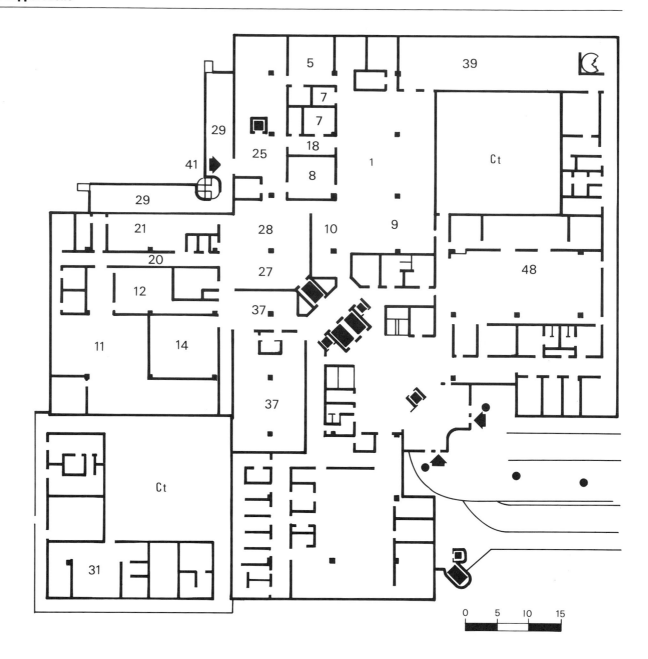

4.11

4.12

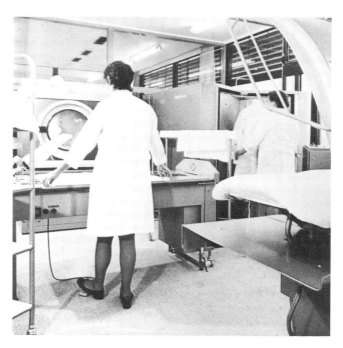

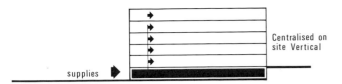

4.10 Nordenham Hospital, West Germany: plan of ground floor. Complete support zone for a small hospital. Manual cart distribution.

4.11 Nordenham Hospital, West Germany: central kitchen with plated meal service in foreground.

4.12 Nordenham Hospital, West Germany: laundry.

4.13 Santa Fe Hospital, Spain: central support zone planned in basement of large 1100-bed complex.

4.14 Santa Fe Hospital, Spain: central sterile supply department.

4.14

4.13

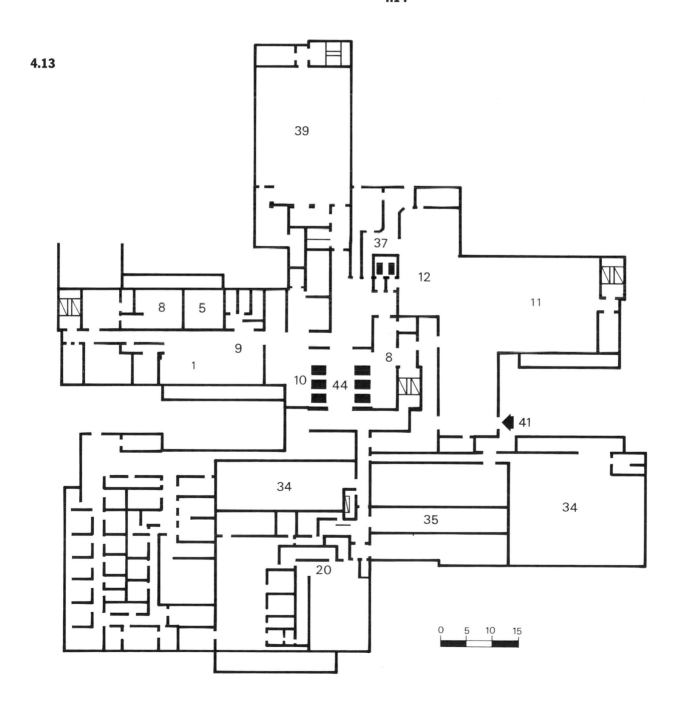

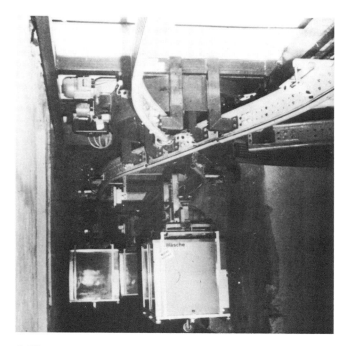

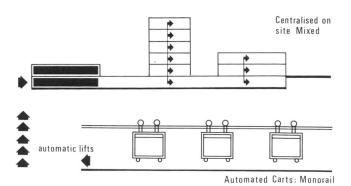

Centralised on
site Mixed

automatic lifts

Automated Carts; Monorail

4.15, 4.16　Hvidovre Hospital, Denmark: schematic section and plan of support zone serving large complex comprising five separate nursing blocks on extensive podium housing the clinical zone. Carts are moved horizontally via a basement duct and then vertically to the required floor.

4.17　Hvidovre Hospital, Denmark: carts moving on monorail in the basement duct.

4.18　Etobicoke Hospital, Canada: basement plan of podium. Highly automated cart system designed by Gordon Friesen, shown as broken line.

4.17

4.15

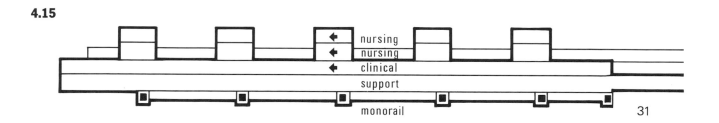

nursing
nursing
clinical
support
monorail
31

4.16

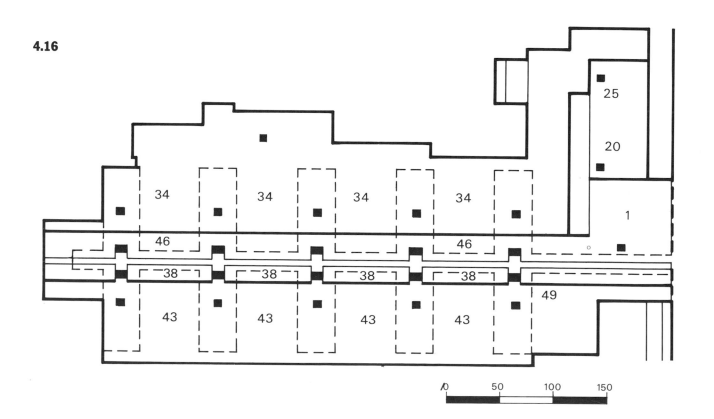

25

20

34　34　34　34

1

46　46

38　38　38　38

49

43　43　43　43

0　50　100　150

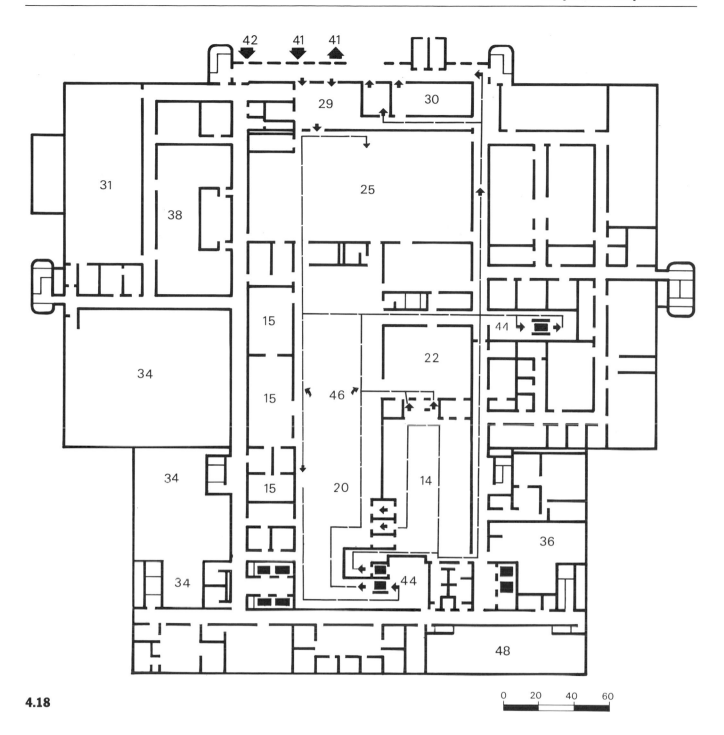

4.18

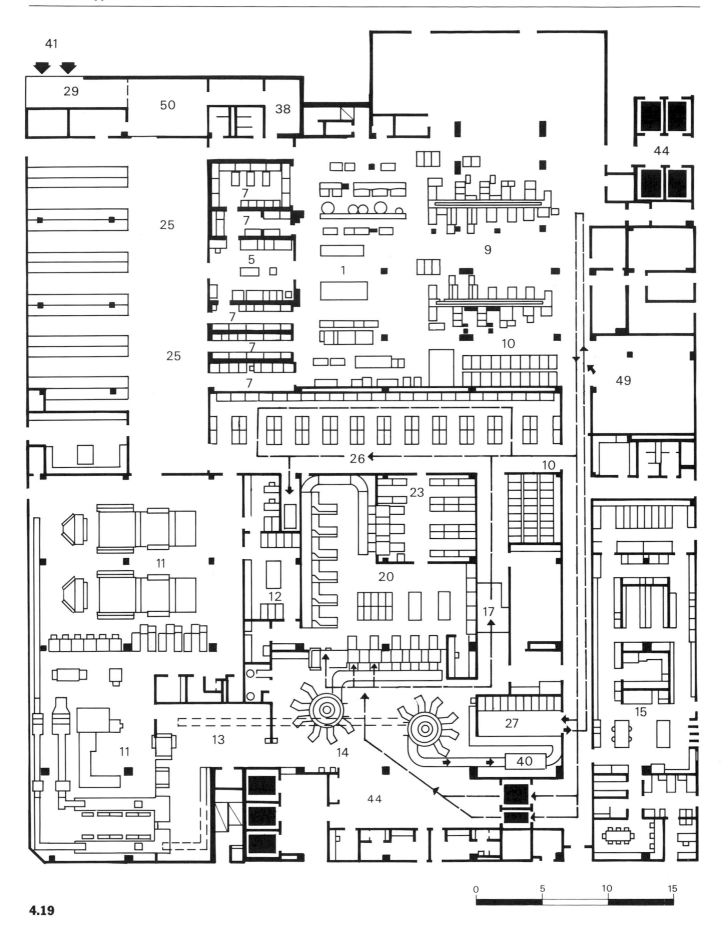

4.19

4.19 Fairfax Hospital, Virginia, USA: part plan of basement supplies centre and processing and storage departments for a 500-bed hospital. The distribution system uses a combination of automatic horizontal and vertical movement, which involves some sophisticated electronic technology. The components consist of a motorised carrier unit or pallet which has a control console, and carries a stainless steel container fitted out for supplies, food trays, drugs, etc. The container has its own retractable wheels and becomes a manually operated cart when not riding piggy-back on the motorised pallets. The pallet and container form a composite module which is guided electrically by a cable buried in the floor. The module moves automatically from the supplies centre along a basement corridor to its programmed floor via a special lift. On arrival, the module leaves the lift automatically, and is then led by one of the ward staff, who by pressing a switch on the console can take over control of the module. The container can be easily detached from the pallet to form a mobile storage unit, while the pallet is returned to the lift and thence automatically back to the dispatch centre.

4.20 Fairfax Hospital, USA. Throughout the journey from supplies centre to user and back, each module is monitored at a central control room.

4.21 Fairfax Hospital, USA: composite module emerging automatically from a lift.

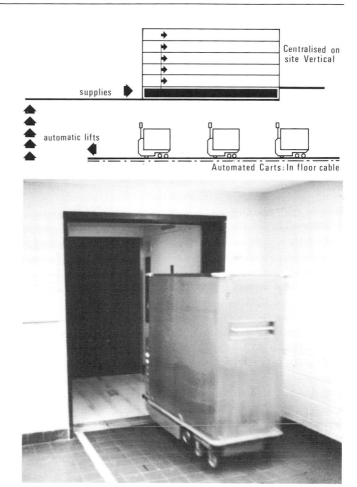

4.21

4.20

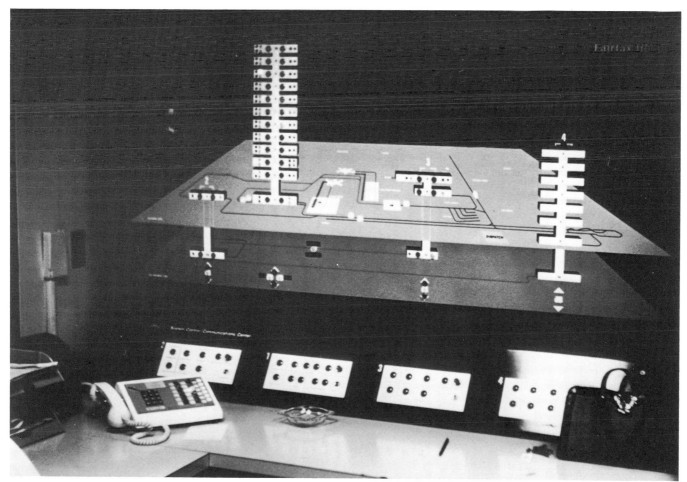

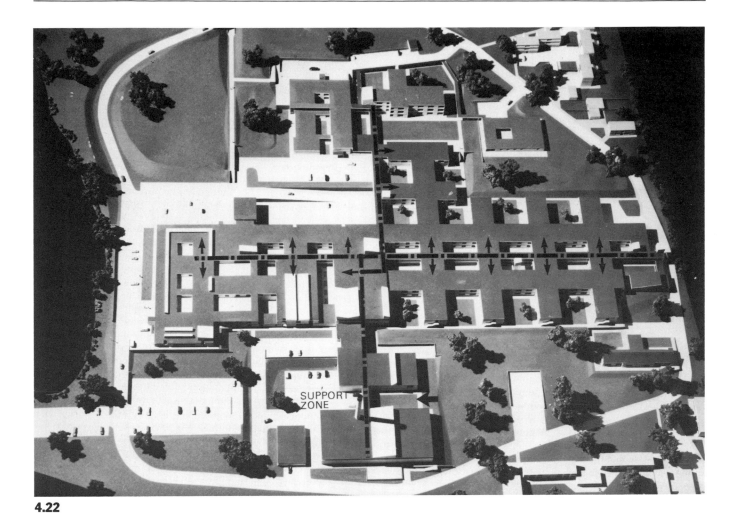

4.22

4.23

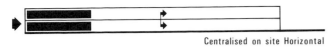

Centralised on site Horizontal

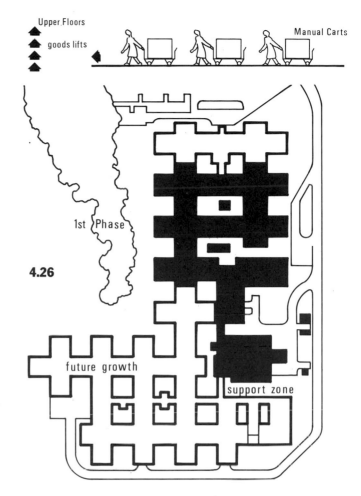

In the typical horizontal scheme developed in the UK in the early 1960s the support zone was a complex of single and two-storey industrial type structures, sited well away from the other zones but linked to them by wide corridors or streets. Large supply trolleys were either manually pushed or pulled by electric tugs. At first this equipment was selected from standard models produced for industrial purposes. The result was extensive damage to finishes and doorways. During the development stages of the Best Buy and Nucleus standard hospitals the design of the equipment was properly co-ordinated with the building.

4.22   Airedale Hospital, UK: model, showing relationship of support zone.

4.23   Airedale Hospital, UK: plan of support zone.

4.24, 4.25   East Surrey Hospital, UK: plans of two-level support zone in a Nucleus hospital (4.24 first floor, 4.25 ground floor).

4.26   East Surrey Hospital, UK: development control plan showing position of support zone and its relationship to present and future phases of a typical Nucleus hospital.

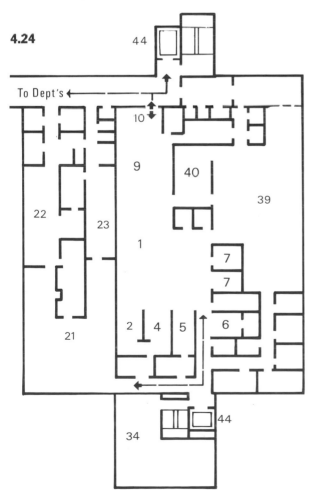

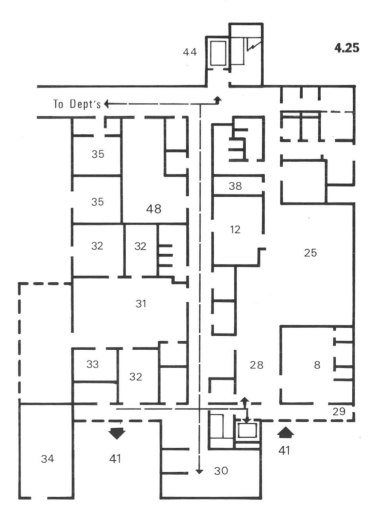

4.28

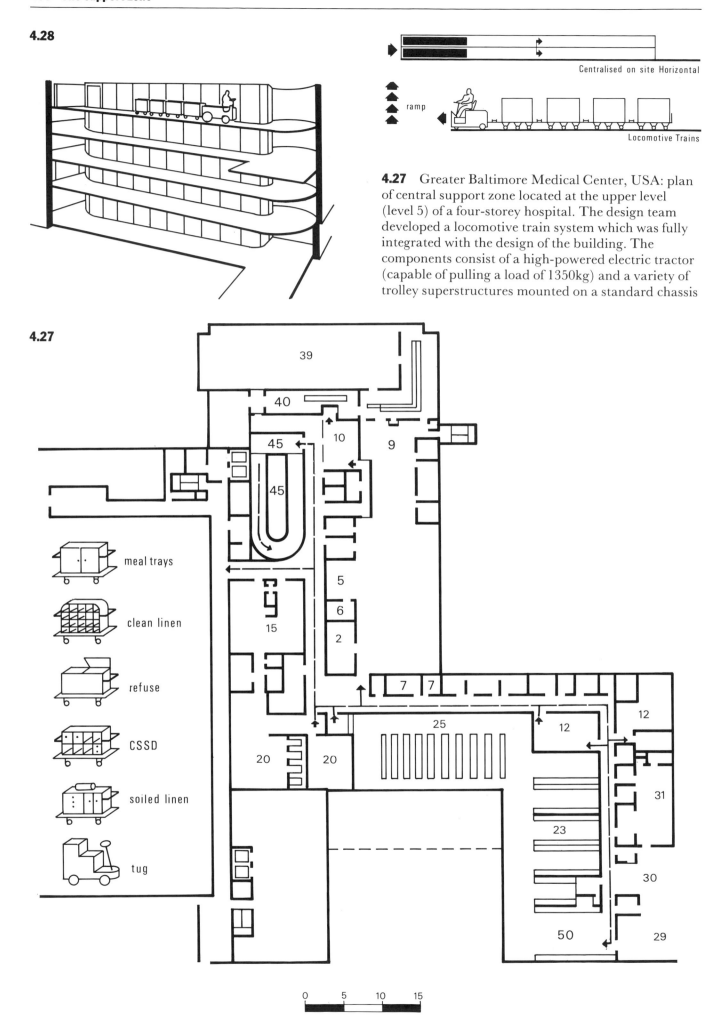

Centralised on site Horizontal

ramp

Locomotive Trains

4.27 Greater Baltimore Medical Center, USA: plan of central support zone located at the upper level (level 5) of a four-storey hospital. The design team developed a locomotive train system which was fully integrated with the design of the building. The components consist of a high-powered electric tractor (capable of pulling a load of 1350kg) and a variety of trolley superstructures mounted on a standard chassis

4.27

meal trays

clean linen

refuse

CSSD

soiled linen

tug

0   5   10   15

150cm×75cm wide. The assembled trains, each comprising a tractor and up to four trolleys, move from the dispatch centre to all four levels via a spiral ramp (4.28) that avoids the task of break-up and reassembly of trains necessary if normal goods lifts had been used. Delivery points at entrances to user departments provide turn-around space so that the train can pull in, drop off and/or pick up the requisite number of trolleys and proceed on its journey.

4.29 King's Lynn Hospital, UK: a Best Buy hospital. Axonometric showing position of support zone and its relationship to the user zones. A locomotive train system was developed for the Best Buy hospital similar to that used at Baltimore. The support zone, conceived as a separate single-storey industrial type building, is placed at a level midway between the two floors of the main complex. Single flight ramps, one up and one down, link the support zone to the ring main corridors at each level. The trains move in a clockwise direction, dropping off and collecting trolleys in the turn-around spaces outside the user department entrances.

4.30 Frimley Park Hospital, UK: a Best Buy hospital: locomotive train negotiating ramp up from support zone.

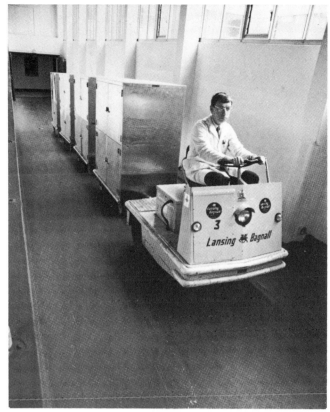

4.30

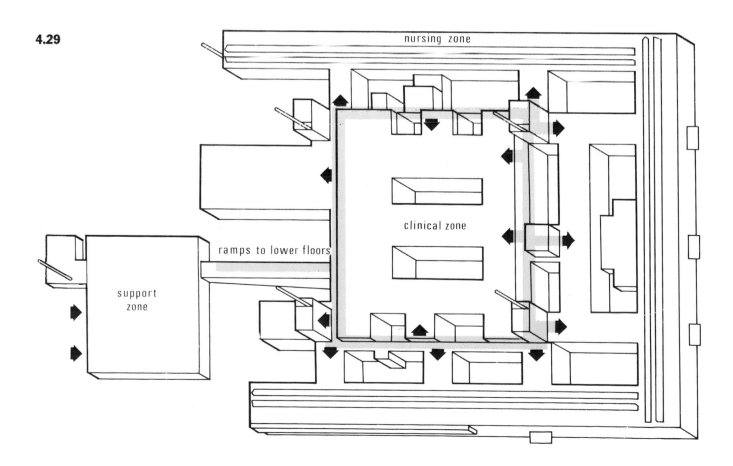

4.29

4.31

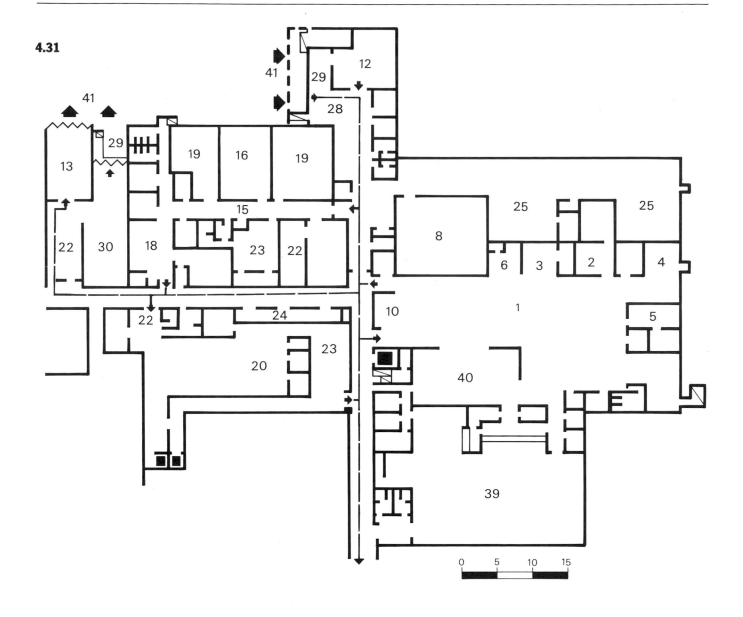

4.32

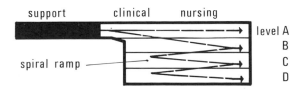

support   clinical   nursing

level A
B
C
D

spiral ramp

4.33

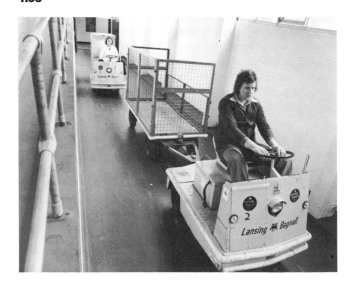

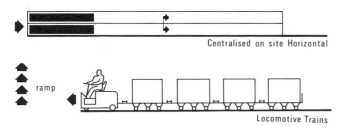

4.36

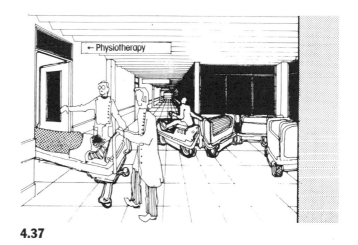

4.37

4.31 Rotherham Hospital, UK: plan of support zone and (4.32) diagrammatic section through ramp. As at Baltimore the support zone is located on the upper level (made possible by sloping site). Loaded trains move down ramp to user departments.

4.33 West Suffolk Hospital UK: train negotiating ramp.

4.34, 4.35 Plan and section of spiral ramp showing critical dimensions.

4.36, 4.37 Nucleus Standard Hospitals, UK: two views showing turn-around space in main corridor outside entrance to a department. Supplies traffic need not interfere with movement of people.

4.34

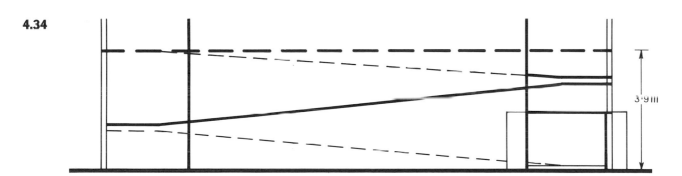

4.35

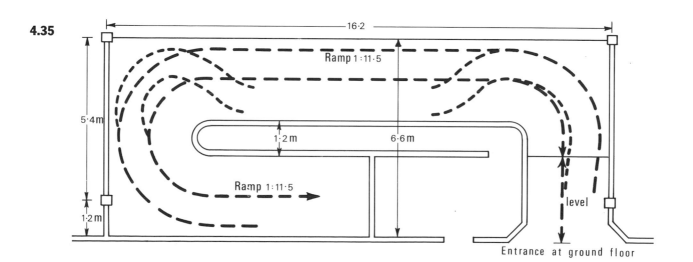

4.38

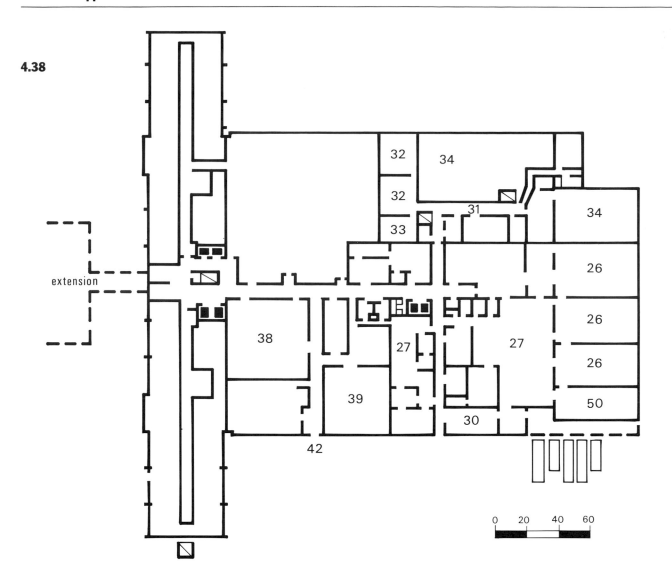

extension

4.39

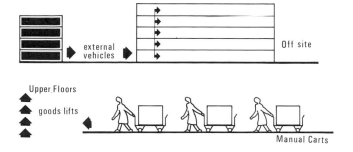

external vehicles

Off site

Upper Floors

goods lifts

Manual Carts

A large part of the materials handling problem in hospitals is created by the need for urgency in delivery of certain items (e.g. patients' meals) and the concentration of deliveries and collections into short periods of time (e.g. linen). If all or most of these fast-moving items could be processed outside the hospital, then much of the need for rapid distribution within the hospital might be removed.

4.38–4.41 Franklin Square Hospital, USA: here policies which virtually eliminate the support zone as a part of the hospital have been adopted. Ready-processed disposable and pre-packaged items such as pre-cooked frozen meals, linen packs, unit dose medications, are received direct from outside suppliers and moved at leisure to the users in the hospital. Gone is the urgent need to get the meal tray to the patient before the food becomes unpalatable. Instead the meal trolley is simply wheeled into an oven at the entrance to each ward unit and the hot meals are available on demand. Slow-moving items such as general stores are delivered in mobile containers parked in the loading dock; when empty these are replaced on an exchange basis by the suppliers.

4.40

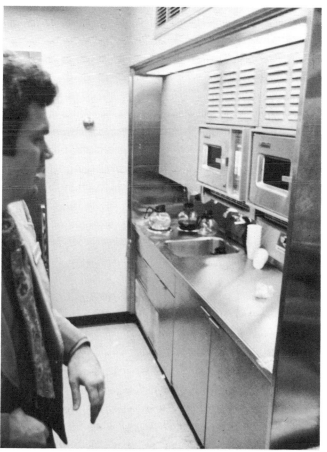

4.41

4.42

4.43

Energy: location and distribution

Early consideration of the location and type of energy source and of the method of distributing energy throughout the building are of vital importance in whole hospital design. They can substantially influence both capital and revenue costs.

4.42 Maidstone Hospital, UK: model, showing the support zone dominated by the central boiler house with its flue stack visible for miles around.

4.43 Sante Fe Hospital, Spain: central boiler plant. In a vertical scheme this is usually located in the basement along with the rest of the support zone. Flues and ducts are taken up through the structure and are often invisible from outside.

4.44 Frimley Park Hospital, UK: here the energy source is detached from the support zone. Four small penthouses on the roof each accommodate an automatically controlled boiler and associated plant. In this way the energy source is placed immediately above the user zones, thereby simplifying the distribution problem.

4.45 Frimley Park Hospital, UK: rooftop boiler house with the primary main services running across the roof behind parapets where they are readily accessible for maintenance or alteration to meet future requirements.

4.45

4.44

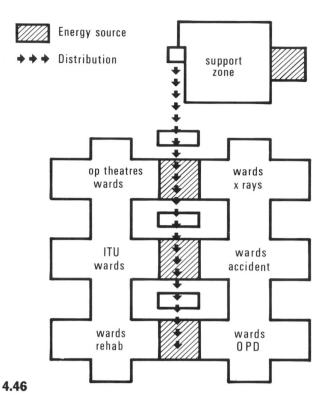

Energy source

→ → → Distribution

support zone

op theatres
wards

wards
x rays

ITU
wards

wards
accident

wards
rehab

wards
OPD

4.46

4.47

4.46 Nucleus Standard Hospital, UK: how decentralised energy sources are related to each pair of cruciform templates. This ensures that the provision for boiler plant follows the modular pattern of development.

4.47 Newham Hospital, UK: phase of Nucleus standard hospital under construction. The rooftop structures housing the energy plant can be clearly seen.

4.48, 4.49 St Mary's Hospital, Isle of Wight, UK: axonometric sketch and schematic section showing the location of the energy source and the method of distribution. Based on the Nucleus standard design, this development project forms part of a series of investigations into energy conservation set up by the UK Department of Health in 1981. The stated objective is to achieve an overall energy saving of 50-60 per cent compared with a conventional hospital.

4.48

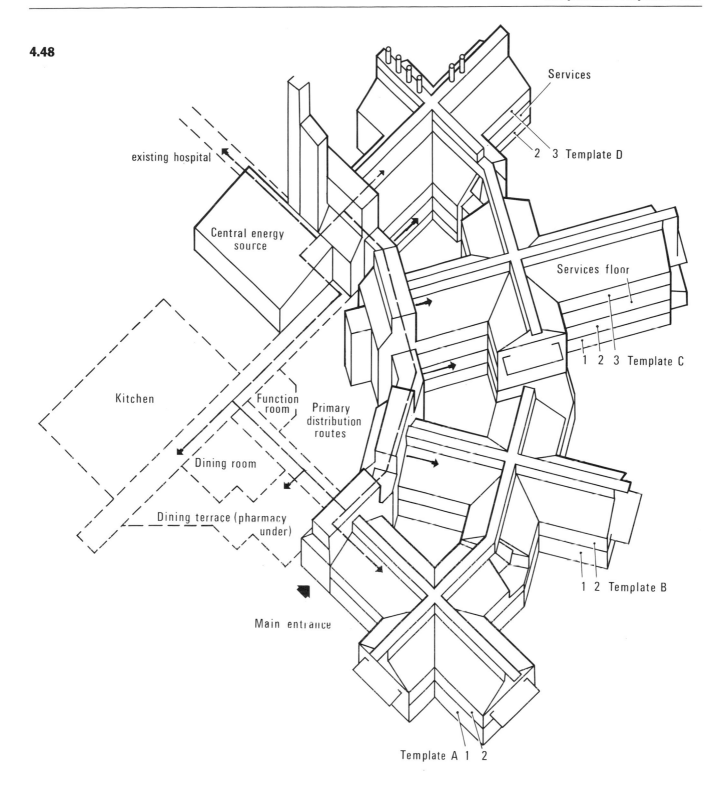

Services

2 3 Template D

existing hospital

Central energy
source

Services floor

1 2 3 Template C

Kitchen

Function
room

Primary
distribution
routes

Dining room

Dining terrace (pharmacy
under)

1 2 Template B

Main entrance

Template A 1 2

4.49

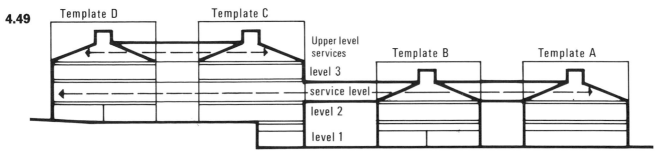

Template D

Template C

Upper level
services

level 3

Template B

Template A

service level

level 2

level 1

PROCEDURES

Procedures for the planning and design, production and delivery of hospitals: a discussion

A   Growth

The 'medical' approach

Traditionally there have always been two quite different approaches to the business of organising the design process; for the sake of simplicity we will here call them the 'medical' and the 'lay'. Each has its merits and drawbacks. The choice between them depends on time, place, and opportunity. In this chapter we set out to show how it is possible to combine the merits of both.

The 'medical' approach starts from the premise that hundreds of hospitals have already been built. They are working acceptably, albeit not necessarily perfectly, in terms of function and cost. It is not necessary to start from scratch every time. We ought to be able to build on what has gone before. On these premises, design is not so much a matter of fresh ideas, but a process of refinement and improvement of solutions already found, with a concentrated attack on any new problems that have arisen. It is a reflection of the Pareto principle: 'eighty per cent of the effort will go into twenty per cent of the product'.[1] Typically, many of the finest European hospitals were designed on this basis. The Herr Professor would say to his architect: 'Go away and design me a hospital. Bring it back and I will show you what is wrong with it.' Perhaps because of his medical training, he was happier diagnosing defective function than when laying down basic principles. The architect would return and he would recommend an excision here and a replacement there, and after the appropriate intervention, the new hospital would emerge, much grander and larger than anything that had gone before.

The 'lay' approach

The 'lay' approach is the exact opposite. It starts from the assumption that a hospital, like any other building, exists to house an organisation. It is an 'inside-out' approach. Design is achieved after a process of logical, rational, sequential thought, starting from a statement of need, a description of the work to be done and the objectives to be achieved. Typically, it flourished in America.

When a community decided it needed a hospital it would hire a planning consultant. His job was to advise on fund-raising, the role of the future hospital, the scale of the 'medical market', likely income and expenditure, the economics of mechanisation of supply and disposal, recruitment and training pro-grammes, residential accommodation etc. In short, before the architect could design a building, the consultant had to design an organisation. This lay approach has the merit of economy of effort. There is less likelihood of abortive work. The risk of having to pay for expensive revisions due to changes of mind or lack of funds is reduced. It is also less exposed to the prejudices of powerful personalities or architectural whims and engineering fancies. An American consultant's report sums up the dangers of relying on the sole judgement of such professional men, however eminent: 'Because of the prestige of their position, chiefs of service (whether salaried or non-salaried) do tend to become very powerful forces in the planning of buildings.' The report also noted that they changed frequently and sometimes had contradictory require-ments. Steps must be taken to combat excessive demands. 'The establishment of objective criteria to relate workloads to space allocations for major hospital services can minimise the effect of such influence and pressures'.[2]

Objective criteria

Such a system of objective criteria was the object of the UK Ministry of Health series of *Hospital Building Notes* and cost allowances which was set up in the 1960s. These were based on the work carried out in the regions and the central department by project teams. Teams comprising a doctor, a nurse, an administrator, an architect, a mechanical engineer and a quantity surveyor were set up along the lines initiated so successfully by Llewelyn-Davies and Weeks in the 1950s (chapter 2). The complex work of planning a hospital of course benefits from a team approach;[4] as an instrument for research or a forum for ideas, the project team can hardly be bettered. A common language is quickly developed. The test of a good project team member is that he should be able to speak for the team without betraying that he is a doctor, an architect, or whatever profession to which he happens to belong. In the early days of the hospital building programme it was an ideal form of education. Whole generations of planners owe the foundations of their expertise to their first few weeks of service on a project team.

Project team's working methods

The project team tradition in Britain is so strong it is worth describing in some detail its method of working,

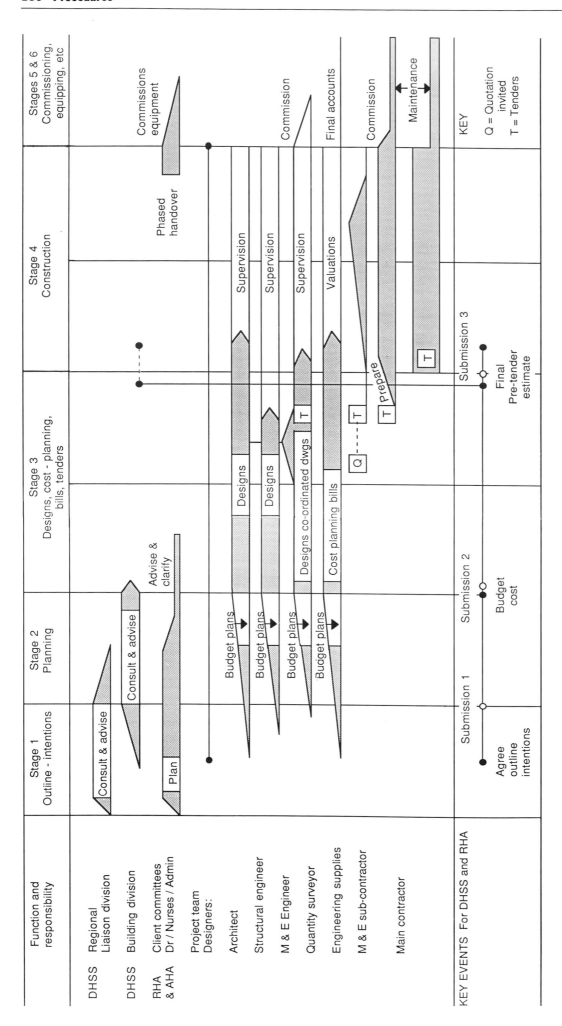

5.1 Capricode diagram. It shows on the left the three committees involved: DHSS, RHA (Regional Health Authority), and AHA (Area Health Authority). Below them come the project team, planners, designers and the various professions, contractors and suppliers whose job it is to get the hospital built and fitted out.

On the right are the six different stages from inception to completion. Note the incidence of workload on the various people involved and the three submissions to the DHSS before the main contractor comes on the scene.

Reproduced from the Department of Health and Social Security *Planning, Design and Construction Process* – the Cruickshank Report 1973, appendix 3a.

as originally conceived. The object is to define what activities will be carried out in every part of a hospital, and how they will be accommodated. This is preceded by a detailed investigation of existing practice. The various specialists in charge of each department are visited in turn and interrogated by the team. They are questioned on a room-by-room basis and notes are taken of the estimated space requirements, and on environmental conditions, sound insulation, sound absorption, daylighting, view out and view in (is overlooking intolerable, undesirable or acceptable?), the type and number of people using each space, the duration, frequency, and times of occupation, the size and weight of equipment used or stored, etc. The standard work-study questions are put: who does it? where is it done? who else could do it? how is it done? why is it done? what other ways of doing it? where else could it be done?

The collection of information has become a highly sophisticated art. Elaborate checklists are prepared to ensure that nothing is missing.[5] As soon as the written collection of data is complete, it is followed by 'room loading sheets' giving engineering requirements, socket outlets, lighting points, etc and 1:50 scale plans and elevations are drawn and returned to the user specialists for checking and initialling. All this often takes a year or more to produce, but it is thought to be necessary if the rooms provided are to be used effectively without some costly last-minute alteration.

For a development project, a rather different system is used, such as that invented by John Green for Greenwich.[7] This concentrates on functions rather than spaces. Before preparing room loading sheets based on existing practice, a more fundamental investigation is undertaken. Subjects studied are 'patient care' rather than nursing units, 'catering' rather than kitchens, and 'supply and disposal' rather than clean or dirty utility rooms. This not only gives the design team a clearer idea of the way the new hospital will be run, it also gives the user a better appreciation of the operational implications of the design proposed. Each person is able to see (sometimes for the first time) the hospital as a whole, and not just his or her own part in it.

The team takes note of alternative operational policies, not only because of the amount of space required, but because of the very different capital and running cost implications. Some hospitals, as we have seen, make up prescriptions in their own pharmacy. Others bring them in ready-packed from commercial sources. Staff cloakrooms are sometimes included on the nursing unit, at others provided in a central area. Teaching facilities may be provided in each department, or alternatively in a joint medical and nursing training centre located in the middle of the hospital or in a separate building.

Origin of cost limits

In the 1950s and early 1960s schemes prepared by project teams in Britain were submitted to the Ministry of Health for central financing. As money became available a trickle of schemes was allowed to proceed. The remainder had to wait. There was no indication when they would start. Money was voted by Parliament on an annual basis and there was no certainty of a continuing building programme.

There was a further difficulty. As the money to be spent by hospitals was not their own money, proposals over £30,000 had to be submitted to the central authority for scrutiny. The Ministry had the responsibility of seeing that the money voted by Parliament was well spent, and spent for the purposes intended. This caused delays while every detail of planning and provision was examined. So the Ministry started to issue cost guidance, department by department, based on what it would expect to find in plans submitted. The accommodation recommended was priced and a system of cost allowances built up, applying the appropriate percentages.

Step-by-step procedure

As the NHS hospital building programme got under way in the 1960s, a step-by-step procedure was elaborated under the name of Capricode. This describes a logical sequence to be followed by project teams from feasibility studies through operational policies, sketch design (schematics), detail design, contract documents, construction, commissioning and occupation, to evaluation and feedback. The number of professions involved and the incidence of workload is shown in diagram 5.1. It will be seen that the key events are the three submissions by the RHA (Regional Health Authority or Board) the agency building the hospital, to the DHSS (Department of Health and Social Security, formerly the Ministry of Health), the authority granting financial approval.

Capricode represents the highest point of what we have called the lay approach. Plans are achieved by a process of logical, rational, sequential thought rather than by inspiration. The step-by-step advance reduces risk of failure through incompetence or inexperience. Safe and slow, it is ideally suited to a governmental machine of financial orthodoxy, regional equity and public accountability. From this point of view, it can hardly be bettered and it has had a wide influence throughout the world.[8,9] But it imposes a delay on the production of hospitals which all the subsequent efforts of the Department of Health have been designed to reduce. We describe them in some detail and give an indication of their effectiveness in achieving the desired results.

Standardisation

The Department was of course aware of the duplication of effort resulting from 15 regional boards simultaneously trying to solve the same problems of form and content. *Hospital Building Notes* were an attempt to reach consensus on content. Standardisation was the obvious answer on form.

The classic aims of standardisation are economy

of professional staff, and concentration of design effort leading to a better product, which in turn increases demand and makes possible mass production and higher output for less cost. The most famous example of hospital standardisation is Brunel's contribution to the Crimean War. In 1856 he designed, manufactured, shipped to the Mediterranean and erected an 800-bed hospital in nine months.[10] A hundred and thirty years later the advocates of industrialised building methods are still trying to equal his achievement.

There are two approaches to standardisation. The first is to produce standard plans (whole buildings). The second is to produce standard components (the bits and pieces). Standard plans have their place in primitive conditions, on flat sites, in virgin country. But with a rapidly changing brief, uneven contours, irregular terrain and complex medical requirements, it is not difficult for a skilled designer to earn his fee producing a purpose-made hospital to solve a particular problem.

Standard hospital components

The approach chosen was therefore to concentrate on standard components, which could be taken up by architects and used in a variety of ways in their individual schemes. An early success was achieved by Jock Kinneir on directional signs.[3] He had already designed the signs used on motorways. The elegant and decorative system he devised for hospitals was rapidly adopted throughout the NHS in old hospitals as well as new. The signs manufactured under regional or central contracts are available on call at local level. Variety reduction led to mass production and lower prices. And the enormous take-up that has resulted produces an added bonus. Visitors can find their way more easily about a hospital without a guide and fewer staff are needed to acccompany mobile patients.

Between 1965–78 the Department of Health in Britain spent some £2.57 million on standardisation.[11] Work was carried out on a whole range of building components, from doors and windows to floors and ceilings. Dimensions were standardised and new products introduced under the title of Manufacturers' Data Base (later renamed Component Data Base)[3].

At the same time, advantage was taken of the change to the metric system to apply the principles of modular co-ordination. The adoption of a 10cm module and a planning grid of preferred dimensions would lead, it was hoped, to a greater demand for components internationally co-ordinated to the same module. In Belgium a complete demonstration of modular co-ordination based on the theory of sets was carried out by J. Delrue in the planning of the Gasthuisberg Teaching Hospital for Leuven, and extended for use by developing countries throughout the world.[12]

The National Building Agency in UK, an independent organisation, carried out a survey of the use made of standard components in a sample of capital schemes for hospitals in 1978/9. It found that out of a potential of 16 per cent of the contract value of buildings being constructed, there was a take-up of approximately 9 per cent over the years 1974–8;[11] a somewhat disappointing result. The expectations of the protagonists of industrialised building methods had proved difficult to realise.

Computers: theory and practice

Far more could be achieved, it was hoped, if the same efforts were extended to the standardisation of all stages of the planning and design process. The advent of computers in the 1960s appeared to make this a feasible possibility.

In 1969 Sir Solly (now Lord) Zuckerman, Chief Scientific Adviser to the UK Government, was charged with the task of re-allocating research funds voted by Parliament for work on weaponry and now no longer needed. It was a swords into ploughshares exercise, and he chose 'computer application to the hospital design process' as one of the recipients. By 1978 some £3.49 million had been spent on developing manual and computer aids for all stages of the planning, design, production and delivery of hospitals in the NHS[11].

The architect whose initiative led to this work was Robert Radford of the UK Department of Health and Social Security. He saw that the logical sequence developed for Capricode (page 181) could be adapted for use on a computer and automated. Once the needs of a community were established, the Design Brief Data Base could translate them into a series of operational policies. These in turn described the activities that would take place and the space requirements to house them, the equipment to be used and the service demands that would be generated. Modular co-ordination, the use of preferred dimensions for floor-to-ceiling heights and service spaces, and a planning grid, enabled the space requirements to be met by a series of standard envelopes. These could then be joined together in different configurations on different sites to suit particular requirements of contour or climate. The resulting plan shapes could be evaluated for ease of access, insulation, heat loss, etc., using computer programmes already developed for other types of building. The architectural concept known as Harness is described in chapter 1. Once a design was accepted, the Production Material Data Base translated it into bills of quantities, schedules of components, standard assembly drawings, and so on. There was thus a fully co-ordinated logical sequence of compatible systems whereby a decision in one stage inevitably led to decisions in the next. Architectural, engineering, and financial consequences followed predetermined instructions fed into the computer. The whole operation was designed to take a fraction of the time required by traditional processes.[13] A pilot project was planned to start at Dudley, in the Midlands of England, to be followed by some seventy hospitals rolling off the production line until about the year 2000.

The timing of the concept was unfortunate. The computer programme was developed in a period of euphoria which affected not only hospitals but universities, new towns and many other fields of human endeavour. Everyone was planning for an expanding future. Generous solutions were adopted wherever possible, to allow for growth and change (chapter 1 page 55). Inevitablly when a limited choice was needed from a range of preferred dimensions, the next size up was always chosen. Floor to floor heights were increased, columns were spaced wider apart. The effect was cumulative. At this time also, medical opinion was swinging away from natural ventilation towards universal air-conditioning. Energy costs soared. The Manufacturers' Data Base of Hospital Building Assemblies tended to reduce competition among suppliers and create monopoly conditions.

Prices rose in an overheated enonomy. The cost per bed worked out at £23,300 compared with the Best Buy figure of £13,500 (both at 1975 prices).

It was unfortunate also that the computer programme was developed at a time when the state of the art favoured a centralised, monolithic operation. Thus, when the red light began to show and everyone concerned in the working party became aware of the danger of increasing costs, it was impossible to alter course. Decisions fed into the system could not be modified, because there was a deadline to be met. Too many people had to be consulted. Each authority that had to agree proposals made revision more difficult. When the oil crisis broke and inflation took off, the whole programme was abandoned. Only a truncated version of Dudley and another at Stafford were allowed to go forward. A prototype was also completed at Southlands Hospital, Shoreham-by-Sea.

Hospital planning information

It would be wrong however to judge the computer programme by the buildings which have emerged. As was shown in chapter 1, Howard Goodman performed a brilliant rescue operation in scaling down form and content, which resulted in the Nucleus concept. But the most valuable legacy has been the wealth of software that is now available. The Department of Health's Works Guidance Index 1982 lists some 144 pages of title headings arranged under subjects, documents and contact points. This comprises a comprehensive and integrated system of guidance for all health buildings. It also includes a range of computer programmes complementing building notes, guidance for costing and performance, planning, design, production documentation, estate management and information retrieval.[14]

Many other countries have built up excellent collections of studies on hospital planning. A list of sources of information is given in Appendix 2. Taken together, they make up the most comprehensive planning data on any type of building an architect may be called upon to design.

The price paid for procedural delays

With such wealth of information built up over the years by the work of dedicated individuals, it seems uncharitable to offer any criticism. It must be admitted, however, that it has not resulted in any general speeding up in the planning, design, production and delivery of hospitals. The average time in most parts of Europe from inception to completion is still about ten years*. Half of this is often spent before the first sod is cut. As planning committees pore over plans, the price of building materials mounts month by month. During periods of high inflation the original estimate may well have doubled by the time the contract is let. Then time becomes even more important. High interest charges on idle capital have to be added to construction costs. In the public sector this is often ignored. But if it were included and aggregated to the hidden costs of postponements and delays, the final price that has to be paid would often bear little relation to the cost of the project as originally conceived.

Effect of on-costs and site selection

Another criticism, with hindsight, may be made of the way on-costs have distorted the basic simplicity of cost allowances. The piecemeal examination of plans, department by department, obscures the major issues of hospital planning discussed in this book. Diagram 5.2 shows two hospitals, A and B, with the same functional content, the same area of nursing and clinical zones. But hospital A is built on an awkward site, involving high foundation costs, an underground car park, a large support zone, high building, air-conditioning and expensive fire precautions. It attracts the maximum on-costs. Hospital B is low-risc, on an open site, with minimum on-costs. Hospital A takes longer to plan and build. Fees and administrative costs are naturally higher. When interest charges (assumed at 10 per cent) and inflation (assumed at 10 per cent) are added, hospital A costs nearly four times hospital B. The final price of hospital A is almost ten times the original figure of cost limits for the functional units comprising the nursing and clinical zones (see Appendix 3).

Some economists would argue that the final price paid has no significance. It merely reflects the extent of inflation. The cost of resources consumed will be the same, whether the hospital takes ten years or three, if they are calculated at constant prices. Others point to the loss in terms of human suffering, waiting for the hospital to be completed. 'Imagine' they say 'the loss that would result if it was a school and a whole generation were deprived of education'.

---

* As an exception, in 1980 the UK Public Accounts Committee enquiry into the *Standardisation of Hospitals, operational procedures and components*, claimed 'something like 18 months saving in time in the client brief and in the design work' as a result of Nucleus.

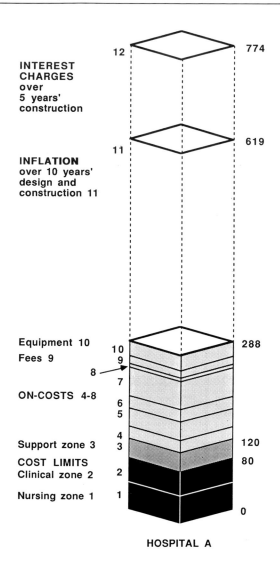

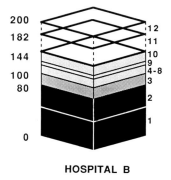

5.2 The financial effect of delay on on-costs. Hospital A and Hospital B perform the same function in the community. The cost limits for the clinical and nursing zones are the same: 80. The support zone at A is 40; and B 20. On-costs* at A are 168 (because of site conditions and location); at B 44. Hospital A takes 10 years to design and build: Hospital B takes three years. Inflation and interest charges (see appendix 3) increase the final cost of Hospital A to 774; Hospital B's final cost is 200.

*Key to on-costs: 8 Height factor
　　　　　　　　 7 Air-conditioning
　　　　　　　　 6 Additional engineering
　　　　　　　　 5 Site works
　　　　　　　　 4 Communications

During the course of this debate, it is easy to see how the main factors making for increased costs – site selection and the choice of appropriate procedures – are lost sight of. As Maria Perez Sherrif[15] pointed out to the World Health Organisation in 1975, 'the cost of administrative delay can far outweigh all the technical or medical savings made by the skill of hospital planners', described in previous chapters, under the heading of Containment.

B   Containment

Questions to be asked

The first question to be asked is: must hospitals always take so long to build and cost so much? And the second is: is there anything to choose between the 'medical' and 'lay' approach? The best way to answer these questions is to look very closely at the various procedures being advocated today and 'observe what happens in practice, as opposed to what is supposed or desired to happen'. This is in fact a dictionary definition of operational research.

Operational research: a classic example

A classic example of operational research was carried out by Aileen Sparrow, a Nuffield Research Fellow working at the UK Building Research Establishment from 1963–67.[16] With the agreement of the Ministry of Health and Regional Hospital Boards she sat in as an observer on various project teams, including one planning the Lister Hospital (page 25). She was thus in a position to see how the planning process worked in practice. It quickly became obvious to her that 'hospitals were expensive, not because of lack of ability, or medical extravagance, but because of the administrative machinery set up under the 1948 Act – the divorce between planning and management already noted. Three independent authorities were concerned with every large building project. This meant that every decision, normally made by a single client, had to be agreed by two and sometimes three specialists (e.g. medical policy had to be agreed by a hospital consultant, a regional medical officer and a Ministry of Health adviser). Similarly two and often three professional men had to agree plans normally prepared by a single professional. There was confusion of responsibilities so complete that no-one could say who was responsible. No one was in charge. There was no chain of command. Authority was not delegated: it was fragmented during the planning stage. Costs were carefully checked by the central authority, after plans had been laboriously prepared, in the only way they could be checked by people remote from management of a hospital, namely by comparing proposed provision with that suggested in the *Hospital Building Notes*. The result was rather unexpected. Maximum provision allowed, became minimum acceptable, and any attempt at economy was dismissed as 'sub-standard'. Hospital Management Committees accepted unwanted accommodation with a shrug saying 'it will come in useful for something.' The Ministry blamed the Regional Boards when estimates exceeded expectations; the Boards blamed the Ministry. The whole process took so long that any revision would have meant losing a place in the queue. The kind of economies which might profitably be made under a different system of control were impossible.

The expert committees that were set up to improve the standard of service made general recommendations that civil servants checking plans interpreted as minimum requirements which could not be questioned even when circumstances changed (e.g. clean and dirty corridors continued to be specified as a means of combating infection after the invention of plastic bags). Diet kitchens were included although the existing diet kitchen at the old Lister Hospital at Stevenage had never been used, because the cooks were so well trained they could prepare special diets in their own main kitchens). Local initiative was thus replaced by a network of rules, recommendations and regulations. Instructions issued in this way were interpreted by specialists to secure maximum provision under every heading. In extreme cases, cost was increased without any practical benefit as a result of one specialist misinterpreting another's requirements, or quite simply making a mistake which other specialists did not feel called on to correct. Opinions expressed by specialist advisers were seldom challenged or publicly refuted. And recommendations made by professional organisations were treated as mandatory unless they happened to conflict with some other regulation, in which case there was sometimes room for choice. As there was no-one in charge, there was no-one to strike a balance between conflicting decisions or to settle differences of opinion if they arose.'

The report concluded 'the method of exercising control over hospital building in operation between 1963/6 appeared to have the following undesirable results:
1   No-one knew where responsibility lay. There was no single identifiable client to relate needs to operational policy and assess design in terms of total cost and performance. This work therefore could not be done effectively and was seldom attempted.
2   Design and approval on the basis of norms was an obstacle to more efficient design and innovation.
3   Each independent specialist, professional organisation, or *ad hoc* body, which had power to make recommendations regarding methods of working, staff rates, standards of accommodation, etc., put up costs, as their recommendations tended to be regarded as mandatory, although they were made in general terms

and without reference to particular building schemes.

4   Each additional authority which had to agree the medical brief, the schedules of accommodation and plans for a new hospital, tended to increase its cost by asking for some provision to be made which might have been omitted had one authority been in complete control.

5   Each authority which had to agree proposals caused delay which increased outlay, as building costs were constantly rising.

6   Each authority which had to agree proposals made revision more difficult. This tended to increase costs, as revision of plans and specifications is the normal method by which costs are reduced when they are found to be too high'.[16]

The Best Buy hospitals experiment

The report was received by the Ministry with a certain amount of incredulity. It was difficult to believe that this was how things were working out in practice. Nevertheless George Wilson, then leading the Building Division at the Department of Health, determined to test out one of its recommendations – that someone should be put in charge. Accordingly he persuaded the Department to appoint one of its own doctors (Dr Harrington) to act as a single client, freeing him from the whole machinery of bureaucratic control. He could bypass the second tier, the Regional Board, and go direct to the people who were going to run the future hospitals. He could also ignore Ministry norms and take short cuts to provide, not the best possible accommodation, but an adequate service without loss of amenity or detriment to good standards of medical and nursing care. Dr Harrington set to work in 1967, and the two Best Buy hospitals resulted, one at Frimley, the other at Bury St. Edmunds. As described on page 7, every possible means of economising space and services was explored. The hospitals were closely integrated with their respective community health services. A lower bed complement, made possible by early discharge, led to a more intensive use of diagnostic and treatment facilities. These medical initiatives were matched by breakthroughs on the design side (page 61). The result was a saving of over 30 per cent on the average cost of District General Hospitals following the Department's normal administrative arrangements.

Both hospitals continue to give satisfactory service, and Frimley, by 1982, was successfully coping with the needs of a population of 220,000, although originally designed to serve 180,000. The Nuffield Report's conclusions have been completely vindicated. The success of the Best Buy hospitals was dependent on:

1   The appointment of a single identifiable client with

2   Direct access to the community whose needs the hospital is intended to serve,

3   Short-circuiting the administrative machinery of consultations, submissions and approvals.

Three case studies – 1: Spain (see 1.59)

By a curious coincidence, just at the time the Best Buy hospitals were being designed in England, a much larger hospital was rolling off the stocks in Spain. Here is a contemporary account by Tatton-Brown reproduced from his internationl news letter no 6: *Rationalisation of Hospital Building* which was circulated from the Department of Health in the UK in June 1970.

Santa Fe Hospital Complex, Valencia

'At the London Seminar, November 1969, architect Florez electrified the gathering with his report of air-conditioned, 14-storey, 1,000 bed hospitals designed and built in 18 months. In April 1970 Dr Harrington and I accepted his kind invitation to inspect his hospital and verify his claim. This letter describes what we saw.

1   The effective dates

The first phase, a 1,100 bed District General Hospital was approved in principle in September 1967. Patients were admitted in February 1969. By February 1971, they will have completed some 2,200 beds in 3½ years at a cost of approximately £6m for the building and £2m fees and equipment.

2   Content

Centre block
17 out-patient suites
Eight X-ray rooms
14 operating theatres (10 in main suite, 2×2 op. room suites).
1,100 beds

Rehabilitation, Orthopaedic and Burns block
400 beds including 17-bed burns unit and wards for paraplegics.
Four X-ray rooms
Large physical medicine department with modern gym, daily living section and hydrotherapy pool.

Nurses' home and school – about 300 places

Mortuary
Maternity 350 beds ⎫ In building, they will be connected. The
                    ⎬ maternity unit will be a double corridor
Children 350 beds ⎭ design.

Total then will be 2,200 beds for 1.5 million insured workers and their families.

Acute beds (including children) 1,850 beds = 1.23 acute beds/thousand (Best Buy norm = 2 beds/thousand).

Maternity 350 beds = 1.23 maternity beds/thousand (British norm = 0.5 beds/thousand).

Area   110,356m²
Date of approval   27 September 1967
Construction period   33 months
Total contract sum   £6m
Hospital beds   2,202
Cost/ft² (includes air-conditioning throughout)   £5.1
Cost/bed   £2,725
Date of occupation of final phase   February 1971
Area/bed   50.1m²

The briefing process

The briefing process occupies 'three or four afternoons'. Dr Santos, the planning doctor of the Seguridad, discusses the latest hospitals with architect Florez and agrees the improvements which they wish to make on their previous design. Dr Santos has been responsible for the hospital building programme of the Seguridad since it was set up twenty-three years ago. He has commissioned some 70 hospitals with a total of approximately 25,000 beds. Señor Florez has a similar length of experience and has completed as a principal in private practice some 30 hospitals. He is one of the four major architects commissioned by Dr Santos over a number of years and they know one another's minds well. The briefing process can be compared with that which took place in the fourteenth century in the Perpendicular parish church programme, which consisted in saying 'we want one like Steeple Bumphrey only five foot higher.'

Planning

Señor Florez has a small office consisting of three architects, two students and seven draughtsmen. They can turn out up to £10m worth of work a year of sketch designs to 1:50 scale. Designs are highly repetitive: 90 per cent of the wards, for instance, consist of two-bed rooms with their own toilet, bedpan washer and shower, in blocks 15.2m wide, 3.50m floor to floor and 2.70m floor to ceiling (Cubith dimensions). Drawings for a £2.5m contract number approximately 70 and follow the American pattern: i.e. they show the general arrangement of building and engineering, leaving the successful contractor to produce production drawings for architect's approval.

Tenders

Public tenders are invited on the basis of these drawings and a very detailed performance specification. They are adjudicated first on the basis of the capability of the contractor, second on speed of construction, 1.25 per cent is notionally allowed for every month saved: e.g. if contractor A claims that he can complete nine months earlier than contractor B, his tender is notionally reduced by 9 times 1.25 per cent, or 11.25 per cent, and if his price is then lower than contractor B, he will get the contract. But if he fails to complete on time he is subject to a double penalty clause of 2.5 per cent for every month's delay.*'

Case study 2: France (see 1.72-1.74)

A 300-bed hospital was completed in 18 months at Beaune[17] in the early 1970s, again by a public authority. Because of 'doctrinal difficulties' – irreconcilable differences of opinion between users, administrators and colleges of medicine – the State decided to intervene. Using techniques successfully employed in the school building programme, the hospital beat all previous records.

Case study 3: England (see 1.85)

In 1982 the 150-bed Alexandra Hospital at Cheadle, Manchester, was built in 12 months, this time by private enterprise.[18] The client was American Medical International. The construction was organised by an American contractor, employing British firms. The construction period was originally envisaged as 21

* By 1982, Dr Santos had commissioned some 110 hospitals for the Social Security organisations, 70 of which had been designed by Señor Florez.

The construction of some 30,000 new acute beds between 1969–80 had taken the heat out of the need for hospitals to be built in double quick time. (The record was 9 months for a Maternity hospital!) The bonus for early completion has been dropped because of natural reluctance to sanction overtime in a period of high unemployment. Hospitals now take 2 years to build and cost about 50 per cent more per m^2 than flats, as compared with 4 years and 100 per cent in UK.

There was one exception to this generalisation: the 1600 bed Ramon y Cajal Hospital in Madrid. For political reasons the briefing of the Architect (Señor Flores) was taken out of the hands of Dr Santos.

months, resulting in an increase of costs from £7m to £12.5m. The phenomenal reduction of time was made possible by changes in function: five wards of 28 beds were replaced by four wards of 36 beds (resulting in a two-storey instead of a three-storey building), in form (travertine was replaced by brick), and in mechanical services. These modifications could be quickly agreed because there was somebody in charge.

Someone in charge

It is obvious from these examples that hospitals need take no longer to design and build than other complex buildings. They were built quickly because there was someone acting as client to give instructions to the architect. There must be a client, to manage the briefing and design evaluation processes and ensure that all the pressures are balanced by an objective authority. The great merit of the 'medical' approach, referred to at the beginning of this chapter, was that this role was played by the Herr Professor. But if there is no one to take on this responsibility, or if he cannot marshal this expertise (and it is an expertise) from his own resources, then he must go out and hire it. It cannot be shrugged off or left to an anonymous project team. The cost of hiring will be repaid many times over by the savings on the capital cost of building, and what is far more important, the functional efficiency and therefore the running costs of the future hospital.

In the case of a complicated building the terms 'client' and 'architect' are used in a collective sense. It is obvious that in all but the smallest projects these individuals are backed by boards and committees and a staff of specialists and consultants and so on.[19]

Who are the clients?

The first question to be asked is: who are the clients? Are they the users: the patients and staff? The managers responsible for running the service? Or the planners of health care, controlling demand and allocating resources? Or the owners, whose principal interest is accountability, the prevention of fraud and a reasonable return on capital investment? Or the Treasury, whose primary aims may be much wider objectives, such as stimulating the economy or restraining inflation? Each client group has a different goal. The patients want a modern hospital here and now, ready at hand to answer an emergency call. The staff are concerned with efficient performance; the management with job satisfaction and staff turnover; the planners with precedents and standards of provision – and so on. All may be subject to fiscal pressures from outside. For instance, in the case of a public service, Treasury insistence on matching expenditure with annual budgets may mean imposing arbitrary cuts which bear no relation to the economic objectives they are supposed to achieve. With this group, speed is seldom a primary consideration. Indeed it may be an embarrassment, because opening a new hospital will almost certainly increase revenue expenditure.

Problem seeking and problem solving

Somewhere a way must be found to reconcile the differences between all these conflicting interests. The approach must be 'rational enough to withstand scrutiny and analytical enough for the information to promote greater mutual understanding'.[19]

In recent years some progress has been made in analysing the nature of the conflict and devising ways of dealing with it. In 1977 William Peña published *Problem Seeking*[19], *an architectural programming (briefing) primer*. He describes the methods used by Caudill Rowlett Scott in over 400 projects ranging from universities, military establishments and town centres to hospitals. We have drawn heavily on his ideas, in this chapter, paraphrasing, with his permission, procedures evolved in solving problems also encountered in the design of weaponry, spacecraft, and almost every field of creative activity involving co-operation between large groups of people with conflicting interests.

The secret of his success is that he has shown a way of combining the authority implicit in the 'medical' approach with the rationale provided by the 'lay'. He has moreover, done this without depersonalising the design process. Indeed just the reverse. He insists on the importance of identifying and appointing a person to represent the 'client' – all the clients – and a person to represent the 'architect' – all the designers.

The project director: combining 'medical' and 'lay' approach

The name used to describe the person in charge will vary from country to country, and the size of the project. He may be called team leader, project director, job captain, or programmer. In a very large medical service centre, approaching the size of a new town, he may be called general manager.

We use the term project director. But some people might prefer job captain, because launching a building project is like taking a ship to sea. Navigational charts such as Capricode are useful, indeed essential, but even with radar and automatic steering you still need a captain on the bridge. No-one knows in advance what hazards will be encountered. There must be some one to guide the ship through the winds of change, past the reefs of political interference, and to avoid collision with vested interests of trades unions or professional associations.

The project director may be an outside consultant, as described at the beginning of this chapter, or an in-house appointment. His background is immaterial. The important thing is that he should have demonstrated marked skills as an entrepreneur. He must be able to command the respect of all parties concerned. In order to preserve the distinction between client and architect, it is better if the project director's role is not played by an architect, or if he happens to be one, that he comes from a different 'stable' from that of the design architect. The two functions are distinct but complementary – analysis and synthesis: problem stating and problem solving: programming and design. They call for different skills and different temperaments. The project director is coldly rational, processing raw data into rational information, stimulating the clients to make decisions. He works with his head. The design architect works with his heart, instinctively translating his brief into form and content.[19]

The appointment of a project director will provoke different reactions in different countries. Feathers will have to be smoothed, and in some cases, a reversal of roles accepted. In Britain, for instance, the notions of 'public accountability' (which resides with the Permanent Secretary) and 'ministerial responsibility' (the Secretary of State for Health and Social Security) militate against such an appointment. But without some delegation of authority there can be no quick decisions. A way must be found to break the deadlock caused by the divorce between building and management, planning and ownership, which as already noted is built into the 3-tier hierarchy of the National Health Service.

A statement of need

The first job of the project director is the preparation of a certificate of need, as it is known in the USA. This sets out the short- and long-term aims, services, costs, benefits and anticipated use of facilities. Once approved by the state or federal authority, the promoter can claim the financial benefits to which he is entitled. From then on the project director is freed from the necessity to submit plans or seek further approvals. He is on his own. The project is launched.

A similar document has to be prepared in the UK, as laid down in the Department of Health's *Health Notice (81) 30.*[20] It comprises a statement of need describing why development is necessary, catchment populations, bed norms, the options open to meet the deficiencies described, and the justification for the preferred option. This is followed by the functional content, location and estimated cost, together with the revenue costs and confirmation that any additional revenue will be available. The major manpower implications, the timetable, and the effects on present services: e.g. decanting, closures, or changes of use. Because of the great public interest and involvement in a new project, it is expected that authorities will want to discuss approval in principle submissions in public. The department will wish to be satisfied that all the options have been fully considered, such as not building on a new site at all, but simply upgrading or changing the use of existing buildings or the development of day or community services. In comparing capital costs, the current value of building, equipment and land must be included, even where the NHS already owns the land. In addition, it is suggested an attempt should be made to quantify any cost imposed on the public or private sector such as travel costs and the cost of increased local authority social services incurred. Against this should be set the social benefits of different options, such as increased throughput of patients or better use of scarce staff resources. There is further advice on discounting, to ensure comparability on an equivalent constant annual sum.

Obtaining consensus

With all the wealth of guidance and documentation now available there is no reason for this to take a long time. The techniques available for obtaining a consensus and reconciling conflicts as described by William Peña can be adapted for use in Britain. After carrying out the usual collection of data and interviews, the project director and his team conduct a series of work sessions. These take place in the client's 'back-yard', and are on the same lines as those conducted by Dr Harrington at Frimley and Bury. They consist of intensive day and night sessions, lasting perhaps a week. All the groups participating are invited to attend. It is important that they should be given an opportunity to express their views. Even if all their wants cannot be satisfied, at least they can feel that they have had a fair hearing. Conflicts between different groups are brought out into the open, and their effect on space allocations and cost illustrated by graphic display. Compromises, which might take years to arrive at if discussions were held with each group separately, can often be agreed before the close of a session. The prospect of getting a real hospital quickly is a strong reinforcement to reasoned argument.

Value for money in form, function and time

The project director has four fields of manoeuvre: form, function, economy and time. In order to achieve best value for money he should be free to operate in at least one, and preferably in all four. From what has been said in chapters 1, 2, and 3, it is clear that hospitals come in many shapes and sizes (high rise, low rise, mono-block etc.) Similar functions can be achieved by many different operational policies (e.g. linen exchange or laundry annexe). Cost consequences and methods of circulation are almost equally variable (e.g. ramps or elevators). He should also be free to decide how and when to let a contract (whether to go ahead immediately or bank his money and wait for a more favourable tendering climate).

As soon as the week of intensive work sessions is over, there is an interval of two to four weeks. During this period of gestation, the project director and his team check the evidence they have received to make sure that it included all the hopes and aspirations of the client groups. He then completes his brief, his statement of the problem to be solved and the parameters within which it must be solved, expressed in terms of form, function, money and time.

During the work sessions the architect and his team of consultants are present. But they play a passive role, answering questions if asked. Their job is to listen and observe, so that they are aware of the problems to be solved and the reasons behind the

project director's decisions. The discipline imposed gives their subconscious free rein, but they take no part in the resolution of conflicts. An explicit and open process conducted in this way at the work sessions, leads to a clear understanding of the project, first by the client and later, by the designer.[19]

On receipt of his brief the architect prepares his sketch designs or schematics – exactly as he would if entering a two-stage competition. The project director (and his jury) calls for alternative solutions from the architect, if necessary, and adjudicates. The selected scheme is then developed into detail designs, and once approved, translated into contract documents. Throughout this stage the project director is available for decisions and all questions are channelled through him.

Fast-track

For reasons stated earlier in this chapter, every means of shortening the production process is worth pursuing: word processors, computer-assisted drafting methods and all mechanical aids at the disposal of the design team. One of the most impressive strategies for saving time is known as fast-track. The aim is to telescope operations that are normally sequential, so that they can be started in quick succession and completed almost simultaneously (see p. 180). In a traditional building operation a quantity surveyor does not start work until he has a complete set of drawings from the architect. The contractor cannot complete his tender until the last item in the bill of quantities has been priced. Fast-track depends on the use of predetermined envelopes such as Nucleus. The number and configuration of these envelopes can be quickly determined at sketch design. Approximate bills of quantities can be prepared in advance and priced, directly or by reference to previous contracts. Tenders can therefore be obtained at a much earlier stage and a contractor appointed immediately. While foundations are being dug, detailed design development is completed and orders placed for equipment. As soon as it arrives on the job the contractor is ready to install it. Fast track can halve production time.

Turnkey

Another time-saving procedure is called Turnkey. It has been especially successful in developing countries. Modern turnkeys combine competitive tendering and design competition in one package. The normal turnkey is contractor-led. The client – government department, public authority or private developer – prepares (or has prepared by his project director) a detailed programme and specification, including in some cases draft schematics. Meanwhile contractor-led consortia are invited to pre-qualify with the client authority. The client then selects a short list of turnkey consortia (which normally include, in addition to the contractor – the medical equipment supplier, architect, mechanical and electrical consultants and cost consultants, all appointed by the contractor, and in effect his sub-contractors). The project director will advise the client on the selection of the short list.

The tender documents (programme and specifications) are given to the selected consortia, who will then bid for the design, construction and equipping of the hospital (often this will include a two-year training and maintenance programme on completion of the work).

Turnkey contractors are usually given a period of from two to four months to complete their bids for a hospital of 300–500 beds. This very tight period makes great demands on the contractors' design consultants, who normally have to produce final design documents to satisfy (*a*) the contractors' need for a firm price base and (*b*) the demands of the project director who, being responsible to the client both for design and supervision, needs to be satisfied that he is getting a sound design. This will usually involve each contractor in an expenditure of up to £100,000: which will have to be written off by all the unsuccessful tenderers!

The successful tenderer is usually given a start-up period of three months before work must commence on site, and it is during this period that his design consultants have to produce working drawings.

The whole design period is thus telescoped into between five and seven months for a hospital of 300–500 beds.

Recent experience in developing countries has indicated that keen competition makes this a very attractive method for funding authorities. Not only will there be a low bid from the contractor but also the design, which is included in the bid price, is being done for an all-in fee of between two and three per cent for all disciplines. All the client pays in fees is for the project director to check the tenderer's work and carry out the supervision on site.

The need for further experiment

Hospitals come in all shapes and sizes. The variety of different ways in which planning, design, production and delivery can be organised would seem to justify further experiment. No one way can be said to be the best. The short cuts of the Spanish solution in the sixties might not be acceptable to Britain in the eighties – nor would Turnkey operations (except perhaps on rare occasions for purposes of comparison) be likely to be widely adopted in the public sector. What does emerge from the few examples described above is the advantages of speed. Quick decisions are best obtained from a knowledgeable client who has discretion, within carefully defined limits, to spend money as if it were his own. Those most likely to be capable of exercising the function of client are those working closest to the patient, or those in a position to get an immediate reaction from users so that they can revise plans or incorporate improvements quickly in subsequent designs. This kind of flexibility is likely to be inhibited by remote control. A better service could almost certainly be provided if the people responsible

for managing hospital construction or reconstruction could be more clearly identified and rewarded. The delegation of powers, previously fragmented between the central authority and regional and area boards, to locally appointed project directors, is one way ahead which is worth pursuing.

Epilogue

In 1985, the British Secretary of State for Health and Social Security issued a circular HC(85)26 accepting all the principal recommendations of Sir Roy Griffiths on management in the National Health Service (see Introduction, p. 1).

His report[22] endorses many of the conclusions set out above and recommends the appointment of a general manager (regardless of discipline) for every unit of management; some measurement of output in terms of patient care; a property function to give a major commercial re-orientation to the handling of the NHS estate; procedures for handling major capital schemes and disposal of property to be streamlined and speeded up and to provide maximum devolution from the centre to the periphery; monitoring experience and perceptions of patients and the community by market research, and by comparison with services provided elsewhere, and so on.

At the same time, in the international field, important developments are taking place. Computer programmes are being developed as an aid to decision-making on larger projects involving heavy investment of capital and human resources.[23] These are being adapted for the planning, design and delivery of hospitals. The wealth of information built up over the years, as described in this book, can be tapped to construct models, predicting what is likely to happen. These models are much more accurate than hunches, because they are based on experience of averages derived from a very large number of projects carried out in different countries.

Thus from a simple decision to build a new acute hospital with 500 beds, the computer will print out what that may mean in terms of cost, area, time and staff. It breaks down each of these categories into great detail. Under cost, for instance, would come the initial capital cost and recurring costs of maintenance and staffing, equipment replacement, catering and so on. The timing of the investment programme and its influence on phasing and recruitment and training programmes are brought out into the open from the start.

As decisions are made on a particular project, local knowledge of prevailing conditions of labour, materials, productivity, wage levels and taxation is substituted for the theoretical values used in the computer model. Gradually a more and more accurate picture of what is involved is built up: see diagram 5.3.

Armed with this tool, the project director can combine the advantages of both the 'medical' and the 'lay' approach described at the beginning of this chapter. He can bring to the intensive work-sessions conducted in the clients' back-yard (described on page 189) immediate numerical consequences of alternative policy decisions in terms of finance, space, time and manpower. The possibility of reducing the number of imponderables and improving the predictability of hospital building should presage a better future for the planning of health services throughout the world – our main object in writing this book.

5.3 Parametric cost model.[24] Starting from a theoretical model (the top configuration) estimates of cost are gradually built up. As more and more local information is accumulated, it is fed into the theoretical model. The forecast of resources becomes progressively more accurate in terms of material, equipment and personnel.

References

General introduction

1 Delande G., 'Coûts hospitaliers et dimension optimale de l'hôpital.' *Santé Sociale, Statistiques et Commentaires*, Paris, Jan/Fev No. 1. 1982.
2 Council for Science and Society, *Expensive Medical Techniques: Report of a Working Party*, 1982, 51.

3 Griffiths R., *NHS Management Inquiry*, Department of Health and Social Security, October 1983.

1 Planning the whole hospital

Note: London, UK, is place of publication, unless any other place is stated.

1 Thompson, J. and Goldin, G., *The Hospital: a Social and Architectural History*, New York 1975, 22.
2 Nightingale, F., *Notes on Hospitals*. 1863, 3.
3 MacCauley, H., *Comparative Study. The Hospital Services of Western Europe*. Report of Conference November 1962, International Hospital Federation in collaboration with King Edward's Hospital Fund for London, 15, 28, 47.
4 Fagin, H., *Technological Impacts on Health Facilities, Analysis and Planning*, University Microfilms International, New York 1973.
5 Department of Health and Social Security, *A Hospital Plan for England and Wales*. Cmnd. 1604, Her Majesty's Stationery Office, 1962.
6 Department of Health and Social Security, Central Health Services Council, *The Functions of the District General Hospital*, 1969 Her Majesty's Stationery Office.
7 McKeown, T., *A Concept of a Balanced Teaching Hospital and the Proposed Application to Birmingham*, The Nuffield Provincial Hospitals Trust, 1965.
8 Tatton-Brown, W., 'Designing the Hospital Community' *RIBA Journal*, February 1965, 88–91.
9 Stone, P., 'Hospitals: the Heroic Years', *The Architect's Journal*, 15 December 1976, 1122–1147.
10 Pütsep, E., *The Modern Hospital, International Planning Practises*, Lloyd-Luke, 1979.
11 Weeks, J., 'AD Briefing: Hospitals' *Architectural Design*, July 1973, 436–463.
12 Department of Health and Social Security. *Greenwich District Hospital*, Descriptive brochure, 1982, 283.
13 Zeidler, E., *Healing the Hospital: McMaster Health Science Centre, its Conception and Evolution*, Toronto 1974.
14 Department of Health and Social Security, *Harness System design reports. The Building system I, Computer aided building II*, June 1972.

15 Stone, Marraccini, Patterson., *Application of the Principles of Systems Integration to the Design of VA Hospital Facilities*. Project No 99 R. 047., Washington DC, 1972.
16 Bridgman, R., *Hospital Utilization, An International Study*. Oxford Medical Publications, Oxford University Press, 1979, 13, 232.
17 Maxwell, R., *Hospital Utilization. An International Study of Health Care Planning*. Lexington Books 1981.
18 Abel-Smith, B. *An International Study of Health Expenditure and its Relevance for Health Planning*, World Health Organisation, 1967, 32. 76–7.
19 Office of Health Economics, *Compendium of Health Statistics*, 1981, 3, 15.
20 Abel-Smith, B. *Value for Money in Health Services*, 1976, 114.
21 Office of Health Economics, *Building for Health*, 35, 1970, 24-6.
22 Department of Health and Social Security, *Rationalisation of Planning and Design. New District General Hospitals: Bury St. Edmunds, Frimley*, March 1968.
23 Department of Health and Social Security, *Works Guidance Index 1982. Nucleus Hospitals*, 124–8.
24 DHSS Hospital Services, *The future pattern of hospital provision in England*, Consultative paper, 1980, 1.
25 Maxwell, R., 'Getting the best value from existing stock', *Hospital Engineering*, April 1982.
26 Howells, S., 'New hospitals from old stock', *Health and Social Service Journal*. 23 November 1979, 1512–3.
27 Department of Health and Social Security, *Enquiry into Underused and Surplus Property in the NHS*, Her Majesty's Stationery Office, 1983.
28 British Association for the Advancement of Science, Shackle, G.L.S., 'Introduction,' *On the nature of business success*, 1968.

2   The nursing zone

1   Abel-Smith, B., *The Hospitals 1800–1948*, 1964, 2.
2   Nightingale, F., *Notes on Hospitals*, 1863, 62–80.
3   Thompson, J. and Golding, G., *The Hospitals: A Social and Architectural History*, New York 1975, 215.
4   Goodale, J. 'Early ambulation', *Lancet* 1951. 43.
5   Pütsep, E., *The Modern Hospital: International Planning Practices*, Lloyd-Luke, 1979, 156.
6   Nuffield Provincial Hospitals Trust, *Studies in the Function and Design of Hospitals*, Oxford University Press 1955, 9, 16, 28.
7   Royal Institute of British Architects, *The Orientation of Buildings*, 1933.
8   Petty, D., 'Hospital Ward Lighting', *Light and Lighting*, 1952.
9   Department of Scientific and Industrial Research, Building Research Board (Acoustic Committee), *Postwar Building Study No 14*.
10   Friesen, G. 'Concepts of Health Planning', *World Hospitals*, Winter 1975, I. 40.
11   Whyte, W., Howie, J., Eakin, J., 'Bacteriological Observations in a Mechanically Ventilated Experimental Ward and in Two Open-plan Wards', *Journal of Medical Microbiology*, Vol II No 3, 1969, 335–345.
12   Lidwell, O., Brock, B., Shooter, R., Cooke, E., Thomas G., 'Airborne Infection in a fully air-conditioned Hospital', *Journal of Hygiene*, Cambridge 1975, 445–74.
13   Speers, R., Shooter, R., 'Shedding of Bacteria to the Air from Contaminated Towels in Paper Sacks. Possible Significance for Operating rooms', *The Lancet*, 5 August 1967, 301–2.
14   Beddard, D., *Comparative Study of the Work of the Professional Surgical Unit in Two Locations at the Aberdeen Royal Infirmary*, Paper for the Scottish Home and Health Department, Edinburgh, 1968–69.
15   Walsworth-Bell, J., 'Under Observation', *Health and Social Service Journal*, 7 January 1982, 10.
16   Burrough, J., A Scandalous Impromptu. Radcliffe Infirmary Oxford.
17   Vaughan-Hudson R., *Lancet* 9 July 1960, 90.
18   Shee, W., personal communication, see also 'An Administrator's View', *Hospital Centre Symposium on the Ward of the Future*.
19   Tatton-Brown, W., 'Owed to the Nightingale', *Nursing Times*, 3 Aug 1978, 1273–8.
20   Noble, A., and Dixon, R., *Ward Evaluation: St. Thomas' Hospital*, MARU, The Polytechnic of North London, 7/77.
21   Noakes, A., 'Ward Design at the Crossroads', *Health Service Estate* 43, January 1980, 46.
22   Williamson, N., 'A ward with a view', *Nursing Mirror*, 27 April 1983, 24–7.
23   Noakes, A., 'Time for a new view', *Health and Social Service Journal*, 26 August 1982.
24   Bobrow, M., Thomas, J., 'The evolving health care system. A framework for design.' *Hospitals and Health Care Facilities*, 2nd edition, Architectural Record Books, New York 1978, 3.

3   The clinical zone

1   Thomson, A., personal communication.
2   'Where Fabricus Taught', *The Times*, 22 August 1962.
3   Summerson, J., 'Sir Christopher Wren', *Makers of History*, 1965, 22.
4   Clare, A., Thompson, S., *Let's talk about me. A critical examination of the new psychotherapies*, BBC, 1981, 53.
5   Abel-Smith, B., *The Hospitals 1800–1948*, 1964.
6   *World Hospitals*, Winter 1976, Ed, xi, 22.
7   Turban, E., *Cost Containment in Hospitals*, Aspen, New York 1980, 584.
8   Florez, F., personal communication.
9   Pütsep, E., *The Planning of Surgical Centres*, 1973, 153.
10   Stephens, F., Dudley, H., *Lancet*, 1961, 10 41.
11   Bobrow, M., Thomas J., *The Evolving Health-Care System. A framework for design*, New York 1978, 4–7.
12   Turban, E., *Special Report: Costs and management at Tucson Medical Centre*, New York 1978.
13   Farndale, J., *The Day-hospital Movement in Great Britain*, 1961.
14   Price, D., *Ambulatory Care Facilities, Functional Planning of General Hospitals*, New York 1969, 185.
15   Abel-Smith, B., 'Value for Money. Health-Care Planning,' *Excerpta Medica*, 1976.
16   Clibbon, S., Sachs, M., 'Creating consolidated clinical techniques spaces for an expanding role in Health Care', *Architectural Record*, New York February 1971.
17   Pütsep, E., *The Modern Hospital*, Lloyd-Luke 1979.
18   Friesen, G., Silvin R., 'Concepts of Health Planning', *World Hospitals*, Winter 1975, xi. 37.
19   Bridgman, R., 'Special requirements of the ward unit in tropical countries', International Hospital Federation Congress, Paris 1963, 54.
20   Scottish Home and Health Department, *Organisation and Design of Out-patients Departments*, Hospital Planning Note 6, Her Majesty's Stationery Office, 1967.
21   Nuffield Foundation Division for Architectural Studies, *The Design of Research Laboratories*, 1961, 48.
22   Zeidler, E., *Healing the Hospital, McMaster Health*

Science Centre. Its conception and evolution, Toronto 1974, 156.

23 Rawlinson, C., Kelly, J., *Space Utilization in Hospitals* MARU 4/78, Polytechnic of North London, 1978, 59–72.

24 *Philadelphia South Jersey Metropolitan Area Hospital Survey*, New York 1969.

25 Department of Health and Social Security, *Space Utilization in Hospitals*, Technical Memorandum 28, 1979.

26 Oxford Regional Health Authority, *Some Facts about the Use of Operating Theatres*, Oxford 1982, 25.

27 Whyte, W., personal communication.

28 Whyte, W., 'Airborne infection in operating rooms and effect of ventilation and clothing' *Japanese Journal of Medical Instrumentation*, Vol 52, Tokyo 1982, 549–556.

29 Lidwell, D. and others. 'Effect of ultra clean air in operating rooms on deep sepsis in the joints after total hip or knee replacement; a randomised study,' *British Medical Journal*, Vol 285, 3 July 1982, 10–14.

30 Cowan, D., *The Clean Operating Enclosure, its effect on the incidence of wound infection and its influence on the design of the operating department of a hospital*, National Building Research Institute, Pretoria 1976.

31 Fagin, H., *Technological Impacts on Health Facilities* University Microfilms, International, New York 1973, 53–69.

32 Chester, T., 'The reorganisation of the NHS blueprint and reality', *World Hospitals*, Winter 1975, I, 12.

33 Bridgman, R., 'Health Care Facilities in Developing Countries', *World Hospitals*, February 1980, xvi, 39.

34 Stolte, J. 'Cost-consciousness as a condition of cost containment in hospital', *Hospital and Health Services Review*, February 1979, 52.

4   The support zone

1 Tatton-Brown, W., 'House without walls' *Topics and Opinions*, Macmillan 1963, 251.

2 Friesen, G., Silvin, R., 'Concepts of Health planning', *World Hospitals*, Winter 1975, xi. 38.

3 Department of Health and Social Security, *Greenwich Hospital*, Polytechnic of North London, 1982, 6.

4 Clibbon, S., Sachs, M., 'Creating consolidated clinical techniques spaces for an expanding role in Health Care', *Architectural Record*, New York February 1971.

5 Mathers and Haldenby, *Interstitial Space in Health Facilities*, Research study report for Department of National Health and Welfare, Ottawa Canada, January 1979.

6 Morris, S., 'Royal Melbourne Central Linen Service'. Hospital Administration, December 1963 (and personal communication).

7 Weymes, C., *Planning and Regional Sterile Supply Service*, McCorquodale 1968 (and personal communication).

8 Department of Health and Social Security, *Guidelines on Pre-cooked Chilled Foods*, Her Majesty's Stationery Office, 1980.

9 Ferguson, P., *The Economic Development of Electrical Services in Hospitals. A Study of the New Lister Hospital, Stevenage*, Electricity Council, 1970.

10 Platts, J., 'Britain's first all-electric hospital.' *Electronics and Power*, August 1978.

11 Department of Health and Social Security, *Low Energy Hospital Study*, 1982.

12 James, P., 'Materials-handling systems in hospitals' *Hospital Engineering*, September 1974, No 11, 5–13.

13 Cochrane, A., *Effectiveness and Efficiency in the National Health Service*, Nuffield Provincial Hospital Trust, 1972.

5   Procedures

1 Steindl, J., *Random Processes and the Growth of Firms, Study of the Pareto Law*, 1965.

2 *Philadelphia South Jersey Metropolitan Area Hospital Survey*, New York 1969.

3 Department of Health and Social Security, *Works Guidance Index*, 23, 89, 91, 111, 112, 113, 130.

4 Moss, R., *The Planning Team and Organisation Machinery*, Draft report prepared for World Health Organisation, MARU Polytechnic of North London, 1975.

5 *Architects' Journal Information Library*, 'Hospital Planning and Design Guide', published in association with the Ministry of Health, *Architects' Journal* 16 November 1966 to 25 January 1967.

6 Department of Health and Social Security, *Activity database. Guide to A & B Activity data sheets and their use in Health building schemes*, 1980.

7 Green, J., Moss, R., Jackson, C., *Hospital Research and Briefing Problems*, Report of Conference at the King Edward's Hospital Fund Centre, London 1971.

8 Ministerio de Sanidad y Seguridad Social, Escuela de Gerencia Hospitalaria. *Catalogo de publicaciones*, Madrid. October 1981. 37–9.

9 National Building Research Institute, Pretoria,

Report of the Committee of Inquiry into Norms and Procedures for Hospital Construction, Pretoria, February 1975.

10 Thompson, J., Goldin, G., *The Hospital 1: A Social and Architectural History*, New York 1975.

11 Committee of Public Accounts Report XI Session 1979–80, *Standardisation of the design of hospitals – operational procedures and components*, Her Majesty's Stationery Office, 1980.

12 Delrue, J., Mikko, E., *Rationalization of Planning and Construction of Medical Facilities in Developing Countries*, World Health Organisation Offset publication No. 29, Geneva 1976, 54–113.

13 Department of Health and Social Security, *Harness System Design Report, I & II Computer Aided Building*, 1972.

14 Department of Health and Social Security, *Health-building Guidance*, Dev. 1, 2. A leaflet describing the range of DHSS guidance material on briefing and design, 1983.

15 Perez-Sherriff, M., 'Calculation, tendering, cost control and organisation of the building phase', *World Hospitals* Vol XI, 2 and 3, 1975, 103.

16 Sparrow, A., 'The Hospital Planning Process 1963–66'. *Internal Note 65/70*, Building Research Station, 4, 15, 21, 22, 28, 30 (A copy is available in the library of King Edward VII Fund, London).

17 Swetchine, J., 'L'hôpital de Beaune' experimental project of Ministry of Health and Social Security *Techniques Hospitalières*, 289, Paris, October 1969, 93–108.

18 'Fast-build Hospitals', *Health and Social Service Journal*, July 1982, 892–3.

19 Peña, W., with Caudill, W. and Focke, J., *Problem Seeking: an architectural programming primer*, Cahners Books International, Boston, Mass., USA, 50, 82, 149, 163.

20 Department of Health and Social Security, *Health Notice*, HN (81) 30, Health Building procedures review of Capricode, DHSS, 1981.

21 Florez, F., Personal communication.

22 Griffiths, R., *NHS Management Inquiry*, Department of Health and Social Security, October 1983.

23 Planning Research Corporation, *Planning and Control of Hospital Developments*, PRC Engineering Inc, 200 Great Dover Street, London SE1 4YB, 1984.

24 PRC Engineering (UK) Ltd.

APPENDICES

List of hospitals and their planners

Hospital	Country	Planner A – Authority/Consultant B – Architect		Figure number
Airedale (General Hospital) Yorkshire	UK	A	Yorkshire Regional Health Authority	1.21, 1.106, 1.107, 2.15, 2.16
		B	Booth, Hancock and Johnson	4.22, 4.23
Alexandra (Private Hospital) Manchester	UK	A	AMI (Europe)	1.84, 1.85
		B	Richard Seifert & Partners	
Algeria (Standard General Hospital) Algiers	Algiers	A	Ministry of Health, Algiers	1.75
		B	Ditto	
Bath Clinic (Private Hospital) Somerset	UK	A	Grand-Met Services	2.72, 2.73
		B	Hospital Design Partnership	3.25, 3.26
Beaune (General Hospital) Beaune	France	A	Ministry of Health	
		B	SEDIM	1.73, 1.74
Beth Israel (Private Hospital)	USA	B	Perry Dean Partners Inc.	3.41
Best Buy Hospitals (Standard General Hospital)	UK	A	Department of Health Consultant – Paul James	1.120, 4.29
		B	Chief Architect, Howard Goodman	
Bromsgrove (Standard Nucleus Hospital) Worcester	UK	A	Department of Health	2.63, 2.65
		B	Hospital Design Partnership	
Bury St Edmunds (Standard Best Buy Hospital) Suffolk	UK	A	Department of Health Consultant – Paul James	1.122, 1.123, 2.32, 2.33
		B	Hospital Design Partnership	3.8, 3.9, 3.10, 3.11, 3.12, 3.13
Central Emergency (General Hospital) Abu Dhabi	UAE	A	Ministry of Health UAE	1.117, 1.118
		B	Jordanconsult and Hospital Design Partnership	2.36, 3.7, 3.39
Chesterfield (General Hospital) Derbyshire	UK	A	Trent Regional Health Authority	2.43, 2.44
		B	Frank Shaw & Partners	
Desert Samaritan (General Hospital) Arizona	USA	A	Samaritan Health Service	1.26, 1.98, 1.99, 1.100
		B	Caudill, Rowlett, Scott & Drover, Welch & Lindlan	
Eisenhower Memorial (Private Hospital) California	USA	A	Trustees (Bob Hope)	1.68, 1.69, 1.70, 1.71
		B	Edward Durell Stone Inc.	
Etobicoke (General Hospital) Toronto	Canada	A	Gordon A. Friesen Inc.	1.27, 1.28, 1.30
		B	Neish Owen Rowland & Roy	3.24, 4.18

Hospital	Country	Planner A – Authority/Consultant B – Architect	Figure number
Musgrave Park (General Hospital) Northern Ireland	UK	A Nuffield Provincial Hospital Trust B Llewelyn-Davies, Weeks.	2.17
Newham (Standard Nucleus Hospital) London	UK	A Department of Health B Hospital Design Partnership	4.47
Ninewells (Teaching Hospital) Scotland	UK	A Scottish Home and Health Department B Robert Mathew, Johnson Marshall	1.103, 1.104, 1.105, 2.20, 2.21
Nordenham (General Hospital)	West Germany	B Weber, Brandt & Partner	1.49, 1.50, 1.51, 1.52, 2.41, 2.78, 3.16, 3.38, 4.10, 4.11, 4.12
Northwick Park (Teaching and Research Hospital) London	UK	A Medical Research Council B Llewelyn-Davies, Weeks.	1.12 2.61
Nucleus Hospitals (Standard General Hospital)	UK	A Department of Health B Chief Architect: Howard Goodman	1.109 2.37, 3.37, 3.46
Ostersunds (General Hospital) Jamptlands	Sweden	B Wirnan-Arkitekterna	3.40
Reinickendorf (General Hospital) Berlin	West Germany	B Tonis & Shroeter	1.127
Rotherham (General Hospital) Yorkshire	UK	A Trent Regional Health Authority Consultant – Paul James B Regional Architect	1.124, 1.125, 1.126, 2.48 3.3, 3.18, 3.19, 3.20 4.2, 4.31, 4.32, 4.33
Royal Free (Teaching Hospital) London	UK	B Watkins, Gray Woodgate International	1.38, 1.39, 3.45, 4.1
Santa Fe (General Hospital) Valencia	Spain	A Institute of Social Security B Florez	1.59, 1.60, 4.13, 4.14, 4.43
St Lukes (General Hospital) Yorkshire	UK	A Yorkshire Regional Health Authority B J.G.L. Poulson Associates	4.5
St Marks (Private Hospital) Utah	USA	A Consultant – Medical Planning Associates B Kaplan and McLaughlin	2.97
St Marys (Teaching Hospital) London	UK	A North West Thames Regional Health Authority B Llewelyn-Davies Weeks	2.101, 2.102
St Marys (General Hospital) Isle of Wight	UK	A Department of Health B Ahrends, Burton & Koralek	1.114 4.48, 4.49

Hospital	Country	Planner A – Authority/Consultant B – Architect	Figure number
St Thomas' (Teaching Hospital) London	UK	A St Thomas' Hospital B Yorke, Rosenberg, Mardall	1.61, 1.62, 2.107 3.30, 3.31
Southlands (Harness Standard Hospital) Sussex	UK	A South West Thames Regional Health Authority B Hospital Design Partnership	1.09 2.34, 2.79, 2.80, 2.92
Stafford (Harness Standard Hospital) Staffordshire	UK	A West Midlands Regional Health Authority B Building Design Partnership	1.108
South Teesside (General Hospital) South Teesside	UK	A Northern Regional Health Authority B George, Trew, Dunn, Beckles-Wilson, Bowes	1.81, 1.82, 1.83
Sundsvaal (General Hospital)	Sweden	B Pütseps Arkitektkonter	1.40, 2.57, 2.58, 3.44
Swindon (General Hospital)	UK	A Oxford Regional Health Authority B Powell, Moya & Partners	2.18
Tembisa (General Hospital)	South Africa	A Transvaal Provincial Hospitals, RSA B Willem Steyn	2.8, 2.9
University College (Teaching Hospital) London	UK	A University College Teaching Hospital B A.W. Waterhouse	1.1
Utrecht (Teaching Hospital) Utrecht	Holland	B Eijkelenboom, Gerritse & Middelhoek	1.86, 1.87
Varberg (General Hospital) Varberg	Sweden	B White Arkitektkonter	1.40, 1.41, 2.11, 2.12, 3.5, 3.6
Walter Reed (Military General Hospital) Washington	USA	A US Army Medical Corps B Stone, Marraccini & Patterson.	1.134, 1.135, 1.136
Weston Super Mare (General Hospital) Somerset	UK	A South Western Regional Health Authority B Percy Thomas Partnership	1.115, 1.116, 2.38
Wexham Park (General Hospital) Berkshire	UK	A North West Thames Regional Health Authority B Powell, Moya & Partners	1.101, 1.102, 2.22, 2.24
Whittington Hospital London	UK	A King Edwards Hospital Fund Jubilee Project	2.99, 2.100
York (General Hospital) Yorkshire	UK	A Yorkshire Regional Health Authority B Llewelyn-Davies, Weeks	1.79, 1.80, 3.21, 3.22

Sources of information on hospital planning

Country	Association/Organisation
Argentina	Argentine Confederation of Private Clinics, Sanatoria and Hospitals Calle Tucaman 1668, 2 piso, Buenos Aires
Australia	Australian Hospital Association P.O. Box 344, Kingston Canberra, ACG 2604 (Tel 062 47 2522) School of Health Administration, University of New South Wales P.O. Box 1, Kensington, N.S.W.
Belgium	Belgian Hospital Association avenue A.J. Slegers 397, Bte 12, 1200 Brussels (Tel: 02/5683200 & 6726033) Association of Public Hospitals rue des Guildes 9, 11 1040 Namur Wallon Hospital Federation rue Notre Dame 9, 5000 Namur
Brazil	Brazilian Hospital Federation Avenida Graca Aranha 19, Grupos 902/3 20 020 Rio de Janeiro
Canada	Canadian Hospital Association 17 York Street, Suite 100, Ottawa, Ontario K1N 9J6 (Tel: 613/238.8005) Health Facilities Design Division Department of National Health and Welfare
Costa Rica	Costa Rican Hospital Association Apartado 745, San Jose (Tel: 21 49 19)
Denmark	National Committee for Danish Hospitals Amstradsforeningen i Danmark, Landemaerket 10, 1119 Copenhagen (Tel: 01/11 21 61)
Egypt	Egyptian Hospital Association Dar El Hekma, 42 Kasr El-Ainy Street, Cairo
Finland	Finnish Hospital League Toinen linja 14, 00530 Helsinki 53 (Tel: 90/7711)
France	French Hospital Federation 33 Avenue d'Italie, Paris 75013 (Tel: 584 3250)

Country	Association/Organisation
German Democratic Republic	Hospital Association of the German Democratic Republic Institut fur Sozialhygiene, Med Akad 'Carl Gustav Carus', Fetscherstrasse 74, 8019 Dresden (Tel: 682853 Cable Medak Dresden) (Telex: 2359)
German Federal Republic	German Hospital Association Tersteegenstrasse 9, 4000 Dusseldorf (Tel: 02.11/43.46.83) (Telex: 8.584.157 dkg.d)
Hungary	Hungarian Hospital Federation Frankel Leo utca 17–19, Budapest 11
India	Indian Hospital Association C-11/72 Shahjahan Road, New Delhi 110011 (Tel: 382 602) Voluntary Health Association of India C-14 Community Centre, New Dehli 110016 (Tel: 383 132)
International	International Hospital Federation 120 Albert Street, London, N.W.1 World Health Organisation 1211 Geneva 27, Switzerland
Indonesia	Indonesian Hospital Association (PERSI) Pertamina Central Hospital, Jalan Kiyai Maja, 2–6 Kebayoran Baru, Jakarta-Selatan (Tel: 775 890)
Italy	National Association of Italian Cities Via dei Prefetti 46, 00186 Rome (Tel: 311540 Cable: Assocomuni)
Japan	Japan Hospital Association 2–14 Kojimachi, Chiyoda-ku, Tokyo 102 (Tel: 03. 265.0077) Japan Municipal Hospital Association Godokaikan 3–4, Kioi-cho, Chiyoda-ku, Tokyo 102
Korea	Korean Hospital Association 782-ka, Jur-Dong, Chung-ku, Seoul (Tel: 261 7066.7)
Mexico	Mexican Hospital Association Queretaro 210, Mexico 7, DF
Netherlands	National Hospital Council Postbus 9696, 3506 GR Utrecht (Tel: 030 73991) National Hospital Institute Hospital Centre, Ondlaan, Utrecht

Country	Association/Organisation
New Zealand	Hospital Boards Association of New Zealand P.O. Box 714, Wellington (Tel: 736 181 Cable: Hosbanz)
Nigeria	Federal Ministry of Health Lagos
Norway	Norwegian Health Services Association Mogens Thorsens GT.10, Oslo 2 (Tel: 02/447410) Norwegian Association of Local Authorities Postboks, 1278, Vika, Oslo 1 (Tel: 02/41 2000 Cable: Kommunebyra)
Peru	Peruvian Hospital Association Camino Real 620, San Isidro, Lima
Philippines	Philippine Hospital Association 14 Kamias Road, Quezon City
Poland	Polish Hospital Association Rutkowskiego Nr. 18–11 00 020 Warsaw
Puerto Rico	Puerto Rican Hospital Association Villa Nevarez Professional Centre 1 Rio Piedras 00927
South Africa	National Association for S. African Provincial Hospitals C/o Director of Hospital Services P.O. Box 517, Bloemfontein, OFS National Building Research Institute P.O. Box 395, Pretoria 0001
Spain	Architectural Section Health Division Ministry of Health and Social Security Alcala 56, Madrid 14.
Sweden	S.P.R.I. Institute for Planning and Rationalisation of Health and Social Services Box 27310, 102.54 Stockholm Swedish Hospital Association Fack, 102 50 Stockholm Federation of Swedish County Councils Box 6606, 113 83 Stockholm (Tel: 08/23.65.60)
Switzerland	Swiss Hospital Association (VESKA) Rain 32, 5001 Aarau (Tel: 064/24.12.22)
Taiwan	Hospital Association of Taiwan 10F No 27 Pao King Road, Taipei

Country	Association/Organisation

United Kingdom

Department of Health & Social Security
Euston Tower, London, N.W.1.*

Hospital Centre
King Edward VII Hospital Fund
126 Albert Street, London, N.W.1.

Office of Health Economics
12 Whitehall, London, S.W.1.

Scottish Home & Health Department
St. Andrews House, Edinburgh

Building Services Research Institute
Glasgow University, Glasgow

Medical Architecture Research Unit
Polytechnic of North London
Holloway Road, London, N.7.

United States of America   Department of Health, Education and Welfare
Washington, D.C.

American Hospital Association
840 North Lake Shore Drive, Chicago, Illinois 60611

*Department of Health and Social Security's *Works Guidance Index* gives a complete list of all the publications issued 1960–1985 by the Works Group.

Financial effect of delay and on-costs computation

1 Inflation (assumed at 10% *per annum*)
After 1 year £100 estimate becomes £110
After 5 years £100 estimate becomes £161.05; say £160
A contract is let and lasts 5 years; assuming payments of $\frac{1}{5}$ of the contract sum $^{160}/_5 = 32$ and inflation continues at 10%

After year	6, £32.00+10%	becomes	35.20
,, ,,	7, £35.20+10%	,,	38.70
,, ,,	8, £38.70+10%	,,	42.60
,, ,,	9, £42.60+10%	,,	46.90
,, ,,	10, £46.90+10%	,,	51.50

Final price paid	214.90
Original estimate	100.00

Increase due to inflation on Hospital A 115%

A contract is let for Hospital B after 1 year at £110 and lasts 2 years. Assuming annual payments of $\frac{1}{2}$ of the contract sum $^{110}/_2 = 55$ and inflation continues at 10%

After year	2, £55.00+10% becomes	60.50
After year	3, £60.50+10% becomes	66.50

Final price paid	126.55
Original estimate	100.00

Increase due to inflation on Hospital B 26.5%

2 Interest charges (assumed rate of interest 10% per annum)

The interest charges are 10% on 0 at the beginning and 10% on the whole contract at the end. The average is 5% per year for every year of the contract.
 Hospital A takes 5 years to build: 5×5=25%
 Hospital B takes 2 years to build: 5×2=10%.

3 On-costs are taken from *Health Building Procedure Note 6*, Appendix 9, DHSS Jan 1974. They are expressed as percentages which can be added to the sum of the basic cost limits of the functional units (e.g. number of operating theatres, consultant sessions, meals served)

4 Fees and expenses, previously aggregated from percentages of the contract sum, as laid down by the different professional institutes. Now they are negotiable and are related to the time involved (see page 190)

5 Summary

	Hospital A	Hospital B
Nursing and clinical zone	80	80
Support zone	40	20
	120	100
On-costs on A 140%	168	44
B 44%		
Sum of functional units and on-costs	288	144
Inflation on A at 115%	331	38
on B at 26%		
Contract sum	619	182
Interest charges on A at 25%	155	18
on B at 10%		
Total Final Cost	774	200

Compiled by R.J. Wynniatt-Husey FCA

Index